Politics and process

Politics and process
NEW ESSAYS IN
DEMOCRATIC THOUGHT

Edited by
GEOFFREY BRENNAN
The Australian National University

and
LOREN E. LOMASKY
University of Minnesota, Duluth

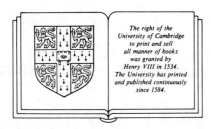

The right of the
University of Cambridge
to print and sell
all manner of books
was granted by
Henry VIII in 1534.
The University has printed
and published continuously
since 1584.

CAMBRIDGE UNIVERSITY PRESS

Cambridge
New York   Port Chester   Melbourne   Sydney

Published by the Press Syndicate of the University of Cambridge
The Pitt Building, Trumpington Street, Cambridge CB2 1RP
32 East 57th Street, New York, NY 10022, USA
10 Stamford Road, Oakleigh, Melbourne 3166, Australia

First published 1989

Printed in the United States of America

Library of Congress Cataloging-in-Publication Data
Politics and process: new essays in democratic thought/edited by
Geoffrey Brennan and Loren E. Lomasky.
p. cm.
Includes index.
ISBN 0-521-35043-3
1. Democracy. I. Brennan, H. Geoffrey, 1944– . II. Lomasky,
Loren E.
JC423.P566   1989
321.9–dc 19   89-517
                                                                                      CIP

British Library Cataloguing in Publication Data
Politics and process: new essays in
democratic thought
1. Democracy
I. Brennan, Geoffrey   II. Lomasky,
Loren E.
321.8

ISBN 0-521-35043-3 hard covers

Contents

Acknowledgments

This volume originated in a 1984 conference entitled "Individual Liberty and Democratic Order" held in Crystal City, Virginia. Earlier versions of several of the essays were originally presented there. We would be remiss not to thank the Liberty Fund for its support of that event – and, indeed, for its consistent promotion of scholarly inquiry into the nature of a society composed of free and responsible individuals. We also thank our research assistant, Kenneth Cust, and the Social Philosophy and Policy Center, Bowling Green State University, for supplying ideal working conditions.

Geoffrey Brennan
Loren E. Lomasky

vii

Contributors

Peter H. Aranson
Law and Economics Center
Emory University
Atlanta, GA 30322

H. Geoffrey Brennan
Faculty of Economics
Australian National University
GPO Box 4
Canberra, ACT 2601
Australia

James M. Buchanan
Center for the Study of Public Choice
St. George's Hall
George Mason University
Fairfax, VA 22030

Jules Coleman
Yale Law School
401 A Yale Station
New Haven, CT 06520

James Fishkin
Department of Government
University of Texas
Austin, TX 78712

Shirley Robin Letwin
3 Kent Terrace
London North West 1
England

Loren E. Lomasky
Social Philosophy and Policy Center
Bowling Green State University
Bowling Green, OH 43403

Dennis C. Mueller
Department of Economics
University of Maryland
    at College Park
College Park, MD 20742

William Nelson
Department of Philosophy
University of Houston
Houston, TX 77004

David Osterfeld
Department of Political Science
Box 896
Saint Joseph's College
Rensselaer, IN 47978

J. Roland Pennock
Department of Political Science
Swarthmore University
Swarthmore, PA 19081

viii

Introduction

Geoffrey Brennan and Loren E. Lomasky

I

Democracy, it may seem, has never been less in need of defense – or even evaluation. Gradually, over the past couple of centuries, it has passed into the catalog of universal virtues. We are *all* democrats now, differing at most only in the qualifier we prefer: "liberal," "workers'," or "people's." Anyone labeled "antidemocratic" or even "undemocratic" has been ostracized from the relevant community of normative discourse. Correspondingly, any urgings in favor of democracy are likely to strike the contemporary ear as platitudinous.

Complacency, however, would be out of place. If "democracy" has become a "motherhood term," it runs the risk of all such: that it become emptied of meaning. If all regimes, whatever their institutional detail and political spirit, claim to be democratic – as virtually all do – then what, we may reasonably ask, is *un*democratic? Is it not a fair bet that charges made in the past against democracy – or for democracy against other regimes – have been answered by mere changes in the meanings of words? What are the defining features of a democratic order? What exactly are the virtues that democracy is supposed to engender? And does democracy really succeed? In some ways it is important that such questions be asked *precisely* when the answers seem to be so widely taken for granted.

Moreover, within contemporary political theory the situation is by no means as clear-cut as the popular imagination appears to have it. We can identify two seemingly antithetical but in fact complementary concerns about the justification of democratic theory: that democratic procedures *fail* to reflect the preferences of the enfranchised citizenry and that they *succeed* in so doing. Let us call the former of these concerns democratic *opacity,* the latter democratic *transparency.* The difficulty posed by opacity is apparent; that posed by transparency less so. In a sense, however, transparency is the more fundamental stumbling block. If the preferences revealed by polling are uninformed, malignant, or basically inconsistent with whatever conditions are taken to make for political legitimacy, then those defects will be transmitted to resultant policy. For example, an

1

electoral majority can coalesce around a program through which its interests will be advanced via dispossession of a vulnerable minority. Only the most extreme democratic enthusiast will maintain that the fact that 50 percent plus one vote for such a program thereby sanitizes it. Unjust political orders are all too compatible with the putative general will.

Social contract theory seeks to ground political legitimacy on the freely tendered consent of political actors. Democracies profess a similar allegiance to the foundational legitimating status of consent. Nonetheless, almost all important contemporary versions of social contract theory reject simple democratic majoritarianism as sufficient to establish legitimacy. Among these accounts, no work has been more influential than John Rawls's *A Theory of Justice*. Rawls goes beyond majoritarianism in two crucial respects: (1) The founding principles of the just regime are stylized as the product of *unanimity* among the contractors rather than simple or special majority; (2) contractors' preferences are filtered by a thick *veil of ignorance* that blocks all particularizing information, including knowledge of an individual's economic or social status, his natural endowments, and even an agent's conception of the good. Rawls maintains that unanimity behind a veil of ignorance elicits principles that are constitutive of a just regime. Minorities are doubly protected against predation by majorities: Since each individual exercises veto power, no agreement will be enacted unless it is of perceived benefit to all; because the contractors know only that they have interests but do not know what those interests are, they lack the capacity to bargain for differential advantage. Unanimity coupled with the veil generates justice as fairness.

Since the publication in 1971 of *A Theory of Justice* there has emerged a vast literature in which its arguments have been subjected to scrutiny from every conceivable angle. It is unnecessary to review that literature here; our concern is not with the theoretical adequacy of the Rawlsian enterprise but rather with its highly qualified endorsement of democratic governance. Though a Rawlsian just regime is democratic, its foundations are not. That is, they are not a cumulation of the de facto preferences of a majority. Indeed, Rawls makes it abundantly clear that no reasonable facsimile of his two principles of justice would emerge from any ordinary procedure of citizens "voting their interests"; that is why the imposition of the veil of ignorance is central to his project. It follows that, for Rawls's contractarianism (and the numerous variants it has sired), the rationale for democratic rule is distinctly derivative. An electorate's various deliverances are always to be constrained by foundational principles that are not themselves the product of democratic choice.

A similar appraisal of the derivative character of democratic institutions had been presented a decade previously by James Buchanan and Gordon Tullock in *The Calculus of Consent*. Like Rawls, Buchanan and Tullock reject majoritarianism as a basis for collective action, contending that nothing short of unanimity is acceptable at a constitutional level. They differ from Rawls, however, in depicting contractors with knowledge of who they are, what they want, and a tolerably clear idea of the means by which they might act to get it. But that difference is not as pivotal as it might at first seem. Buchanan and Tullock maintain that, because the effects of the operation of a set of rules is uncertain even in the present and more so over time, individuals will be largely unable at the level of constitutional choice to maneuver for direct political advantage. Unanimity and natural (as opposed to Rawlsian hypothetical) ignorance combine to establish the preconditions of mutually acceptable collective action.

If the rule of unanimity were also employed at the postconstitutional level, such that each individual possessed an effective veto over every collective determination, exorbitant bargaining costs would ensue. Because rational contractors know this, and know also that collective action can provide to the community goods otherwise inaccessible, they will, at a constitutional level, endorse in-period decision procedures other than unanimity – and do so unanimously. Balloting thus emerges as an efficiency-enhancing device itself resting on a foundation that eschews majoritarianism. Even more noteworthy is the insistence by Buchanan and Tullock that the rule of simple majority is just one among an indefinite number of collective decision procedures that could reasonably be adopted. No special virtue resides in majorities, and no moral defect attaches to institutions that empower minorities to block policies viewed as inimical to their interests. If one takes "democracy" to be synonymous with "majority rule," *The Calculus of Consent* expresses no more than indifference toward democracy.

Several of the contributors to this volume address concerns surrounding democratic transparency, among them Buchanan himself. He reiterates his prior insistence that the ultimate model of politics be contractarian and proceeds to develop a tripartite classification of political action: (1) enforcement of laws previously enacted, (2) collective provision of goods and services, and (3) constitutional alteration. Buchanan argues that conflation of these distinct activities comes at the price of social and intellectual confusion. Majoritarian determination has, he claims, no place at levels (1) and (3) and is by no means a unique solution to level (2) decisions. He labels the "electoral fallacy" the notion that, so long as democratic decision rules are guaranteed, anything goes. To the contrary, the first normative principle of contractarianism is that state authority be *limited by law.*

Priority of the rule of law is also central to Shirley Letwin's argument. Periodic election of officeholders and open conduct of public affairs are, she maintains, necessary conditions for the existence of a genuinely democratic polity, but are not themselves sufficient. The indispensable basis of a free, democratic society is a system of law that is general, impersonal, and noninstrumental. Letwin derives this result from the telos of political association: peaceful resolution of disagreements over a domain in which indisputable knowledge is necessarily absent. Nonviolent resolution of problems of communal association requires authoritative law that does not dictate outcomes to be achieved but rather sets conditions within which individuals are at liberty to act to achieve whatever ends they happen to hold. Substantive disagreement is thereby resolved through procedural agreement. Law, so conceived, is fundamentally different from the commands of an omnipotent sovereign. Letwin's conclusion is that, paradoxical though it may seem, the morality of democracy assigns priority to the rule of law even over the democratic way of constituting a government. Between democracy without the rule of law or the rule of law minus democracy, she would opt for the latter.

James Fishkin argues from within a contractarian framework but criticizes the models presented by Rawls and Buchanan and Tullock. Rawlsian thickly veiled contractors know too little to arrive at significant results; Buchanan and Tullock contractors know too much to establish unanimity as uniquely preferable for constitutional solution of the collective action problem. Fishkin claims that because our pretheoretical notions of impartiality and fairness can be modeled in a variety of nonequivalent ways, no single imaginary choice situation enjoys moral jurisdiction. Therefore, the Rawlsian original position is just one among many plausible ways in which one can hypothetically represent the derivation of political principles. Hypothetical contract is thus inconclusive, but a theory that takes its bearings from the actual preferences of individuals is vulnerable to transmission of unfair advantages present at the inception of bargaining. Fishkin suggests that the dilemma may be avoided by construing agreement as predicated on actual but *refined* preferences. He describes these as the political understandings of a culture insofar as they are filtered through a process of unmanipulated debate. Although the proposal requires further development, he contends that it affords prospects of a greater rapprochement between contractarianism and democracy than that which emerges from either Rawls or Buchanan and Tullock.

William Nelson builds on a contractarian formulation introduced by T. M. Scanlon in which the ideal of unanimous agreement among all individuals is replaced by a conception of consent among all and only those motivated to find principles of free agreement. The alteration is significant, because it affords a filtering mechanism similar to that endorsed by Fishkin. On this account, not all preferences have equal moral weight. Specifically, those inconsistent with the aim of establishing principles of free, general agreement are inadmissible. Nelson proceeds to characterize representative democracy as a decision-making procedure in which policies are openly debated and adopted only when they can be defended by good arguments. Although there exists no guarantee that any particular system of democratic institutions will rigorously hew to the normative ideal of producing legislation that can be justified to everyone, democracy is attractive because it is a decision-making procedure predicated on public deliberation. It is worth noting that the proffered justification is *procedural* rather than substantive. No preordained set of property rights is – or should be – beyond the purview of political adjustment. It is the democratic process itself, claims Nelson, rather than any list of alleged natural rights that has moral priority.

Jules Coleman is more skeptical about the possibility of an adequate proceduralist justification of collective action. He is concerned to evaluate two common lines of justification for collective action – one that he describes as "contractarian," and the other as "procedural" (a third, termed "consequentialist," is mentioned but not discussed in any detail) – and to relate these lines of attempted justification to the rational-choice framework that they share. Coleman's discussion centers, in the proceduralist section, on social choice theorists, of whom he regards· William Riker as an archetype. Coleman's exemplary contractarian figures are Douglas Rae and Buchanan and Tullock. The nuanced discussion identifies several intriguing justificatory problems without attempting to draw a "bottom line" conclusion. We are left instead with guarded claims, and a strong sense that some lines of reasoning are more promising than others and deserve to be pursued.

In Roland Pennock's essay we find a synthetic statement of the considerations that weigh in justifying one form of political organization against others and Pennock's own characterization of what he terms "ideal democracy." He attempts to exhibit conceptual and psychological connections between institutions of liberal democracy and a rich conception of a human nature embracing both individualistic autonomy and the essentially social nature of the species. Because Pennock has written his essay in the light of others in the collection, he is able to address some of the issues that they raise – though, of course, his aim is not so much to provide a summary of others' positions as to meet some of the arguments presented. Because the chapter attempts to traverse the whole justificatory territory, it affords a very fitting leadoff to the volume.

II

The essays introduced in the preceding section tend to scrutinize democratic procedures from a perspective of transparency. That is, they are willing to assume, at least for purposes of argument, that vote tabulations more or less accurately reflect underlying preferences of the electorate. The basic issue these authors confront, therefore, is the adequacy of a political mechanism that translates into collective action a morally mixed lot of preferences. However, there exists alongside this strand of the critique of democracy another whose basic motif is examination of distortions contained within the translation mechanism itself. In the late eighteenth century, the Marquis de Condorcet demonstrated that there may be no equilibrium result in an electoral contest among more than two alternatives. In this century, related anomalies have multiplied exponentially. Within *public-choice theory* these results have coalesced into a wide-ranging and effective critique of democratic political institutions. Such criticism has not been overt in the sense that public-choice theory has rarely directly addressed the case for democratic as against other forms of political order. But public-choice theorists have had as a major part of their agenda the comparison of democratic decision-making processes with the *decentralized* decision-making processes characteristic of markets. The comparison has not exactly been flattering to the former.

A little doctrinal history may be helpful here. Public-choice theory arose, at least in its modern guise, as an integral part of the economic theory of the state. The latter theory took as its point of departure the standard theories of welfare economics concerning the optimality of decentralized market institutions, theorems refined by Edgeworth, Pareto, Arrow, and Debreu from origins in Smith and Ricardo. The economists' theory of the state sought to argue a role for government, over and above the minimal one of establishing and maintaining the institutional fabric of the market, by developing a theory of *market failure* to set against the more traditional theory of market success. The resultant accounts of "public goods," "externalities," "consumption jointness," "natural monopoly," and the like were all elaborations and refinements of a single idea: that the independent, decentralized decision-making processes of the market did not always make possible the full appropriation of potential gains from exchange. Equivalently, individual action coordinated by the market mechanism could, under certain circumstances, give rise to outcomes that were valued less highly by all agents than was some other feasible outcome.

Where those circumstances could be identified, a role for governmental action to correct for market failure was taken to be established. On this basis, the case was made for public provision of such goods as defense, law and order, pollution control, public health, and academic research, as well as intervention through subsidies and/or regulations in relation to a wide range of other activities such as education, housing, transportation, and communications. Indeed, the public role in "managing the macroeconomy" and even in determining the distribution of income could, it was argued, be articulated in generalized market failure terms.

Implicit in all this, however, was the assumption that, where markets "failed," government was likely to do better. As a purely logical matter, however, market failure considerations are not sufficient to establish a case for government activity. Additionally required is a *comparative* assessment of alternative institutions, including an assessment of their respective inefficiencies. Thus, the economists' theory of the state remained incomplete until a systematic treatment of the normative properties of majoritarian/democratic decision making could be developed on all fours with the welfare economics of markets.

Public-choice economics was that resultant theory. Two aspects of its ambitions should be emphasized. First, its explicit object was to overturn the so-called benevolent-despot model of politics that dominated welfare economics generally and public finance orthodoxy specifically. The notion that governments had the power and inclination to pursue the "public interest" was explicitly to be questioned. Any public-interestedness in political outcomes could not simply be assumed: It had to be *proved* – and proved in terms of essentially the same analytic method and by appeal to the same repertoire of underlying assumptions that economists had used to establish market failure. Anything else would be to load the dice. In particular – and this is the second matter that requires emphasis here – agents in their political roles were to be endowed with precisely the same motivations as agents in their market roles. Specifically, since the assumption of self-interest was used in modeling individual behavior in markets (and in demonstrating the propensity of rational agents to free-ride in the market provision of public goods), consistency demanded that the same assumption be made in modeling the behavior of politicians, voters, and bureaucrats.

This importation of the self-interest assumption into political analysis has proved controversial – on both empirical and ethical grounds. The empirical dimensions of the argument are complex and need not occupy us here. The ethical argument is more relevant. The claim is that some sort of basic faith in political process – and political agents – is necessary if democratic order is to survive. Indeed, public-choice theorists are often charged with professing profoundly antidemocratic sentiments.

There are two things to be said about such charges. The first is that, on the face of things, these are strange arguments to bring in defense of democracy, since democracy, with its characteristic features of institutionalized opposition and competitive electoral constraints, might seem *Madison ?* to be based on precisely the sort of appraisal of human nature that the self-interest assumption can be taken to embody. The second observation is, however, that the anxieties do seem justified: The main results in public-choice theory represent a major attack on the processes of democratic collective decision making. If public-choice theorists have had, as a major ambition, that of undermining naive faith in collective decision-making institutions, they appear to have been gloriously successful. In fact, it is not *naive* faith only that they have undermined – one wonders rather whether there is room for any faith in collective decision making *at all.*

Several of the contributors to this volume are fideists, others skeptics. Dennis Mueller assesses thirty years of public-choice theory as it bears on the related problems of *preference revelation* and *rational abstentia.* The former is the question, first raised by Samuelson, of how one can get individuals to volunteer accurate information concerning their preferences for public goods. The latter stems from the fact that a realistic balancing of narrowly self-interested inducements to participate in electoral contests against costs thereby incurred generates the conclusion that rational individuals will choose to abstain. Neither difficulty can be dismissed out of hand, but, suggests Mueller, each may be of more theoretical than practical concern. In part that is because there is reason to believe that individuals give greater scope when in the polling booth than when engaging in private activity to their ethical preferences. Mueller further claims that recent analytic developments in the literature of public choice strongly suggest that the propensity of social choice to yield disequilibrium outcomes was vastly overestimated by earlier authors. Democratic regimes can be expected to do a tolerably good job of giving effect to individuals' preferences and will do better yet if several reforms are instituted: more public provision of political information, a shift from single-member districts to proportional representation, more finely tuned preference revelation procedures.

Peter Aranson draws rather different conclusions. He identifies four major problems besetting representative democracy. The first of these is the rational-abstention difficulty addressed by Mueller. It is closely akin to the second, *rational ignorance*. Even if an individual chooses to vote, it will rarely be in his economic interest to devote any significant quota of his resources to garnering the information that would make his ballot well informed. The third problem concerns the conditions making for electoral disequilibrium, as exhibited in the Condorcet result and its descendants. The last problem is the phenomenon of *rent seeking:* investment of resources by interested parties to secure the provision at public expense of essentially private goods. Aranson's overall appraisal will be unsettling to enthusiasts of democracy: Each of the four introduces serious distortions into collective choice procedures and, worse still, attempts to ameliorate some one of these will likely exacerbate others. Aranson does, however, cautiously endorse several reform measures, including the passage of a balanced-budget amendment to the Constitution and devolution of authorization for funding programs from the federal level to states and localities.

The latter theme receives close examination by David Osterfeld. There has not been anything in traditional political theory that has insisted that democracies *must* be federally structured or indeed that has seen federalism as anything more than perhaps a useful adjunct to democratic institutions. Osterfeld's position is more "radical" (as his title suggests). His view is that the virtues of democratic institutions are to be seen in terms of the constraints they place on the behavior of politicians. However, these constraints are tenuous at best. Potentially of considerably greater effect on the behavior of officeholders than periodic voting with ballots is the ability of citizens to "vote with their feet." Even an absolute dictator will find his predations sharply checked by the circumstance of individuals who can easily "take their business elsewhere." This ability is enhanced when there exists a large number of small, accessible societies to which an individual can relocate. Accordingly, Osterfeld advances the strong proposition that federalism is a necessary articulation of the democratic ideal of rule by the people – more so even than are democratic institutions as standardly conceived.

Brennan and Lomasky also accept the claim that regime size is an important political parameter, but for reasons different from those advanced by Osterfeld. They argue that a characteristic feature of electoral choice to which political theorists have been insufficiently attentive is the voter's *indecisiveness*. Whether – and how – one votes will almost never alter the outcome of an electoral contest in a populous jurisdiction. By way of contrast, individuals acting in their private capacities are routinely decisive: If they "vote with their dollars" for an item, they both get that item and bear the associated costs. Therefore, as a purely logical matter, political explanatory theories directly modeled on market behavior lack coherence. Like Mueller, Brennan and Lomasky contend that voter choice will involve a more significant appeal to ethical considerations than does consumer choice. However, they take this to be more of a mixed blessing than does Mueller, arguing that one traditional justification of democracy – namely that it is government *by the people* and thus reflects the public will – is basically misconceived and has to be radically recast if indeed it is to survive at all.

CHAPTER 1

The justification of democracy

J. Roland Pennock

1 Political justification and metaethics

How does one go about justifying a form of political ideals and a form of government? Moral philosophers are broadly in agreement. Those who support anarchism are exceedingly scarce. Some form of democracy enjoys a wide degree of support, as does the ban on slavery. So also does the requirement that people who drive automobiles observe rules calculated to facilitate the movement of traffic and to protect the safety of those using the highways. Yet if one ventures into the field of metaethics, it soon becomes apparent that agreement on principles of political ethics by no means implies agreement on the method of arriving at, and substantiating, those principles. On that point the doctors are in sharp disagreement, and James Fishkin, for example, finds this discord disturbing. The first step for one who would justify a form of government, he believes, is to select the proper "moral decision procedure." Yet this is the very matter on which disagreement is rife. It is not just as a philosopher that this lack of agreement concerns him; he fears the practical consequences. From his own empirical studies he has concluded that the person in the street believes in moral absolutes. It follows, in Fishkin's view, that anything that casts doubt upon those absolutes and all that is derived from them tends to lose legitimacy, leading him to conclude that liberal democracy faces a "crisis of legitimacy."[1]

For several reasons Fishkin's argument is not persuasive. First, the

11

cognitive dissonance that he assumes would disturb the person in the street and lead him or her to doubt the legitimacy of democracy assumes a degree of philosophical knowledge and sophistication that is quite unrealistic.[2] Most people, I believe, are unaware of the differences, say, between consequentialists and deontologists and would not be much concerned if they were. Further, the argument, if it proves anything, proves too much. It is common for philosophers to argue that the metaethical theories of certain other philosophers are invalid, while being in agreement with these philosophers on many, often most, matters of practical ethics. That is to say, they concur as to conclusions but not as to supporting arguments. But why, then, are the commonly held moral concepts like truth telling, promise keeping, and avoidance of harm to innocent people not facing a similar crisis, for in these cases, too, philosophers, while concurring in the result, differ sharply regarding their first principles? Fishkin's overkill is self-destructive.

More generally, are the political theories of philosophers determined by their metaethical theories? The evidence seems to support a negative answer to this query. Probably the most obvious example of common political conclusions (justifications) arrived at by theorists of differing ethical and metaethical persuasions is that of the justification of the coercive power of the state itself. Plato, Aristotle, Thrasymachus, Stoics, Epicureans, Church Fathers, St. Thomas, Hobbes, Locke, Rousseau, Bentham, Hegel – the roster of philosophers of widely diverging ethical theories all in agreement on justifying the coercive political power of the state goes on and on.[3]

When we turn from the justification of coercive government to that of particular forms of government, much the same situation prevails. Thinkers as far removed from each other with respect to metaethical beliefs as Thomas Aquinas and Thomas Hobbes support monarchy, whereas the utilitarian J. S. Mill and the neo-Hegelian T. H. Green find common ground in liberal democracy. The same is true of deontologists like John Rawls and Alan Gewirth, on the one hand, and utilitarians like Mill and R. M. Hare, on the other.

Incidentally, when it comes to questions of public policy, I do not claim that ethicists of all persuasions agree on such political issues as whether the state should permit women to have abortions at their discretion. What does seem to be true, however, is that they do not divide on this and other questions along the same lines that divide them with respect to ethical theory.

If, as I have been arguing, political philosophers' conclusions about political ethics are not dictated by their metaethical principles, what does determine them? Some would say that they are determined by their environment or their training, that insofar as they reflect rational processes at all, they are simply rationalizations. We need not decide to what extent this is true; I am concerned with what determines their *rational* thought.[4] It is my belief that the kinds of disagreements among thinking people we are here concerned about, especially as they apply to the justification of forms of government, generally arise out of differences as to matters of fact – generally quite complicated matters of fact. For instance, the question may be whether a much more steeply graduated income tax will so retard investment that the incomes of members of the most disadvantaged class will be reduced.[5] Another, and perhaps more important, complicated matter of fact has to do with human nature. Does political participation have the self-improving tendency that Mill supposed? If people enjoy the franchise, do they *enjoy* it? If they are denied it, do they suffer psychologically? Do people behave in the voting booth in the same way, vis-à-vis their self-interest, as they do in the marketplace? If they do, is this destructive of civic virtue? And so on. (It is worth noting that Fishkin's assumption, on which his conclusions depend, that the common person will be alienated by the discovery that philosophy does not give an unchallengeable justification for the form of government under which he is living, also rests upon a factual assumption, albeit one derived from survey data.)

Again, let us look at some particular political theorists. Consider, for instance, the question of why the form of government Plato advocated in *The Laws* was quite different from that outlined in *The Republic*. It was not that his metaethics had changed. Rather it was that (either because of the differing purposes of the two works or because his own views of the facts had changed) the assumptions he made about human nature in *The Laws* were different from those he made in *The Republic*. In the earlier discussion about those who support coercive government, no anarchists were named; but a glance at the basis of their position is highly instructive. Contrary to the others, they believe that human nature is such that people can live together, whether communally or in highly individualistic fashion, without being reduced to a war of all against all. It is this belief about a factual matter – what humans are like or can be made to be like – that accounts for, or at least provides their justification for, their belief in the feasibility and desirability of anarchy. Even the Church Fathers, departing from the communistic ideal of primitive Christianity, came to the conclusion that the Fall made reliance on political institutions a necessity for checking selfishness and concupiscence.

On examination, then, it appears that disagreements on matters involving political justification generally arise from differing views of the facts or divergent calculations of probable consequences. (The generality of this statement exceeds what can be proved in the available space, but I believe its validity will be evident to the informed reader, on reflection. In any case, as will be seen, my argument does not depend on its universality.) Even when, for instance, it appears that the argument is about the *meaning* of a key term, investigation generally reveals that it can be traced back to disagreement as to what will be the consequences of selecting this or that definition. Those who wish to define liberty narrowly, as absence of direct interference, tend to believe that, with a minimum of protection of life and property, the individual can do best for himself and for society by being left to his own devices; while those who would define this key concept in terms of enablements as well as protections doubt the validity of this factual proposition. Similarly, different concepts of equality can generally be reduced to divergent views of the facts. Some believe that legal equality is sufficient because the large amount of liberty it allows will so greatly increase production that even the least advantaged will be better off than they would be under another system. (This was Locke's belief, at least as far as concerned the move from primitive to more fully developed economies.) Others, unconvinced that this would be the case, believe that the relatively unchecked individual liberty would lead to gross inequalities of fortune that would themselves be unjust and, because of the power they gave to the rich, would result in exploitation of the weak.

The important point is that utilitarians can logically take either position; and the same is true of Rawlsian deontologists. Godwin's utilitarianism led him to a far different position than that of Jeremy Bentham. Hegel's followers divided sharply between the Right and the Left. Robert Paul Wolff, a Kantian deontologist, supports anarchism, in opposition to Kant himself as well as to most other deontologists. How much these differences owe to disagreements of a factual order and how much to varying ethical intuitions is impossible to say, but each pair of contrasting political–theoretical conclusions grew out of the same metaethical theory. And if the same metaethical theory leads philosophers to opposing political–theoretical conclusions, and if the same political–theoretical conclusions are grounded by various philosophers on opposing metaethical theories, how can it be argued that a political philosopher's conclusions are dictated by his metaethical beliefs?

Note that I say "dictated." Whether certain metaethical theories may *predispose* philosophers to accept one view of the facts of human nature rather than another is a different question from the one I have been discussing. It is *logical* connections with which I am concerned. Even regarding dispositions, however, it is worth noting that their common acceptance of radical individualism did not prevent Hobbes and Bentham from moving in opposite directions regarding the best form of government. Moreover, a holistic view of society in earlier periods seemed to favor nondemocratic forms (e.g., Hegel), whereas in more recent times a similar outlook as to the nature of the individual and society inspires Marxian and many other collectivists.

With these considerations in mind, let us turn to the question immediately at hand. In long-term perspective the justification of democracy seems less in need of discussion than ever before. Since the seventeenth century we have seen a complete reversal of attitudes toward this institution. As John Dunn has pointed out, even Leibniz, writing about the best form of government, declared that "today there is no principle so bad that it would not be better than to live in a democracy."[6] Today one can scarcely find a government that does not claim to be a democracy, with or without some qualifier, such as "people's." It is a universal term of approval. The first problem in justifying democracy, then, is to define what it is we are seeking to justify.

The general outline I shall follow, after dealing briefly with the definition of "democracy," is to discuss, in order, what I call "hybrid" justifications, my own justification of ideal democracy, an evaluation of formal democracy in the light of arguments that the linkage between it and the ideal is weak or nonexistent, and a conclusion.

2   Definition of democracy

The democracy I shall discuss is "political" democracy. It pertains to the government of a state, a polity. "Social democracy," "economic democracy," and the like are not my present concern. Democracy has two definitions, perhaps better conceived as two aspects of the same thing. First, it is a practice or method of government, a set of forms and procedures. Second, it relates to ends rather than means, to an ideal or set of ideals.

When the person in the street is asked what he thinks about democracy, I daresay the former is what comes to his mind. He, I believe, has in mind a form of government in which major policy decisions are made by office-holders selected by periodic popular elections or by persons subject to the control of those so elected. These elections must be open to participation by all adult citizens, barring those who have been legally adjudged insane or (possibly) who have committed infamous crimes. Further, each voter has one, and only one, vote; and the person or issue receiving the most votes wins (except that for certain purposes more than a bare majority may be required).[7] Refinements of this generally understood definition I shall abjure.

Some would leave the definition of democracy at this point, insisting that democracy is a form of government having nothing to do with aims.[8] But questions about what forms (fixed terms of office or not, for instance) and what procedures (absolute or qualified majority rule) are constantly arising; and the ensuing discussion is likely to take the form of an argument about what procedure is more "democratic." It is not a matter of what procedure more accurately fits the definition of "procedural democracy"; rather an appeal is being made to what that definition *ought* to be. We need, and in fact in common usage we assume, an "ideal" definition or aspect of democracy. This second concept refers to a government that not only is democratic in form and procedure but also has certain objectives or goals. It respects above all, equally, the autonomy and freedom (overlapping and integrally related concepts) of the individuals who comprise the state in question. Many things follow, including most of the rights included in our Bill of Rights; but I will not spell out this reasoning here. "Popular elections" plus "one person, one vote" implies majority rule in one sense – that of no rule over a majority by a minority – together with appropriate institutions to ensure that this requirement is met. (For instance, if votes are to be equal, they must not be coerced; voters must have freedom of expression and be free to organize; opponents of the party or parties in power must not be subject to arbitrary arrest; and so on.) The matter of extraordinary majorities is left open. Although I have ruled out social and economic democracy as part of the definition of democracy, I leave open the extent to which one or both is a necessary condition for its successful functioning, one that achieves some reasonable approximation to the ideal. It is implied in what has just been said, but it will do no harm to stress it, that what I am aiming to justify is liberal, constitutional democracy. I have no desire to justify every government that *claims* to be a democracy; nor do I attempt to justify government by the unconstrained rule of the majority.

3   Hybrid justifications

Consent

One of the most venerable justifications, still frequently heard, is that democracy rests on the "consent of the governed." As a major support, however, it does not hold water and is seldom advanced by those who have given the matter much thought. I shall deal with it briefly, and largely by raising questions that seem to indicate its vulnerability, without detailing the answers. How is this consent to be expressed? By voting? If so, does a vote against those in office count as support for the regime, the form of government? If so, how can we answer the charge that it might indicate only that the voter was expressing a desire above all to defeat the program of this government, while actually opposing the form of government as well?

Further, how many voters must freely express approval? A majority of those voting? Suppose only a minority of the enfranchised actually vote. Or suppose that in some way all are given an opportunity to vote for or against continuance of the democratic form of government, and only a plurality favors it, no majority favoring any particular form (which probably was the case, for instance, in Weimar Germany in its later days).

Still further, does it matter how a minority is being treated, or whether many members of the minority feel sufficient opposition to the regime to resort to guerrilla warfare?

The preceding neither fully explores the question of what constitutes *free* consent, nor denies that if I freely consent to something I incur an obligation. The most that could be said on the positive side of the original proposition, it appears, is that, *other things being equal*, a government that is clearly consented to by a majority, or at least a plurality, of eligible voters has a weak prima facie claim to the allegiance of all.[9]

Peaceful change

Let us turn, then, to the more sophisticated and more plausible claim that democracy provides the only known method for achieving peaceful change, an idea often expressed by the statement that it substitutes ballots for bullets. Hayek espouses this position, saying that "it is the only convention we have yet discovered to make peaceful change possible."[10] Hayek does not rely solely, for his defense of democracy, on the proposition quoted here. That statement was preceded in his text by the claim that "the true value of democracy is to serve as a sanitary precaution protecting us against an abuse of power."[11] This much sounder proposition will be discussed later.[12] That democracy does normally have the highly desirable effect of enabling peaceful change, at least in well-established democracies, is true and constitutes a strong argument for it. But the case of the Soviet Union, and even that of China, raises serious doubts about the contention that a free election is the *only* way to bring about a peaceful change of regime, although where the conditions for democracy prevail it is certainly the most likely one. Even countries lacking democratic institutions sometimes shift peaceably to democratic regimes, as in the cases of Spain and Portugal in recent times. Moreover, coups d' état often involve little or no violence. Finally, civil wars break out in democracies, as our own case illustrates.

Not only is the linkage between democracy and peaceful change less complete than Hayek would have it, but the argument also assumes that resort to violence to bring about change is always worse than any injustice or harm that might occur under democratic forms and procedures. To say the least, this assumption is highly questionable. In short, the argument provides some support for democracy, but it cannot claim to be a sufficient justification for it.

Fairness

The argument is sometimes made that democracy is justified because it is fair. But a fair procedure may yield bad results. It may be fair to treat preferences equally, but as Nelson remarks, not all preferences are good.[13] From this fact one might conclude, as Nelson does, that the use of fair procedures cannot be a sufficient condition for a good government; but, if only because governmental procedures will not gain legitimacy unless they are *seen* to be just, procedural *un*fairness would be a weighty negative consideration in the evaluation of any form of government. Belief in the fundamental fairness of a regime's forms and procedures goes a long way toward producing that emotional attachment without which no government is likely to endure in the face of inevitable vicissitudes.

Not only this. It is right, within limits, that procedural fairness should command our loyalty to the resulting decisions regardless of their merits. Contrary to what has sometimes been argued, this is not paradoxical. Any decision arrived at by a fair procedure creates a prima facie obligation to obey it. That does not mean that the decision is right, but only that one ought to obey it ceteris paribus. If the decision is fundamentally wrong, if, for example, it commands me to kill an innocent person (in a civilian context), it may be my right, indeed my duty, to disobey it.

What is a "fair" procedure depends upon the context. Flipping a coin is a fair means of settling some questions, but certainly not all. The determination of what procedure is fair in a given context entails an evaluation of the context, including the purposes in view. (Should a judge decide whether to sentence a person convicted of murder to death or to life imprisonment by flipping a coin?) The context by which the fairness of governmental procedures should be judged involves an evaluation of the *ends* to be achieved, including the recognition of fundamental rights.

4   The justification of "ideal" democracy

I call the justifications discussed in the preceding section "hybrid" because they combine justification of democratic ideals (ends) with that of democratic forms (means). The justification of democracy appears to me to be a more manageable task if one separates the case for the democratic ideal from the argument for the institutions of formal democracy as the best way to realize that ideal. Let me consider first, then, the justification of the democratic ideal.

Human nature

The life and welfare of its inhabitants must be the starting point for the justification of democracy, as of any form of government. It exists for the good of humankind (that portion of humankind that falls within the state's jurisdiction); not humankind for the good of the state. *Why?*

What is this "humankind?" Certain minimum assumptions may be specified. They are, I believe, hardly controversial; but they are fundamental to the subsequent argument. Humans are rational animals. They can think inductively and deductively; they can conceptualize and formulate abstractions; they can envisage consequences, both by calculation and by reference to experience; they can deliberate, make choices and decisions, and act accordingly.

The rational beings that can do these things are said to be "autonomous" or, more precisely, capable of autonomy in the absence of overriding coercion. Their actions respond to their desires, aversions, hopes, fears, goals, and the like, to their ideas, however formed, and to their determination, after some calculation and reflection, to act in a certain way. Action from this process of reasoning, as distinct from reflexive, thoughtless, or coerced behavior, is what I am calling "autonomous" – a widely accepted usage. If one wishes to say simply that one of the distinctive features of rational beings is that they act from *reasons*, that makes my point. How this fact relates to the philosophical controversy over free will and determinism need not concern us here. The democrat does not deny that human beings are subject to external causes; that would be absurd. The claim that humans are autonomous does mean that the processes enumerated above mediate the lines of causation that affect them and are typically transformed in the process. We speak of the result as an act of "will."

Not only are human beings rational and capable of autonomous action; they are also moral, in the sense that they have the capacity and the tendency to develop ideas of the way they and others ought to behave – a morality, including a sense of justice, a belief in a kind of equality.[14]

Humans also have needs, psychological as well as physical. The former include psychological security, a sense of identity, and a desire for some control over events. For the last one in particular, they require freedom, just as they do for autonomy. For a sense of identity they also need a feeling of accomplishment through both competitive and cooperative activity. Finally, human beings are social animals. They achieve their self-consciousness and their sense of identity in, and because of, society. They are happy in society, other things being equal, and unhappy without it. Ostracism is a dreaded form of punishment. As an individual values his self, so he values these fundamental characteristics and strives for and values institutions that tend to preserve and promote them. At certain stages of societal development a minimum of physical security is the dominant need, for which a nearly absolute form of government may be a necessity. But when more favorable conditions prevail and when absolute government rules arbitrarily, oppressively, and in other ways contrary to the needs and desires inherent in human nature, claims for greater freedom and justice develop and usually eventuate in a struggle for their attainment.[15] The demand for individual as well as group autonomy is at least implied at an early date, as is exemplified by such statements as those of Pericles (as recorded by Thucydides) and Col. Rainborough.[16]

It is upon these facts of human rationality, autonomy, and the other characteristics mentioned earlier that the democratic ideal is justified. For democrats they provide the starting place. The intervening linkage between these facts and the moral claim of right may be variously supplied by the will of God, self-evidence, intuition, contract, what rational persons would agree to, utility, or whatever. My own reasoning in making this move from fact to value will be set forth in the following paragraphs.

The relation of ideal democracy to individualism

Before dealing directly with the question of why we should place a high value on the democratic ideal, however, it will be helpful to say a word about its relation to individualism. Whether democracy as here defined is "individualistic" calls for consideration partly because individualism is today under attack and, even more, because addressing this question will cast further light upon the nature and justification of the democratic ideal. It is important to be extremely careful about the use of the term "individualism." Often it is identified with an atomistic concept of the individual – with "economic" man or with Hobbesian "political" man. We need not become involved in a debate over the definition. We need consider only certain democratic propositions, without reference to whether they add up to something tagged "individualism." The first of these is that the democratic ideal places an extremely high value on the life and well-being of all individual human beings. It holds that no individual's life or well-being should be sacrificed for the sake of others, living or yet to be born, without some powerful justification. (Some may hold that life, as contrasted with well-being, should *never* be sacrificed for the sake of others. Liberals are doubtless divided on this question, depending, for instance, on whether they would, under any circumstances, countenance capital punishment or compulsory military service; or on the question of whether cannibalism is justified when it is clearly the only alternative to the starvation of all who share their predicament.)

In speaking of both life and well-being, I am embracing a continuum that extends from the loss of life through many intermediate points to some loss of liberty, enjoyment, or opportunity for the development of the self. (The last of these values, self-development, is one to which I shall return at a later stage.) It is also arguable (*pace* Rawls) that in considering what is a sufficient justification one must take account of the number of potential winners and losers as well as the likelihood that the consequences envisaged will actually occur. We are inevitably dealing here with matters of degree.

The supreme value that democracy places on individual autonomy, thriving, and all that contributes to a person's well-being is fundamental. Without autonomy the individual is degraded. An individual capable of autonomous behavior, and aware of that fact, possesses something of great intrinsic value. It is good in and of itself. As one writer has aptly described it, following Brandt, it is like the rapturous joy of a child swinging.[17] (This is by no means to deny that it is also instrumental, making our lives "our own" and being conducive to self-esteem. Nor is it to deny that autonomy may be exercised in evil ways, even in ways so evil that the disvalue they cause exceeds their value.)

Critics of liberal democracy sometimes attack its ideal of individual autonomy as nonexistent and unattainable, because the reigning ideology in a person's society determines his values, and any notion he may have of his own self-determination comes under the heading of "false-conscious- *can you say "exist"?* ness."[18] A full rebuttal of this argument would take me far beyond the limits of this essay. The chief point to be noted, however, in addition to what has already been said about autonomy, is that the influence of conditioning factors is by no means denied, but that to hold that these factors eliminate all individual autonomy is a self-defeating argument, *Thank you JRP (* undermining the foundation of all rational discourse.[19]

It is also argued that liberal democratic theory errs in placing the individual at the center of its value system, on the ground that the individual is a creation of society. Liberal democratic theory holds that the value of society or of community is not a thing in itself apart from the individuals that compose the entity in question. Of course, any community has value for each of its members; and in fact the individual is in large measure what he is because he lives in society and because of the nature of the society in which he lives. The perceived value of his society may be an important part of a person's self. He may feel fulfilled in contributing to it; he may wish to "sacrifice" his own (narrowly conceived) interests for it. He may take an interest in its continuance and its quality beyond his own lifetime; but it is *his* interest. That is all that I mean. I call it "basic individualism," but the tag is unimportant. What is important is that the individual whose liberty, well-being, and further development are the objects of democracy's concern is the individual as he is – not the individual as he may have been at some prior period, and not an imagined, atomistic individual, untouched by those around him and unconcerned for their welfare.

Finally, with respect to the individualism of the democratic ideal, the theory embodies a strong (but sometimes overstated) presumption in favor of each individual's judgment about what contributes to his well-being. Three reasons support this presumption. First, there is the old "shoe-pinches" argument: We can know our own feelings, our states of mind, our "well-being," indeed the way no one else can. Second, making choices contributes to our development and our sense of being real persons. (Of course, our decisions may prove to be mistaken, in which case they at least contribute to our education.) Third, democrats trust the individual because of a strong *dis*trust of what others will decide when they are in positions of unchecked power. It is important to note that all three of these aspects of individualism are related to, indeed are dependent upon, the most fundamental element of democratic theory: the rationality and autonomy of the individual, as defined earlier.

Implications: liberty and equality

Two of the most fundamental elements of the democratic credo are liberty and equality. Autonomy itself entails liberty, both political and civil, at the same time that in another sense it flows from liberty. Without the capacity (liberty) to take purposive action, individuals could not be autonomous; but if outside forces prevent this capacity from being exercised – if those who have the capacity are coerced into making decisions they cannot feel are their own – their autonomy and freedom are diminished. This includes their freedom to decide that certain areas of their lives should be free of intrusion – in short, their privacy.[20] In the absence of a large measure of liberty the capacity of the individual to develop his distinctively human capacities would be virtually nullified. J. R. Lucas has put it well:

Freedom is a necessary condition of rationality, of action, of achievement. Not to be free is to be frustrated, impotent, futile. To be free is to be able to shape the future, to be able to translate one's ideals into reality, to actualize one's potentialities as a person. Not to be free is not to be responsible, not to be able to be responsive, not to be human. Freedom is a good, if anything is.[21] Without liberty the high value placed on the individual would be a mockery.

Equality. It is not just certain individuals or certain kinds or classes of individuals on which democracy sets the highest value; it is the individual person per se. Of course, this does not mean that all individuals must be treated alike. It does mean, however, that their dignity would be violated if they were treated unequally without justification, that is to say in a way that failed to show equal concern for their claims to liberty, justice, and well-being. In short, as rational beings capable of autonomous action and of indefinite self-development, they are entitled to equal consideration. Like should be treated alike, similars similarly. Discrimination is invidious unless it passes a severe test. The presumption is always against it and in favor of equality. I call this the principle of "presumptive equality." The equality of the vote, the hallmark of democracy, is so not only because it gives each citizen, equally, a substantive power with which to protect and advance his interests, but also, perhaps preeminently, because it symbolizes that equality of respect to which each individual is entitled. People who are denied political equality, symbolized by the vote, feel themselves second-class citizens and tend to be treated as such.[22]

Whether symbolic equality and equal suffrage are enough to meet the test of the democratic ideal or whether that ideal demands that each citizen's *substantive* political power be as nearly equal to that of every other citizen as is possible (requiring equality of resources) is a hotly contested point. If the consequence of such egalitarianism were to diminish production to the extent that even the least advantaged would be made worse off, it is doubtful whether anyone would support it as a requirement of the democratic ideal. At the other extreme, if the result were to make everyone better off, it would probably be a generally acceptable ideal, although this is less certain. Philosophers who hold that desert (perhaps measured by effort) should be rewarded might feel it unjust; so also might those who believe that *relative* equality is what counts, if in fact the gap between rich and poor were increased. In these hypothetical situations, what is at stake is not whether formal democracy is in principle justifiable; rather it is the extent to which the democratic ideal demands that it minimize economic inequality.

Caveats

Certain caveats are called for at this point. The theory defended here does not hold that human nature is fixed, the same everywhere and for all time, except within broad limits (e.g., limited altruism). Presumably, however, these broad limits are sufficient to avoid the "lapse into arbitrariness," that, it is alleged, "the deontological self is unable to avoid" because it admits of no "constitutive attachments," no "relative fixity of character" prior to the individual's freedom to construct his own moral principles.[23] To be sure, it may come to pass that bioengineering will abolish even those limits, but I will not explore the problems with which that eventuality would present us.

Also, basic individualism does not require either capitalism or the maximum use of the market, although it is arguable that these institutions are essential to the effective functioning of democracy or even to its preservation. It may also be contended that some of the same considerations that justify liberal democracy also support capitalism and maximum use of the market system; and this position may be used either to support the latter or to condemn *liberal* democracy. Neither conclusion follows as a matter of logic. These are matters to be settled by investigation, calculation, and experience.

5   Relation of formal to ideal democracy

The ideals of democracy are fine, it may be said, but what assurance do we have that the institutions of liberal democracy will be an effective vehicle for realizing them? Here we are inevitably involved in the calculation of probabilities rather than with proofs of necessary connection, or inevitabilities. I shall turn immediately to consideration of one of the most serious challenges that has been advanced against the proposition that democratic voting has or can have the desired result.

Voting: crucial link between practice and ideal

The most fundamental procedure of democracy is that of majority rule as defined earlier. The subject is the principal focus of other chapters in this volume; but it is so central to democracy and has been subjected to so much critical analysis that no justification of democracy worthy of the name can escape discussion of it, however condensed. A host of writers, beginning in the modern period with Duncan Black and Kenneth Arrow, have shown that majority rule, contrary to the assumptions of early and possibly many current democratic theorists, has been unable to solve the problem of aggregating preferences. This is a matter of logic.[24]

It might seem to follow that the concept of ideal democracy cannot embody or justify this procedural principle as the normal method for determining all major policies,[25] although – and this is extremely important – it would remain a crucial means for providing equal consideration for all persons and their preferences. But William Riker takes a different line. He concludes that (1) populism (the theory that all decisions should be made in accordance with unconstrained majority preference) is logically impossible, and (2) liberalism (and therefore liberal democracy) requires only that the negative vote of a majority may *possibly* (not necessarily) bring about the defeat of an official or policy of whom (or of which) they disapprove.[26]

I believe that more can be said for liberal democracy within the limitations Riker outlines. First, anyone who gives much thought to the effect of voting (actual or prospective) on Presidents Johnson and Nixon must have a clearer and more positive comprehension (from the point of view of linkage between public perception and political effect) of what the defeat of the abuse of power, or of what has come to be thought of as an evil policy, may mean. A second approach is to take another look at the effects of the instability to which majority rule – and perhaps any alternative voting system – is subject. How serious are the probable consequences? One answer appears to be that they may even be good. In the case of voting in a legislature, where the situation is most likely to be found, various practical constraints (rules, time, weariness, etc.) bring the matter to a halt, sooner or later. Where it stops may indeed be accidental or the result of manipulation. But, especially if one group of losers cares about the matter with an intensity that was not reflected in the outcome, this result need not be final. It may rather be the prelude to a period of persuasion, maneuvering, and regrouping that leads to an eventual modification or reversal of the original policy decision. The fact that this can and sometimes does happen gives support to the belief that the technical instability of rational decision making may in fact lead to support for long-run political stability.[27]

Another point may be even more persuasive. It is that legislation that was feared by certain groups often turns out not to be so harmful to them as they had anticipated. Possibly they had miscalculated; or the law may have been administered in such a way as to protect or foster their interests. In short, it is by no means clear that the logical possibility of cyclical majorities means that the use of majority rule to implement the democratic ideal need be destructive of the latter or of the stability of the regime that is committed to that ideal.

A more fundamental approach, however, is to attack Riker's positivistic assumptions. Before considering this line of reasoning, I must make a few remarks about another and different attack, also coming from social-choice theory. I refer to the arguments propounded by Geoffrey Brennan and Loren E. Lomasky in their essay in this volume (Chapter 2). Their argument is of a different order from that of most of what has been written on this aspect of the subject. They do not concentrate on the frustrating problem of the aggregation of preferences (as expressed by votes). Their chief concern relates to an earlier stage of the political process: behavior in the voting booth. This conduct, they argue, may be selfish, altruistic, or duty-bound, but the rational actor perceives it to be inconsequential. For this Schumpeterian conclusion they provide an elegant mathematical demonstration. It follows that the ballots cannot be assumed to represent deep convictions. Essentially, as Brennan and Lomasky put it, the problem with the elective process is the separation of cost from outcome.

This position has great merit and, as the authors suggest, probably has more practical significance than the problem of cycling. Certain points, however, may be suggested by way of qualification or addition. First, making the economist's assumption of individualistic rational behavior, it is not in all situations true, even with a large number of voters, that, when it is a question of apportioning costs and benefits, the aggregation of votes leads to antisocial results. When the costs will obviously fall upon the beneficiaries, voters' calculations of costs and benefits will not lead them to the support of economically unjustified expenditures. In other words, when costs and benefits are both particularized and fall on the same group or groups, individualistic rationality does not lead to social irrationality. Whenever an activity is to be supported by user costs – as exemplified by toll roads and national parks if user fees cover the costs – this situation prevails. Much special-district legislation also falls in this category.[28] In many situations too the costs and benefits are both generalized. If they are spread more or less equally – expenditure for national and personal security is an example – it may again be true that voting is not biased against the general interest, or is only moderately so.[29]

My second point is simply to emphasize, perhaps to give greater weight to, a consideration that Brennan and Lomasky also take into account. The rational individualist (according to the "economic" mode of reasoning) would not vote. The probability of his vote determining the outcome is miniscule, much too small to equal the cost of taking the time to vote, let alone trying to learn enough about the candidates and issues to know how he *should,* by any standard, cast his ballot. Of course, not all individuals may consider these items "costs." In fact, many people do vote, for one reason or another. Many feel that they *should* vote – that, as Brennan and Lomasky say, it is their "civic duty" to do so. And, I would hazard, they feel this way because they believe (perhaps because of the way they have been brought up) that they should not behave in a manner that would be seriously harmful to society *if everyone did likewise.* This (Kantian, if you like) argument appears to me to have considerable effect both in leading people to vote and in determining how they should vote. It may be derivative of the "you-wouldn't-like-it-if-Johnny-did-that-to-you,-would-you?" line of reasoning that most of us have encountered in our childhood. Or it may be that a sense of fairness, of not letting the side down, makes one feel a moral compulsion to vote one's convictions and one's known preferences, regardless of a recognition that it is a hopeless cause. In any case, however derived, common observation attests to the effectiveness of *some* kind of moral motivation. I offer this not only as a partial explanation of why people do vote but also as a qualification of the Brennan–Lomasky demonstration that "between altruism and malice, democratic procedures differentially favor the latter."[30]

Further, I would suggest that the economist's rationality, even as Brennan and Lomasky modify it, tends to omit or underrate an important segment of human behavior. And it does so in a way that also distinguishes between market behavior and voting behavior, but in the opposite direction from that of the economist's assumption. The ethical environment of public actions, including voting, is different from that of private actions – less so than I would like, but still, I believe, significantly so. Market theory holds that each person is out to get the most for the least; and we feel nothing wrong about behaving accordingly. Even socialists and communists in capitalist countries can and do justify their own market-type behavior as long as they are in a market society. On the other hand, not all the rhetoric in discussion about the commonwealth that is cast in terms of the public interest or welfare is fraudulent or hypocritical. Individuals in society do have concern for their society. Moreover, when it comes to outward-oriented, altruistic behavior, the public arena has a distinct advantage over the private one. Even in the private arena, many people respond to appeals to contribute of their substance to the welfare of others whose need is greater than their own. But one would expect their willingness to do this to be greater if they knew that others were going to do likewise rather than to be free riders on the contributions of the more public spirited. Thus, other things being equal, they would be more willing to vote for a public (governmental) grant that would cost them $100 than to make an equal private donation.[31]

What weight should be given to these qualitative considerations I am in no position to say. I wish primarily to call attention to them. My own belief is that they are of sufficient importance to blunt the edge of the Brennan–Lomasky knife, to prevent it from *completely* severing the linkage between voting and significant achievement of democratic ideals.

In view of the fact that Brennan and Lomasky go on to maintain that, when decisions must be made collectively, voting may be the best procedure, since any alternative would give an advantage to "some self-serving elite,"[32] this may be not so much a qualification of their argument as a reinforcement of one aspect of it.[33]

Now I return to the alternative line of reasoning I referred to before considering the Brennan–Lomasky thesis. This consists of a criticism of the positivism underlying Arrow's famous theorem. That theorem consists of a series of propositions each of which is claimed to be intuitively reasonable and essential to the majority-rule principle, but which taken together are logically incompatible. Hence, the "paradox of voting." One of these propositions, as interpreted by Amartya Sen, is the rule of Unrestricted Domain. In Sen's words, that rule reads, "Every logically possible set of individual orderings is included in the domain of the collective choice rule."[34] As Sen points out, this rule is incompatible with "even minimal liberalism." Since Arrow's rules embody and rely upon the Pareto principle, it is that principle with which liberal values have been found to conflict.[35] In short, that principle comes into conflict with such liberal democratic values as freedom of expression, freedom to organize political parties, freedom from arbitrary arrest and detention, and fair trial. It clashes with liberal *democratic* values because these provisions are essential to the protection and implementation of democracy itself. Not just freedom but equality would be endangered, for if these rights are not protected they may be permitted to some and denied to others. This points to Riker's conclusion that populist democracy (unrestricted majority rule) is a logical impossibility. Riker's reaction to this problem is to redefine liberalism in such a way as to make it compatible with at least part of what the liberal democrat wants, while at the same time jettisoning populist democracy. His unstated reason for taking this course is to preserve his purely positivistic method, refusing to make normative judgments, and relying on the Pareto principle in order to avoid the necessity of making interpersonal comparisons. Another possible way of treating the problem is to retain liberal democratic theory as previously understood and jettison both populism *and* positivism.

One trouble with positivism arises out of its tendency to identify rationality with self-interested conduct.[36] When, to avoid this unrealistic, self-directed narrowness, all preferences, self-directed or other-directed, are included in the concept of rationality, it tends to lose all usefulness for either prediction or understanding, beyond what is available to common sense. This is especially true, if, contrary to usage, it includes among preferences duties, obligations, our sense of moral responsibility. It seems plausible on the basis of common experience, as was suggested earlier, that our marketplace behavior and our public behavior tend to be divided along these lines, with self-interest almost monopolizing the former, with goodly amounts of altruism and sense of duty prevailing in the latter. To this we may add the proposition that our sense of moral responsibility to the public is greatly enhanced if we feel ourselves a contributing part of the public.[37] Jettisoning both populism and exclusive reliance on positivism may be arrived at in other ways, as their conflict with various liberal rights calls to mind. Liberal democratic theory and constitutionalist theory have always incorporated a (normative) theory of rights. I will not now embark upon a justification either of rights in general or of the specific fundamental rights embodied in liberal democracy, except to note, importantly, that they may all be derived from the democratic ideal, from the individual's entitlement to autonomy, liberty, and equality. That the institutional counterpart (formal, procedural democracy) of the democratic ideal must include the assurance of these rights is basic to its justification. They are as essential to equality as they are to liberty.

The statement just made calls for this qualification: What in the final analysis is critical is the *behavior* of governments, not their institutional arrangements. The United Kingdom is a classic example of a government lacking a written constitution, with minimal institutional protections of liberal rights, that yet has maintained an enviable record of respecting liberal rights.[38] In contrast, many regimes, democratic and otherwise, have admirable bills of rights but pay scant regard to them. All of this reminds us of Rousseau's assertion that the constitution that counts is the one that is written in the hearts of the citizens.

Finally, in this connection, it might be argued that setting apart fundamental rights, giving them special protection from majorities, does not completely solve the problem. Other policy decisions would presumably still be made by majorities and thus be subject to the irrationality of the voting paradox. The first point made earlier (regarding positivism's tendency to rely on an assumption of narrowly self-interested behavior) spoke to this concern at least in some measure, but I believe more may be said.

As has been shown by Miss Anscombe and is also stated by Riker, the problem of the voting paradox is not specific to any voting system or indeed to democracy. It applies even to a benevolent despot.[39] This fact might seem to be a sufficient answer to the objection; but though it refutes a claim, on this ground, that any other form of government is superior to democracy, it fails to get to the heart of the matter. The voting paradox, since it points to a problem that characterizes *any* method for aggregating preferences by *any* form of government, does not invalidate the case for democracy; but neither does it validate it. For that we must look to other considerations. In part, that has already been done by reference to democracy's institutionalized protections of autonomy, liberty, and equal respect. Partly, too, Brennan and Lomasky's argument that any alternative to majority rule gives power to a self-interested elite is much to the point here. In part, still other reasons apply. They will be discussed in the next section.

Other considerations

Do democratic institutions in fact protect individual autonomy and liberty more effectively than do other types of political organization? In part, the answer is definitional. If the forms of democracy are a mere façade, existing on paper but not being put into effect, if, that is to say, they are not *working* institutions, they are not worthy of the name. We speak of countries with such institutions as democracies only in quotation marks, or as "so-called" democracies.

Empirical evidence

Beyond this, we can appeal to empirical evidence. Probably little more than common observation is needed. Is respect for individual liberty and political equality more widely experienced in countries that enjoy democracy as we have defined it, or among those that do not meet this test? But we can do better than this. Freedom House, a widely respected organization whose concern is announced by its title, monitors freedom throughout the world and publishes its findings in *Freedom at Issue*. Some of its most recent findings are tabulated in the following fashion. One hundred and sixty-seven states are classified as to whether or not they have a political party system, and if so whether it is a one-party, dominant-party, or multiparty (competitive) system. Each is given a rating of from 1 to 7 with respect to "political rights" and likewise with respect to "civil rights." These states are then categorized as "free," "partly free," or "not free." These are rough summary terms used to cluster much finer gradations of "freedom." "Freedom" itself is a term that includes both "civil liberties" and "political rights," the latter defined to entail a "fully competitive electoral process" and clear rule by those elected. The factor of "political rights" is also graded so as to take account of the "effective equality of the process."[40] Of the sixty-nine states with multiparty systems, fifty-six are classified as "free" and thirteen as "partly free." Of the nineteen "dominant-party" system states, eighteen are partly free and one not free. The remaining seventy-nine states, either one-party or nonparty, include three that are free (Kiribati, Tuvalu, and Nauru, both nonparty, nonmilitary), twenty-four partly free (most of which fall in the nonparty category), and fifty-two nonfree.[41]

Causal relationship

The correlation between the elements of liberal democratic institutions and the democratic ideal certainly suggests a strong linkage. But, it may be asked, are these institutions the causal factors, or are they merely reflections of the firm public regard for democratic ideals that characterizes the countries in question? Space does not permit even a summary of the work that has been done on this difficult question. It is notable, however, that where dominant groups of people have this respect for liberal ideals it is to the institutions of liberal democracy that they turn when attempting to embody their ideals in a framework that will effectively implement them. And they make use of them. Two striking instances in recent American history strongly suggest that an institution such as our Supreme Court may be particularly important for advancing democratic ideals. I refer to the *Brown* case, the culmination of a series of decisions leading up to it and serving to educate the country on the implications of democratic rule, which played a key role in the battle against racial segregation. My second instance, also a Supreme Court decision, is that of the establishment of the principle that legislative apportionment must give substance to the rule of one person, one vote.[42] I select these examples among many because in them the Court so clearly played a leading, not just a reflecting, role. Moreover, whatever one may think of certain recent judicial trends, a reversal of those two decisions and the changes they brought about is practically inconceivable.

It will be noted that both of my examples involve the Supreme Court, an institution that is often said to be undemocratic. My selection was deliberate. These decisions demonstrate what no democrat should forget: that without institutions not themselves easily subjected to popular control, effective popular control may suffer.[43]

Legitimacy

To be generally accepted as fair, just, or otherwise good, though not a sufficient justification for a governmental procedure, is nonetheless essential for it's justifiability. The idea that a majority rather than a minority should govern, in the circumstances appropriate for making a decision, provides major support for the acceptance as right – support for the legitimacy of – a regime adopting that principle. That this is so today derives partly from tradition and partly from what appears to most people to be intuitively obvious. Insofar as it is the latter it foreshadows the second point I would make: Rule by the majority, more precisely the denial of minority rule over a majority, constitutes a recognition, an acceptance, and an implementation of the individual's autonomy, of his equal right to exert that autonomy.

A further consideration in this connection is that the process of voting and all the campaigning, debate, and so on that go with it – whether it be voting for representatives or voting in the representative body – permits and encourages the exercise of free speech and of cooperative activity aimed at the accomplishment of political purposes.[44] It both provides an opportunity for the exercise of autonomy and does so in a situation that strengthens the linkage between that exercise and the realization of informed voter preferences. Voting that violated the equality principle would of course be contrary to the democratic ideal itself.

Individual development

It is true, then, that the liberal element in democracy insists on protections for the individual beyond that of the franchise. The vote is arguably the most important single protection the individual citizen of a democracy possesses; but it is not enough. Majorities may tyrannize. However, the franchise contributes to another virtue of democracy (although it does not monopolize this contribution): the development of the individual. Only as they develop their powers, their capacities, do individuals become self-respecting and happy. Here, as elsewhere, liberal democratic theory depends upon a theory of human nature. In this case, the element of human nature in question is what Rawls has called the "Aristotelian Principle."[45] It holds that people enjoy the exercise of their realized capacities increasingly as the capacities are developed or become more complex. This principle has played an important role in all liberal democratic theory at least from the time of J. S. Mill.[46] It plays that role in two different ways, one relating to the procedural aspect of democracy and the other to its ideal or substantive aspect. A few words about each are in order.

The procedural aspect relates to the franchise. It is Mill's well-known argument and need not be treated at length here. In thinking about how to cast their ballots, citizens are compelled to exercise their intellectual faculties (and thus to develop them) and are at least encouraged to consider their personal interests in the context of the public interest, not just because this is what in theory they are supposed to do, but because their votes are more likely to be effective if they coincide with a general interest which a majority of voters are likely, by the same reasoning, to adopt.

Against this line of argument it is often objected that, whatever may have been true in Mill's time, today the thought of being less than one-hundred-millionth of a sovereign gives little encouragement to either thought or sympathy. Political apathy in the United States, as measured by nonvoting, appears to support this contention. However, even if only half of the eligible voters freely cast their ballots in competitive elections, that is a substantial improvement over the nondemocratic alternatives. Also, many citizens today are members of organizations that are to various degrees politically oriented. Insofar as they participate in the activities of these organizations, they are likely to experience the same kinds of effects that Mill attributed to the exercise of the franchise itself. Moreover, they will be bombarded by these organizations with arguments about how they should vote, write to their representatives, and so forth. The result is that these citizens will be encouraged to vote, for two reasons: (1) because they have more clearly articulated arguments for supporting certain policies and (2) because they have grounds to believe that they will not be a voice crying in the wilderness but will be joining in a cooperative endeavor with many others, an endeavor that is pleasurable in itself, while increasing the chances of success.

Substantively, and perhaps more importantly, liberal democracy contributes to the development of the individual's capacities. Here I have in mind not just specific liberal rights, such as that of freedom of expression and association and the right to privacy, but also the general priority given to liberty – not an absolute priority, of course, but a presumption. Many specific rights, not normally enumerated in constitutions, fall under this heading: for instance, rights to choose a mate, to enter an occupation (subject to certain regulations), to move about freely, and to make enforceable contracts. Belief that these opportunities will, on balance, lead to personal development and not simply to romantic posturing or whimsical acting on impulse depends again on the Aristotelian Principle. Further, the development of complex capacities is normally enhanced by, if not completely dependent upon, being part of a cooperative, harmonious society. Thus, the socializing effect that Mill attributed to the franchise is also and perhaps more significantly produced by the substantive liberties fostered by democracy.

Policy outcomes

Not all, but most, of what has been written here about the arguments in favor of democracy relates directly to the individual. What about the society as a whole, the quality of governmental outputs? It would be wrong to make this contrast too sharp, for what harms or helps the one does likewise for the other; but it is worth emphasizing that, as political participation contributes to the intellectual and moral development of citizens, it tends to improve the quality of governmental output. What is valuable, to be sure, is not just *any* participation – for example, voting – but discussion, debate, organization for political purposes, and all that contributes both to the education of citizens concerning the issues surrounding policy decisions and to voter influence on policy.

Something more than the Millean argument is relevant here – something that does more than educate and broaden the sympathies of the individual. This is Rousseau's contention that when the individual is placed in a position where he must persuade others of the rightfulness of his cause, whatever it may be, he must appeal to a broad, general interest if he expects to gain a wide following. In fact, if his motive is simply concern for his reputation, the same logic applies – assuming in this as in the previous case that he is "clear-sighted."[47] Nor is consideration of the general interest prompted only by the necessity for winning widespread support. Real concern for the welfare of a community or a state, either as a matter of morality or as one of sympathy, is a fact of life that any thinking person must recognize, while at the same time realizing that it is by no means universal and that it varies greatly in degree from one person to another.

A related but distinct line of reasoning deriving from Rousseau is that arguments rationally related to a visible public welfare reinforce each other, whereas those that are fallacious, used to support differing private interests, tend to cancel each other out. No unifying force, such as concern for the general interest, serves to pull them together.[48]

Further support for the normal democratic use of the majority principle may be derived from probability theory. It requires the assumption that the average voter or legislator is more likely to be right than wrong, as judged by the public interest. If we assume further that errors, ignorance, and self-interest are as likely, on the average, to influence his vote in one direction as the other, then even a modicum of knowledge, understanding, and concern for the public welfare will do the trick. (Clearly this assumption, if valid at all, as I believe it is, would apply only to the long run – and thus especially to constitution makers – not to each particular decision.) With a body of 100 individuals, each of whom is likely to be right (or more nearly right than wrong) 51 percent of the time, it follows that a 51 percent majority of the vote has a 51.99 percent chance of being right and a 60 percent majority will be right 69 percent of the time. With 10,000 voters, the probability of 51 percent being right rises to 99.97 percent![49]

6   In conclusion

My thesis has been that the democratic ideal is justified as an ideal and that democratic institutions (forms and procedures) are justified because they normally realize that ideal to a greater degree than would any known alternative form of government. (The ideal, of course, includes such conditions for its realization as the provision for peaceful change and the avoidance of extreme abuse of power.) The probability referred to assumes that the conditions for democracy (not discussed here) are reasonably approximated. This makes the justification of any particular regime contingent. The contingency relates to numerous economic, historical, and political–cultural considerations, which, taken together, normally determine whether a democratic regime can be sustained.

Certain implications of these statements should be made explicit. Questions of judgment are inescapable. To what degree is respect for persons upheld? How complete is political equality? How probable is it that a change of form or procedure would improve the situation? It must be borne in mind, too, that our subject is the justification of democracy, a form of government and its ideal, not particular policies. And, finally, "justification" is not identical to "obligation to obey." One may be obligated to obey an unjust government, for instance, if the likely alternative would be even more unjust.

These matters of contingency and probability are not matters for which the democrat need apologize. They would apply as well to the justification of most, if not all, human institutions.

In addition to the Liberty Fund, which supported the conference from which this essay derives, I thank the editors of this volume as well as anonymous reviewers for Cambridge University Press for helpful criticisms. I owe a similar debt to John W. Chapman and Charles R. Beitz, both of whom made useful suggestions regarding an earlier version of this chapter.

The opening section, "Political Theory and Metaethics," is reprinted almost verbatim by permission of New York University Press from my contribution to *Justification in Ethics, Law, and Politics,* NOMOS 28, pp. 291–6, edited by J. Roland Pennock and John W. Chapman. Copyright © 1986 by New York University Press.

Notes

1   James Fishkin, "Liberal Theory and the Problem of Justification," in J. Roland Pennock and John W. Chapman, eds., *Justification in Ethics, Law, and Politics,* NOMOS 28 (New York: New York University Press, 1986), pp. 207–31.

2   Hereafter I shall assume that "he" and its cognates are gender neutral, unless the context indicates otherwise.

3   To be sure, the *extent* of political power they justify is not the same for each of these political philosophers, but the reason for these differences is other than their differing metaethical theories, as I shall point out in a moment.

4   Incidentally, insofar as they are *not* the product of rational thought, they are presumably not susceptible to the kind of ratiocination that Fishkin fears will lead to severe problems of legitimacy. See Barry Holden, "Liberal Democracy and the Social Determination of Ideas," in J. Roland Pennock and John W. Chapman, eds., *Liberal Democracy,* NOMOS 25 (New York: New York University Press, 1979), chap. 12.

5   This, of course, is a matter of the form of government only if the form in question is democratic and if it is assumed that democracy calls for a low degree of inequality of incomes.

6   John Dunn, *Western Political Theory* (Cambridge University Press, 1973), p. 3.

7   This definition leaves open the possibility of direct as well as indirect democracy. I shall, however, confine my discussion to the latter, *representative* democracy, which is what we have and what is most frequently attacked.

8   See F. A. Hayek, *Law, Legislation and Liberty* (University of Chicago Press, 1979), vol. 3, p. xiii; also William Nelson, *On Justifying Democracy* (London: Routledge & Kegan Paul, 1980).

9   For comprehensive treatments of this subject, see P. H. Partridge, *Consent and Consensus* (New York: Praeger, 1971); A. John Simmons, *Moral Principles and Political Obligations* (Princeton, N.J.: Princeton University Press, 1979); and idem, "Consent, Free Choice, and Democratic Government," *Georgia Law Review,* 18 (1984): 791–819.

10   Hayek, *Law, Legislation and Liberty,* vol. 3, p. 137.

11   Ibid.

12   Ibid., pp. 47–50.

13   Nelson, *On Justifying Democracy,* p. 92. It should be recognized, however, that the denial of a preference does constitute a *limitation* of individual autonomy, even if it is justified by reference to the "real" or the long-run interests of the person whose autonomy is restricted or by consideration of the interests or rights of others, unless that person is voluntarily persuaded of its justification. Absolute autonomy is not a requisite of democracy or any other form of government. Its logical conclusion is anarchism. See Robert Paul Wolff, *In Defense of Anarchism* (New York: Harper & Row, 1970), whose argument rests upon the strong (absolute) definition of autonomy (p. 40).

14   In stating it as a fact that humans tend to develop a belief in a "kind" of equality, I am recognizing that, in Aristotle's terms, it may be either absolute ("numerical") or relative ("proportionate") and that in the case of the latter people differ as to the elements of the required proportionality.

15   Obviously, this capsule history leaves much unsaid. It is not meant to

imply, for instance, that political development is either linear or inevitable.

16   Thucydides reports Pericles in his famous funeral oration as having made it a virtue of the Athenians that they valued their private as well as their public life and that they did not "feel called upon to be angry with [their] neighbour for doing what he likes, or even to indulge in those injurious looks which cannot fail to be offensive, although they inflict no positive penalty. But all this ease in our private relations," he continued, "does not make us lawless citizens." *History of the Peloponnesian War*, revised Crawley translation (New York: Modern Library, 1982), p. 108. Col. Rainborough, in mid-seventeenth-century England, made it even clearer. "Every man that is to live under a government," he declared, "ought first by his own consent to put himself under that government," adding in his next speech that this right to political equality derived from the fact that "the main cause why Almighty God gave men reason, it was that they should make use of that reason, and that they should improve it for that end and purpose that God gave it them." Quoted from the Putney Debates in A. S. P. Woodhouse, ed., *Puritanism and Liberty* (University of Chicago Press, 1951), p. 53.

17   Robert Young, "The Value of Autonomy," *Philosophical Quarterly*, 32 (1982): 35–44 at 43.

18   The concept abounds in Marxist literature. See, e.g., Karl Marx, *The German Ideology*, in Robert C. Tucker, ed., *The Marx–Engels Reader*, pp. 136–137. It has been further developed and applied in the extensive literature of "critical theory."

19   For a compelling treatment of this argument, see Barry Holden, "Liberal Democracy and the Social Determination of Ideas," in Pennock and Chapman, eds., *Liberal Democracy*, NOMOS 25, chap. 12.

20   See Stephen Lukes, *Individualism* (New York: Harper & Row, 1973). In Chapter 9 Lukes deals with the right to privacy, tracing its origin in general back to the Epicureans and, later, the Romans and documenting its place in liberal theory back to the origins of European liberalism. It is true that it did not find an explicit place in U.S. constitutional law until recent times, but the famous article by Warren and Brandeis (*Harvard Law Review*, 4 [1890]: 193) derived this right from the more specific law of libel and the right not to be subjected to unreasonable searches and seizures, all adding up to a "right to be let alone." It is reflected also in the British principle that "a man's house is his castle." When the right was recognized (or federalized) by the Supreme Court in 1965, reliance was placed on a variety of arguments, including earlier Court dicta and the reference in the Ninth Amendment to certain unspecified "rights . . . retained by the people."

21   J. R. Lucas, *The Principles of Politics* (Oxford: Clarendon Press, 1966), p. 144.

22   Bentham gave priority to this fundamental equality with the phrase "each to count for one and nobody for more than one" and Kant with

the dictum that each should be treated as an end in himself and never as only a means. Both liberty and equality are treated more fully in my *Democratic Political Theory* (Princeton, N.J.: Princeton University Press, 1979), chap. 2.

23   Michael J. Sandel, *Liberalism and the Limits of Justice* (Cambridge University Press, 1982), pp. 175–83. All of the quoted phrases are from page 180. With regard to the "broad limits" referred to in the text, see Jerome Kagan, *The Nature of the Child* (New York: Basic Books, 1984), p. 152.

24   The works of Black and Arrow referred to are especially Duncan Black, *The Theory of Committees and Elections* (Cambridge University Press, 1958), and Kenneth J. Arrow, *Social Choice and Individual Values*, 2d ed. (New York: Wiley, 1964). The literature, including the proofs, is admirably summarized in William H. Riker, *Liberalism Against Populism: A Confrontation Between the Theory of Democracy and the Theory of Social Choice* (San Francisco: Freeman, 1982).

25   It must be recognized that much that is essential, but obvious, must be here left unsaid for lack of space. We are dealing with *representative* government, so of course majority opinion, even majority voting, does not *directly* determine policies. Also many important policies are set by appointed officials, adding another step to the process by which opinion is brought to bear on policy. These considerations, however, are quite different from those raised by the analysis of the logical problem of aggregating preferences.

26   Riker, *Liberalism Against Populism*, pp. 239–46. Thus, he holds that the only *logical* constitutional restraint for democratic regimes is that of regular elections for those who determine major policies. He goes on to argue, however, that other restraints, including the Madisonian checks, are in practice necessary for the preservation of democracy (pp. 248–9). Various writers have taken issue with Riker, especially with his contention that the problems of vote aggregation defeat the claims of populists while the case for liberal democracy remains sound. Thus, Jules Coleman and John Ferejohn ("Democracy and Social Choice," *Ethics*, 97 [1986]: 6–25) argue that Riker's points against populism may have equal application to liberal democracy and conclude that we need "a fuller understanding of the likely performance of democratic institutions" (p. 25). Since my own position does not depend upon Riker's reasoning, fuller discussion of their arguments is not called for here. In the same symposium, Joshua Cohen is likewise concerned to defend populism, but he does so by redefining the term so that it admits the necessity of restraints upon majorities in a way that makes one wonder whether his "epistemic populism" might not be extended to include most if not all of liberal democracy (pp. 26–38). Albert Weale has written in a vein that, for present purposes, is similar to that of Coleman and Ferejohn. See his "Review Article: Social Choice Versus Populism? An Interpretation of

Riker's Political Theory," *British Journal of Political Science,* 14 (1984): 369–85.

27   Nicholas R. Miller, "Pluralism and Social Choice," *American Political Science Review,* 77 (1983): 734–47.

28   How numerous and important are the cases that fall in this category I cannot say. It is also undoubtedly true, as Lomasky has suggested to me in his helpful editorial capacity, that frequently opportunity costs would fall on individuals other than the beneficiaries. At the least I believe it can be said that whenever costs, in the form of user fees or special taxes, can be substantially laid upon those who benefit from the project in question, the inequities that would otherwise be entailed by voting systems are modified.

29   I have discussed this and related issues much more fully elsewhere. See *Democratic Political Theory,* chap. 9; "Another Legislative Typology," *Journal of Politics,* 41 (1979): 1205–13; and "The 'Pork Barrel' and Majority Rule: A Note," *Journal of Politics,* 32 (1970): 709–16.

30   See Chapter 2. How much of a qualification it is I am unable to judge. Like them I would, in any case, wish to rely on such constitutional restraints as are embodied in the Bill of Rights (most, if not all, of which I believe can be defended as being essential for the enforcement of the democratic ideal) for identifying interests "too highly charged to be left to the vagaries of majoritarian decision making" (Chapter 2).

Further, motivational differences between marketplace behavior and voting-booth behavior do not solely favor the former, in terms of consideration of the public interest. It is true, of course, that if, because of failure to look it up in *Consumer's Research,* or wherever, I buy a bad product, I am the one who pays the price, whereas if my candidate wins and turns out to have been a bad choice, the cost is widely spread. Thus, as Brennan and Lomasky argue, "voting tends to divorce preference from cost" (Chapter 2).

31   The "other-things-equal" qualification is made to exclude such considerations as fear of adding to public deficits that they may consider to be already of dangerous proportions.

32   See Chapter 2.

33   If I am right, however, the statement that "between altruism and malice, democratic procedures differentially favor the latter" does call for qualification. (See Chapter 2.)

34   Amartya Sen, "The Impossibility of a Paretian Liberal," *Journal of Political Economy,* 78 (1970): 152–7, at 153.

35   Ibid, p. 157.

36   Russell Hardin's summary remarks on this point are of interest and accord with my argument:

> The argument of the logic of collective action is based on the strong assumption that individual actions are motivated by self-interest – or on the assumption of what I will commonly

call narrow rationality, or, more briefly, rationality. Obviously, individual actions are motivated by concerns in addition to self-interest. But collective action for mutual benefit is, in an analogous sense, narrowly rational for a group or organization. Hence, it should not surprise us to find that many of those who want their collective interests to be served may weigh their own self-interests heavily, even too heavily to cooperate in serving their collective interests. (*Collective Action* [Baltimore Md: Johns Hopkins University Press, 1982], pp. 9–10)

37   Discussion of these ideas can be found, among other places, in Stanley I. Benn, "Problematic Rationality of Political Participation," in Peter Laslett and James Fishkin, eds., *Philosophy, Politics and Society*, 5th ser. (New Haven, Conn.: Yale University Press, 1979), chap. 13, esp. secs. 2 and 3; and in Nelson, *On Justifying Democracy*, pp. 128–9. Howard Margolis has discussed an interesting way of dealing with altruistic behavior while remaining in the realm of positivist theory. *Selfishness, Altruism, and Rationality* (Cambridge University Press, 1982).

38   It is true, however, that the British government is experiencing increasing criticism at home for insufficient protection of these rights. See David G. Smith, "British Civil Liberties and the Law," *Political Science Quarterly*, 104 (1986): 637–60.

39   See G. E. M. Anscombe, "On Frustration of the Majority's Will," *Analysis*, 36 (1976): 161–8, and William H. Riker, "Implications from the Disequilibrium of Majority Rule," *American Political Science Review*, 74 (1980): 432–46.

40   Raymond D. Gastil, "The Comparative Survey of Freedom, 1987," *Freedom at Issue*, no. 94 (January–February 1987): 19–34. "Effective equality" is measured by such factors as "extreme economic inequality," "illiteracy," and "intimidating violence" and also the "weakening of effective competition that is implied by the absence of periodic shifts in rule from one group or party to another." Further details regarding the classification and the methodology used can be found in the article.

41   Ibid., p. 33.

42   See *Brown v. Board of Education of Topeka*, 1954, 347 U.S. 483; and *Baker v. Carr*, 1962, 369 U.S. 186, which paved the way for subsequent decisions pronouncing and implementing the one-person, one-vote rule.

43   I say not "easily" controlled because popular controls over the Court do exist. The Constitution may be amended, the Court may be brought to heel by cutting appropriations for its effective operation, and the president may "pack" it. The failure of the last attempt to do so reflected the Court's popular support.

44   See Brian Barry, "Is Democracy Special?" in Laslett and Fishkin, eds., *Philosophy, Politics and Society*, pp. 155–96. Nelson makes essentially the same point in *On Justifying Democracy*, chap 7.

45   John Rawls, *A Theory of Justice* (Cambridge, Mass.: Harvard University Press, 1971), pp. 426–8.

46   See Gerald F. Gaus, *The Liberal Democratic Theory of Man* (New York: St. Martin's Press, 1983), esp. chap. 4.

47   *The Political Writings of Jean Jacques Rousseau*, ed. C.E. Vaughan (Oxford: Blackwell Publisher, 1962), 1: 482.

48   See Rousseau's discussion of the "pluses and minuses" (in the "will of all") that cancel one another, thus leaving the General Will as the "sum of the differences." *The Social Contract*, bk. 1, chap. 3.

49   The calculations are taken from Brian Barry, "The Public Interest," in Anthony Quinton, ed., *Political Philosophy* (New York: Oxford University Press, 1967), p. 122.

CHAPTER 2

Large numbers, small costs: the uneasy foundation of democratic rule

Geoffrey Brennan and Loren E. Lomasky

1 Introduction

During the fall of 1973, as Watergate lurched toward its denouement, automobiles along the eastern seaboard began to sprout bumper stickers proclaiming, "Nixon 49 – McGovern 1: Don't Blame Me. I'm From Massachusetts." This novel plea of innocence raises problems. If McGovern voters from Massachusetts (and the District of Columbia) merit exculpation from the Nixon reelection, who deserves blame? All voters from all other states? Nixon voters from all other states? Massachusetts voters who cast a ballot for Nixon? Does the fact that no one vote could have altered the outcome by the slightest degree *and that this fact was known with a high degree of assurance before the election* mean that no one bore any responsibility at all for the outcome?

Ascribing praise or blame to individual electors may have little practical importance. (Although, if voters regard themselves as morally responsible for the quality of the vote they cast, moral considerations will weigh in determining how they vote.) What is decidedly nontrivial is the relation between voter responsibility and the justification of democratic governance. If there is something distinctive about rule that stems from democratic processes compared with that which is exercised by a nonelected elite, it may be said that in the former case the enfranchised populace bears *direct responsibility* for which candidates gain office and somewhat

42

less direct responsibility for policies that are enacted. (If ballots include referenda questions, then responsibility for policy can also be direct.) Voters are responsible because they are not merely the passive recipients of decisions made on high but rather themselves *bring about the outcomes* that are attained.[1]

Implicit in this understanding of a democratic order is the conception of some parity between private action and collective action. An individual's responsibility for his private conduct rests on his ability to act voluntarily to produce intended results. To the extent that the collectivity can be satisfactorily viewed as itself a choice-making entity that selects "social outcomes" in essentially the same way as an individual chooses private outcomes, the parity is complete: Society intends certain outcomes and acts to bring them about. This organic model of the state currently enjoys much less popularity than it has in the past – an eclipse that we do not regret and will not attempt to reverse in this essay. Instead, we shall restrict our attention to the claims of the methodological individualist, one who treats individual human beings as the only authentic choice makers. The weak parity that a methodological individualist sees between private action and collective action involves a two-stage analysis of collective action. Each act of voting by an individual is construed as a private choice intended to increase the probability of the occurrence of a preferred outcome. To these items of individual choice is applied an aggregation rule which transforms the several expressions of preference into a collective choice of policy or candidate.

Unless otherwise indicated, we shall assume that the aggregation rule being applied is majority rule. Certainly no other one has enjoyed as long a history of acceptance within democratic theory. Indeed, "democracy" and "majority rule" have acquired very much the same meaning within popular consciousness. It should be noted, however, that other aggregation rules can be devised and are in fact observed within democratic polities. Some require less than a majority – for example, simple plurality among three or more alternatives. Others, such as the complex rules for changing the U.S. Constitution, require more than a majority and that from more than one voting body. Majority rule may or may not have some distinctive and significant property,[2] but it surely is not the only feasible aggregation rule for collective decision making. Our analysis is applicable to these other rules, provided that in each case they are taken to be devices for merging individual preferences into collective undertakings.

We shall argue that there are grave – we believe insuperable – difficulties confronting any attempt to base a justification for democratic procedures on their responsiveness to the preferences of the electorate.

What people do in the voting booth is so unlike what they do in the marketplace (and in other arenas of uncoerced private action) that it is equivocal to call them both instances of "choice." It will be shown that the sense in which a voter who pulls the lever for A rather than the lever for B can be said to *prefer* A to B is very different from that in which a shopper who chooses product A rather than B or a worker who accepts employment A rather than B can be said to prefer A.

Our analysis rests in part on phenomena that emerge when the number of voters is large, a situation that obtains in all democratic nation-states and in many of their political subunits. The difference the number of voters makes is developed in Section 2. More fundamental, however, than a large number of voters as such is the separation that occurs within the voting context, even when the electorate is relatively small, between *expressing support* for an outcome and *bearing the costs*, pecuniary and otherwise, of that outcome. We shall demonstrate that voting tends to divorce preference from cost. An elector is led to choose as if costs were largely absent or as if their incidence were otherwise than is in fact the case. Preference for outcome A when its costs can be shed is markedly different from choosing to bring about A *and* to bear its costs. It will be shown in Section 3 that what emerges through democratic procedures may not be the will of the majority, and may not have been desired by a single voter. Thus, justification of democracy as adherence to popular preference fails.

The argument developed here differs significantly from those more familiar in economic analyses of collective choice. In the analysis of electoral outcomes there are two separable elements: The first is concerned with the calculus of the individual voters in deciding how their particular votes shall be cast; the second is concerned with the way in which individual votes are aggregated to yield an electoral "decision." The major focus in public-choice theory has been the second of these elements. Emphasis has been placed on the peculiarities of majority rule as an aggregation device – on how majority rule may fail to yield a stable equilibrium[3] or on how it may involve outcomes that leave all voters worse off.[4] We do not denigrate these results in any way. However, our focus is on the former element, and the considerations with which we are concerned arise independently of the aggregation rule employed. Although we restrict our attention to two-option/candidate elections under majority rule, the result can be generalized to other electoral situations.

Our argument reveals a sharp contrast between action in private arenas, in which the individual can be presumed to act in order to *bring about* a desired outcome, and action in electoral contexts, in which case such a presumption is illegitimate. This result is more than a scrap of theoretical fallout, curious to behold but not encountered in practice. Rather, it systematically distorts the results achieved by regimes and institutions grounded on democratic procedures. It is not claimed that there neither are nor can be valid reasons for resorting to decision making by ballot; in Section 4 we tentatively suggest what they might be. Democratic rule may be, over a wide range of situations, the least bad of several flawed alternatives. If that seems a lukewarm endorsement of democracy, so be it.

2   Large numbers

Consider an individual in a voting booth facing levers A and B. They may represent either policies, exactly one of which is to be adopted, or candidates, exactly one of whom is to gain office. In order to skirt interesting but not directly relevant questions concerning the nature of representation, we can assume that candidates stand for determinate policy packages,[5] thus making the two cases identical. When the voter pulls the A lever, he thereby expresses support for A.

Support for A can be expressed in numerous other ways: making speeches for A; wearing buttons saying "I like A"; donating money to the A campaign fund; praying in the privacy of one's bedroom that A will win. Note that each of these activities could go on in a regime in which choice between A and B was not democratic but rather determined by the decision of one person, the dictator. It is true that nondemocratic regimes are not noted for the tolerance with which diverse expressions of policy preference are met. This, however, is a contingent feature of such regimes. What may be held to be an essential distinguishing feature of democracy is that, whereas in the latter case the dictator brings about the outcome, under democratic rule each of the voters equally shares in bringing about the outcome.

Let us return to our voter in the booth. Because he is a citizen of a democracy, not a dictatorship, his pulling lever A is to be construed as *both* expressing support for A *and* acting to bring about A. More precisely still, it is *intentionally* acting so as to bring about A. If all levers were unmarked, frequency of pulls could still be used as a decision procedure, but no one could be said to intend the outcome that emerged. A "voter" in such circumstances might have a fondness for pulling one lever rather than the other, but such fondness could not be rationally related to an attempt to bring about the desired outcome.

When levers are identified, however, voters can act in order to produce results. That they can do so does not mean that they in fact do so. They might be motivated by pure lever preference, pulling the one that they do irrespective of its role in producing a particular outcome. This possibility may seem too far-fetched to merit any consideration as a realistic description of people's actual voting behavior. We believe that appraisal to be mistaken. Persons' voting behavior may have many explanations, but one that must usually have relatively *little* weight is the intention to produce a favored outcome. The larger the electorate, the less important a motivation to produce outcomes becomes.[6]

Consider an "electorate" of one person. His vote is certain to be decisive. If he cannot impose his choice on anyone else, he bears all the benefits as well as all the costs of his choice. This limiting case is equivalent to market transactions involving the purchase of purely private goods. The consumer who "votes" with his dollar to purchase pinto beans rather than lima beans secures the benefits of the former at the cost of one dollar's worth of lima beans forgone. Moreover, he is aware of the cost–benefit alternatives that confront him and so can accurately be said to bring about the desired outcome intentionally.

Now expand the electorate to three. If all votes are independent, and if the prior probability of each other voter choosing A is .5, then each voter has a .5 probability of being decisive. In those cases in which the other two split their vote (two of the four possible cases) his vote carries the decision; when the other two agree, his vote has no effect on the outcome. Generalizing to all cases of $(2n + 1)$ voters, an individual's vote is decisive if and only if the other $2n$ voters are equally divided between A and B; otherwise it has no effect. If we let $v_i(A)$ and $v_i(B)$ stand, respectively, for the value placed on A by the ith voter and the value placed on B by the ith voter, then the payoff to the ith voter for a vote for A is

$$v_i(A) - v_i(B) \quad \text{if he is decisive}$$
$$0 \qquad\qquad\quad \text{otherwise}$$

His expected payoff R is

$$R = h[v_i(A) - v_i(B)]$$

where h is the probability that the other $2n$ voters will divide equally between A and B.

Clearly, as the number of voters increases, h becomes smaller. The probability of a tie occurring is the number of ways in which $2n$ voters can be arrayed such that A receives exactly n votes, divided by the total number of ways in which $2n$ voters can be arrayed. This is

$$h = {}^{2n}C_n/2^{2n} \tag{1}$$

More generally, if the probability that a random voter will vote for A is p, the probability of a tie occurring is

$$h = {}^{2n}C_n \cdot p^n(1-p)^n \tag{2}$$

Using Stirling's approximation for large number n, (2) becomes

$$h = \frac{2^{2n+1/2}}{\pi \cdot 2n}(p)^n(1-p)^n \tag{3}$$

and when $p = .5$, the corresponding approximation to (1) is

$$h = 1/\sqrt{\pi n} \tag{4}$$

Therefore, the expected payoff to voter i in casting a vote for A is

$$R = \frac{1}{\sqrt{\pi n}}[v_i(A) - v_i(B)] \tag{5}$$

In elections where the number of voters is large, h is small, and thus the expected payoff for a vote for A will be trivial except where A is intensely valued over B. For example, consider a voter choosing between candidates A and B in a gubernatorial election in which 1 million people vote. Suppose that the voter values A's election at 100 dollars; that is, if he were the sole determinant of who will become governor, he would pay up to 100 dollars to bring it about that A win. Substituting into (4), we find that h approximately equals $1/1253$, and so from (5), R amounts to slightly less than 8 cents. If the primary motive for voting is simply to increase the likelihood of the preferred outcome, R will surely not compensate the voter for the time and trouble incurred in voting. Indeed, if the cost of voting is as little as 1 dollar, he will not vote unless $v_i(A) - v_i(B)$ is greater than 1,250 dollars! If we make the realistic supposition that such intensity of preference is quite uncommon, it follows that any explanation of voting behavior as attempts to bring about preferred results is highly dubious.[7]

The extent to which persons are or are not concerned about the welfare of others has some bearing on the result. Someone for whom choice of policy matters only insofar as it affects himself directly may have a smaller stake in the outcome than someone whose concerns include the welfare of other persons. (It is also possible that other-regarding preferences may tend to cancel out self-interest, moving the voter closer to indifference.) If either altruism or malice runs high throughout the voting population, the attempt to bring about outcomes could be more relevant to voting behavior than the preceding calculations seem to indicate.

However, those calculations considerably overstate for most cases the probability of an individual being the swing voter. Recall that they are based on the assumption that the prior probability of each of the other voters selecting A is precisely .5. Typically a random voter will not be equally likely to pick A as to pick B. Preelection polls, voting history, and other data can provide evidence that p deviates from .5. (Even the total absence of all such evidence does not constitute counterevidence for the judgment that $p = .5$.) Let m stand for the expected majority for A (which can be positive, negative, or zero); then the prior probability of a random voter casting a ballot for A is

$$p = \frac{n + \frac{1}{2}m}{2n} \tag{6}$$

and the prior probability that he will vote for B is

$$q = 1 - p = \frac{n - \frac{1}{2}m}{2n} \tag{7}$$

Substituting (6) and (7) into (3) yields

$$h = \frac{2^{2n} \cdot 2\frac{1}{2}}{\sqrt{\pi} \cdot 2n} \left(\frac{n + \frac{1}{2}m}{2n} \right)^n \left(\frac{n - \frac{1}{2}m}{2n} \right)^n \tag{8}$$

or

$$h = \frac{1}{\sqrt{\pi n}} (1 - j^2)^n \tag{9}$$

where j is the expected proportionate majority for A, that is, $m/2n$.

Even when j is very close to zero and $(1 - j^2)$ very close to unity, $(1 - j^2)^n$ is very small when n is large. The somewhat involved mathematics are inserted simply to provide some of the analytic structure supporting a fact known intuitively by most voters: The chance of one's own vote being decisive in a large election is vanishingly small.[8] This means that the expected payoff to a vote for A is also minute. Suppose again that the ith elector will vote only if the return to that vote is 1 dollar or greater. For an electorate of 1 million, if the expected proportionate majority to either side is only .005, he will not vote unless $v_i(A) - v_i(B)$ is 340,000,000 dollars or greater; if j is .01, the figure becomes approximately (6.5×10^{24}) dollars. Since this sum is comfortably greater than the world's total product for the previous century, it seems safe to conclude that even a person of remarkably intense preferences will not be pulled into the voting booth by a realistic appraisal of the impact he can expect to have on the outcome.

This is not intended to be a demonstration of psychological truths about voters. For all we know, it may be that some people do cast ballots in large elections in order to maximize their return. But if our figures are accurate within one or two orders of magnitude, and if voters are not uniformly prey to gross delusion about the efficacy of a single vote, the "natural" understanding of voting behavior as the deliberate attempt to bring about a preferred outcome cannot be assumed generally to obtain. Also, normative assertions to the effect that a person ought to vote because he thereby has a nonnegligible impact on political outcomes are either misinformed or duplicitous or both.[9]

Even without an extensive psychological examination of voters, there is some empirical evidence that desire to affect outcomes is not the only or primary motive for voting. For example, the result of the 1980 Reagan–Carter presidential election was announced by all three of the major television networks well before the polls had closed on the West Coast. This early announcement was subsequently deplored in hundreds of editorial pages on the grounds that it discouraged voters in those states from casting a ballot. Why it should be supposed desirable that persons abandon the comforts of home in order to cast a vote that would not and could not affect the final outcome was not widely discussed in those pages. (Would it be equally salutary, one wonders, to reenact the election of 1928 so that new generations could provide their deliberative judgments concerning the respective merits of Herbert Hoover and Al Smith?) And though it was noted that voting lines thinned after the network announcement, what deserves more attention is why anyone at all remained to cast a ballot for the presidency. Given a conception of voting as an exercise in bringing about outcomes, such conduct is irrational to the point of perplexity.

We maintain that voters are not predominantly irrational, and thus they vote as they do for reasons *that have little to do with an intention to affect outcomes.* Consider an analogous case: Jones sends the hospitalized Smith a "Get Well Quick" card. Jones may incur the cost of sending the card because he believes that Smith will thereby receive some therapeutic benefit and Jones values the expected benefit to Smith more than he does the out-of-pocket cost. This is a possible explanation – but an awfully far-fetched one. It remains so even if it turns out that there is some discernible benefit from receiving cards. Or consider the sports fan who goes to the stadium to cheer on his team. It is barely possible, but no more than that, that he does so in the belief that the marginal return to one more scream from the bleachers sufficiently enhances the probability of his team's winning to justify the time, energy, and money expended. We do not deny that the aggregate cheering of hometown fans influences the outcomes of some ballgames; that fact, however, does not explain the cheering. And though it is true that votes in the aggregate actually determine election results, it does not follow that individual voters act in order to bring about those results.

The results heretofore obtained are essentially negative. We have not stated why persons vote for a candidate or policy, but have instead argued against one particular explanatory theory. It could be, and we suppose is, the case that there is no single reason underlying nearly all voting behavior. One factor that will receive more scrutiny in Section 3 is the *expressive* function of voting. Just as one expresses the desire that one's friend will recover from an illness or that one's team will win the game without explicitly aiming to bring about either result, so too can one's vote for A be a bona fide expression of support for A even in the knowledge that the effect on outcomes is miniscule.

In addition we suspect that people vote in order to fulfill their civic duty, in order to be *seen* fulfilling their civic duty, to avoid pangs of guilt, to break the monotony of the day, because they judge that the consequences of everyone not voting would be disastrous and that this generalization test has moral force for them, in order to be able to say even if hooked up to a lie detector, "I voted for A, not that scallywag B," some combination of these, or still different reasons. It was lightheartedly suggested earlier that some voters might exhibit pure lever preference, that they vote as they do because of the location of the levers. Even that possibility is not as outlandish as it might first appear to be; political professionals maneuver to get their party's candidates put on the top row because they judge that this affords them a differential advantage.

Where so many factors may be present, we have no wish to commit ourselves to some one positive theory of voting behavior. Nor does our argument require such commitment. It has been noted that justifications of democracy typically rest on some claim that democratic procedures afford the citizenry a *choice* of rulers and policies; the citizens are the ones who *bring about* political results. However, when the number of citizens is moderately large, this attempted justification collapses. Neither the electorate as a whole *nor any single voter* can be described as choosing an outcome. Choice is not the idle expression of a wish,[10] but rather action intended to eventuate in an outcome. Because the probability that a single vote will alter the result is, for all practical purposes, zero, voting for A is not choosing A.[11] That A is victorious does not mean that anyone *chose* it. Nor, as will be shown in Section 3, is the victory of A an especially reliable indicator that the majority of voters prefers A to B.

3   Small costs

The opportunity cost of a dollar spent on groceries or an hour devoted to listening to music is the next most highly valued use of the dollar or the hour forgone. Because acting to achieve ends is costly, it is senseless to speak of an agent's preferences among alternatives without bringing in their relative costs to him. This truth applies equally to altruistic and selfish actions. One may wish in the abstract that some impoverished person had an extra dollar, but the cost of directly bringing about that state of affairs is one dollar of personal consumption forgone. That is why someone who thinks that the alleviation of poverty is desirable in principle might not do much of it himself. He prefers a dollar of his own consumption to a dollar of poverty relief. Of course, if the cost of a dollar's worth of poverty alleviation dropped to a dime, he might allocate his resources differently.

Counterbalancing the gloomy fact that altruistic action is not free is the cheering reminder that indulging one's malice also imposes costs. Tracking down one's bête noire in order to stomp on his toes takes time and exposes one to retaliation. Hiring a mercenary toe stomper requires the outlay of cash. The bigoted storekeeper who refuses to trade with blacks thereby forgoes all economic benefits such trade would bring. Again, as the cost of malicious actions varies, so too do individuals' effective preferences for malice. A society's structure of law and punishment can in large measure be viewed as an attempt to raise the costs of malicious acts.

Expressing support for an outcome can be much less costly than actually bringing about that outcome. Voicing pleasantries about the desirability of charity or muttering under one's breath imprecations concerning one's boss comes easier than giving away substantial sums or walking away from a lucrative job. In a democracy, one important way in which one can express support for an outcome is by voting for it. When the number of voters is even moderately large, voting is a low-cost way to give vent to sentiments that would, in other contexts, lie dormant.

Consider a voter confronting the choice of whether to vote for or against a proposal involving his being taxed 100 dollars, the proceeds going to the poor. He will vote, let us suppose, as he prefers. It is a mistake to conclude that, if he votes yes, he prefers the imposition of the tax to its nonimposition. All that can be concluded is that he *prefers to vote* for its imposition. The distinction is crucial. It hinges on the difference between the cost of a policy and the cost of voting for that policy.

Again, numbers enter the analysis. In the limiting case, an electorate of one, a vote to be taxed is decisive. It brings about 100 dollars' worth of poor relief at the cost to the voter of 100 dollars. It is, of course, precisely equivalent to private charitable allocation.[12] As the size of the electorate increases, the opportunity cost of a vote decreases. It is the probability of being the decisive voter multiplied by the amount of the tax. This will be a few cents when the electorate is even moderately large. Therefore, it is entirely illegitimate to conclude that a yes vote reveals a preference to have 100 dollars transferred to the poor; rather, it reveals a preference to express support for a policy where that expressive act comes virtually free of cost.

Why would someone vote for such a policy unless he were genuinely willing to be taxed? Many of us subscribe in some measure to moral principles maintaining that those who are financially well off ought to transfer some appreciable part of their assets to the poor. For better or worse, most of us are loath to forgo attractive opportunities for private consumption. However, guilt at not acting on one's moral convictions is itself a psychic cost; it is not pleasant to recognize oneself as weak willed or a hypocrite. The collectivization of transfer decisions provides relief from cognitive dissonance. One can "do the moral thing" by voting with relative ease for a tax because the cost of that vote is trivial.

This hypothesis has explanatory power in some surprising areas. Clergy, especially of the mainline Protestant denominations, have responded to increasing secularization by making fewer demands on the private behavior of their parishioners. On the other hand, they have eagerly embraced political solutions and political activism. We hold that this response is rational. A leader of enormous personal authority can demand with some success, "Give all you have to the poor!"; one with less authority, "Give ten percent of your annual income to the poor"; one whose authority is marginal, "Vote to be taxed ten percent for the poor."

Suppose that everyone in an electorate were to cast a ballot motivated by such moral considerations.[13] The result would be that each would provide 100 dollars of poor relief at the cost to himself of 100 dollars. By hypothesis, each would prefer instead to keep the money. The curious result is a multiperson Prisoner's Dilemma arrived at by democratic procedures. Each of the voters would be better off had he and all the others (or, under majority rule, half the others) voted no, but the dominant strategy for each is to vote yes. They are taxed, although no one prefers that result.

The basic resemblance to the familiar Prisoner's Dilemma game can be indicated by appeal to Table 1. The complications arise because in the remote case of a tie (which occurs with a probability of at most 1/1250 in an election with 1 million voters) the "vote-against" strategy gives the higher return; but since this case *is* so remote, it has insufficient effect on the expected net benefit of "voting for" to be decisive. The net benefit of voting for the tax transfer project is

$$q(1 - 0) + \left(1 - q - \frac{1}{\sqrt{\pi n}}\right)(101 - 100) + \frac{1}{\sqrt{\pi n}}(1 - 100)$$

$$= q + (1 - q) - \frac{100}{\sqrt{\pi n}} = 1 - 0.08 = 92 \text{ cents}$$

Table 1. *Returns to expressive voting*

Each voter	Vote for probability q	Majority of others		Expected return
		Vote against probability $(-1 - q - 1/\sqrt{\pi n})$	Tie probability $1/\sqrt{\pi n}$	
Vote for project	1	101	1	$q + 101 (1 - q) - 100/\sqrt{\pi n}$
Vote against project	0	100	100	$100 (1 - q)$

where q is the probability that a majority will vote for the project. In other words, the prospect of a tie can be ignored, and we can focus on the basic Prisoner's Dilemma interaction of the first two columns. Each voter will be led to vote *for* the project for a payoff of one dollar each; yet all would prefer the *outcome* whereby the project does not go ahead, in which case they receive a payoff of 100 dollars each (in taxes not collected).

To the extent that the normative case for democracy rests on the claim that democratic procedures give force to the preferences of the people, or at least the majority of the people, this result undermines that case. Majority vote for A rather than B does not reveal majority preference for A rather than B. We believe this to be of more practical importance than some other anomalies of voting that theorists have uncovered. Cycling majorities may emerge more often in learned journals than they do in actual elections. By contrast, the separation of cost from outcome is a routine feature of elections with a large number of voters. If collective action were restricted to the provision of goods valued by all or most voters above the cost of their provision, this separation would be less important. However, modern democratic policies engage in extensive wealth transfers that are not homogeneously valued by most sectors of the citizenry. Majority rule cannot be assumed to reflect accurately majority preference for such policies.

An enthusiast for democracy might, at this point, shift his ground. "All the better if voters vote more morally than they act! Political decision making will then produce morally better outcomes than would result if decisions were left to individuals acting in their private capacity."

Leaving aside comment on the conception of morality presupposed by this remark, it is erroneous in its assumption that voting behavior unequivocally encourages the expression of altruistic sentiments. As was noted earlier, voting also renders malice cheaper. A German voter in 1933 who cast a ballot for Hitler was able to indulge his anti-Semitic proclivities at lower cost than he would have borne by organizing a pogrom.

Table 2. *Returns to voting for persecution*

	A majority	
Each	Vote for	Vote against
Vote for persecution	-10^a	10
Vote against persecution	-15	5

a Equilibrium outcome.

A Prisoner's Dilemma problem in expressing negative preferences exactly analogous to the one indicated earlier with respect to public philanthropy emerges. Let us suppose that the individual relishes the symbolic act of thumbing his electoral nose at the Jews while not in any way desiring their destruction, for either moral or instrumental reasons. Here (in Table 2) the dominant strategy for each voter is to vote for persecution, and the persecution outcome emerges. Yet the best *outcome* is one in which there is no persecution. Electoral decision making yields a payoff of -10 to all voters, when each might have had a payoff of $+5$. Or again, in the context of military engagement, each voter may wish to express his patriotism and his determination before the potential enemy, yet not at all desire an outcome in which he has to go to war. The dominant strategy (in Table 3) for each voter is to vote "expressively" for bellicose policies; the final outcome is that all vote for war, which no one wants.

Because voting is essentially cost free, it is conducive to extremes of altruistic and malicious expression, both of which tend to be dampened by the cost structure of private undertakings. Even if there were an equal chance that malicious and altruistic inclinations might motivate individuals' votes, we might still be concerned to limit the political domain. A cautious maximin strategy calls for removing from the arena of direct democratic control high-risk decisions whereby the intrusion of malice could severely damage the interests of some group. This is exactly what is accomplished by constitutional limitations on the scope of majority rule. A bill of rights identifies certain interests as too highly charged to be left to the vagaries of majoritarian decision making.

A maximin strategy is not the only reason for endorsing, when feasible, the privatization of choice. There is, in addition, presumptive reason to suspect that the extreme most favored by voting is *malice*. Voting altruistically is less costly than acting altruistically, but the return to it is lower. Because a vote is anonymous, the recipients of altruistic concern will be unable to identify and express gratitude toward their benefactors. If someone places value not only on helping other persons but also on having that

Table 3. *Returns to voting for aggression*

	A majority	
Each	For	Against
Vote for aggression	-80^a	20
Against	-100	0

[a] Equilibrium outcome.

altruistic deed acknowledged, he will receive a greater return from a dollar of direct giving than from incurring an equal expense through his vote. There is then at least some tendency for persons to channel their altruistic impulses into private transactions rather than through an impersonal governmental welfare program.

The reverse is true for malice. Here anonymity is a benefit rather than a cost because it insulates one from the reproach of one's victim. Admittedly, the sadistic and the vengeful may not only desire to harm someone but also desire that their target know whence his harm comes. We believe this to be the exception: More people will vote for capital punishment than will volunteer for duty in the firing squad; many Germans noted with equanimity the disappearance of the Jewish population from their community without desiring to become more deeply involved in the machinations of the Third Reich. Between altruism and malice, democratic procedures differentially favor the latter.[14]

4   New foundations for democratic rule?

It may seem as if our argument is designed to be a categorical indictment of democratic governance. Not so. Our argument has rather been put forth as a corrective to adulatory treatments of democratic political processes that are blind to any blemish. Our object has been to expose proffered justifications of democracy that inaccurately represent the nature of the voting decision or the authority of electorally revealed "preferences."

The critique should not, however, be oversold. It does suggest that, when decision making can be "privatized," outcomes will tend to reflect more accurately the relevant costs (and benefits) to individual agents. It also alerts us to the folly of relying too heavily on collective cures for collective ills – it is by no means obvious how the problems intrinsic to large-number voting can be solved by yet more large-number voting. But it does not indicate that, when collective decisions *are* to be made, non-democratic procedures are to be preferred. The choice among possible political institutions is necessarily one among *imperfect* alternatives, and it seems likely that the determination of outcomes by aggregating votes will often be a preferable procedure to other options.

One of the prime virtues of majority rule is precisely the obverse of the earlier argument. If the collectivity does not *choose* the emergent outcome, then equally no particular individual is producing a favored result. Unlike monarchy, dictatorship, or oligarchy, no one is situated so as to bend results in order to advance his own interests at the expense of others. If there is no way we can design institutions so that electoral outcomes reflect the interests of everyone, then, one might argue, it is better that the outcomes reflect the interests of *no one* than that they spin to the tune of some self-serving, self-styled elite.[15]

This may seem like scant praise indeed. Democracy would have no stronger justification than would flipping a coin to select outcomes – a procedure that is equally free of corruption. We do not find this comparison particularly disturbing. Resorting to chance is not necessarily an irrational procedure: Athenian democracy used lots to fill various offices; random selection is currently used to select jurors and, until recently, was used to conscript American armies. One might be prepared to endorse it more extensively if one could be sure that the procedure *were* genuinely random (which it may not be if the options are selected by some agent with an interest in the outcomes). But voting processes have at least one advantage over random selection: They afford an opportunity for the expression of sentiments in the same forum that also leads to (unchosen) outcomes. Because many people do go to some trouble to vote in spite of the negligible probability that an individual vote will be decisive, it can be inferred that they value this expressive possibility.

It is both tempting and easy to decry the egregiously limited political information that voters carry to the polls. It is true that the representative voter does not rival Walter Lippmann for political sagacity; however, the results achieved in Section 2 suggest that electors invest far more resources in securing political information than can be explained by the expected payoff to them of a better-informed vote. That indicates that expressive support evinced by voting is more highly valued as it is better informed. (Reverting to a previous analogy, the most vociferous baseball fans also tend to be the ones best informed about the makeup of the roster, batting averages, etc.) So outcomes that emerge through voting reflect more and better information than does decision by random selection.

Moreover, although votes do not infallibly express preference over outcomes, it would be foolish to deny the existence of any association. People's natural affection for themselves leads them to regard favorably candidates and policies that further their own interests. Expressions of support for such candidates and policies will tend to produce outcomes roughly congruent with those genuinely preferred – although frequent small deviations and occasional gross ones are to be expected under democratic procedures. Nonetheless, this fact undeniably suggests some support for outcomes democratically arrived at compared with those that result from random procedures.

It should be noted in closing that voting is not the only arena in which valued expressive behavior concerning political matters can occur. The writing of this essay – and your reading it – are expressive activities engaged in outside the realm of collective choice and with no intention to alter outcomes. (We did not choose to write it on the basis of some calculation of the probability that it will produce our favored political arrangements multiplied by the value we place on those arrangements.) In a free society, there are many valued forms of political expression that do not carry the associated cost of gendarmes breaking down one's door. Uncoerced private choice is a path by which outcomes can emerge, and we have given some reasons for favoring it when both private choice and collective choice are possible.

To be sure, private choice through market arrangements also suffers from imperfections. Most of the welfare economics of this century has been devoted to demonstrating "market failure" in which externalities and public goods intrude. In response, public-choice economics has emphasized that government is peopled not by perfectly benevolent saints but by individuals who, like the rest of us, engage in self-interested conduct. They have demonstrated that there exists "governmental failure" that corresponds to market failure.[16] Our essay, although it has nothing to say about the motivations of politicians and bureaucrats, is continuous with the public-choice critique. What we have tried to demonstrate is that familiar problems such as free riding, Prisoner's Dilemma, and undesired spillover effects are not only encountered in private choice; they are inextricably woven into the fabric of democratic decision making.

Notes

1   A useful overview of normative and empirical democratic theory is that of J. Roland Pennock, *Democratic Political Theory* (Princeton, N.J.: Princeton University Press, 1979).

2   The issue of which decision rule is appropriate and whether majority rule has any claim to uniqueness is addressed explicitly by James Buchanan and Gordon Tullock, *The Calculus of Consent* (Ann Arbor: University of Michigan Press, 1962).

3   See, e.g., Duncan Black, *The Theory of Committees and Election* (Cambridge University Press, 1958), and William Riker, "Voting and the

Summation of Preferences," *American Political Science Review* 55 (December 1961): 900–11.

4   See Richard McKelvey, "Intransitivities in Multi-Dimensional Voting Models and Some Implications for Agenda Control," *Journal of Economic Theory* 12 (June 1976): 472–82, and Steven Slutsky, "A Voting Model for the Allocation of Public Goods: Existence of an Equilibrium," *Journal of Economic Theory* 14 (April 1977): 1027–81.

5   Typically, campaigns do not make vividly clear the positions to which candidates subscribe; and the record of postelection fidelity to campaign promises would not gladden the heart of Immanuel Kant. Moreover, officeholders will find themselves confronting issues that could not have been anticipated during the campaign. For these and other reasons, voting for candidates is unlike voting for policy packages. These dissimilarities, to the extent that they affect our argument, tend to strengthen it. That political conventions go to the trouble of producing platforms and pundits learnedly upbraid candidates who do not sufficiently emphasize "the issues" may be taken as evidence that the legitimacy of democratic rule is tied to the ability of electorates to associate candidates with policies. If that cannot be done, elections look embarrassingly like the choice of to whom to cede one's political autonomy.

6   For a large variety of situations in which the number of those involved is very large, one's own contribution to a desirable or undesirable state of affairs amounts to only a miniscule fraction of the totality. For example, whether or not I disable the catalytic converter on my car will have no perceptible effect on the city's pollution problem. However, it will have some slight effect. The voting case is different in that one's vote will either have zero effect (nearly all of the time) or substantial effect (rarely). Voting will be more nearly akin to pollution, world hunger relief, etc., for one who subscribes to a *mandate theory* of elections; i.e., the value of the victory of A is enhanced by each vote above a bare majority that A receives. We assume in our argument that there is no mandate effect. If, as seems reasonable, the supramajority mandate effect is very small compared with the threshold effect of casting the swing vote, a mandate theory will be susceptible to basically equivalent results.

Two important treatments of the implications large numbers have for moral obligation are James Fishkin, *The Limits of Obligation* (New Haven, Conn.: Yale University Press, 1982), and David Lyons, *Forms and Limits of Utilitarianism* (New York: Oxford University Press, 1965).

7   Virtually all modern "public-choice theory" (i.e., the application of economics to political theory) makes just this assumption. See Dennis Mueller, *Public Choice* (Cambridge University Press, 1979).

8   Nonetheless, boosters of civic virtue often proclaim the insidiousness of this belief. While leafing through the October 1982 issue of the magazine United Airlines provides to its passengers, we found the following editorial comment by Richard J. Ferris, the airline's chairman and chief

executive officer: "Why do so many Americans take for granted the right to vote? Perhaps it's because they are politically apathetic, distrustful of the system, unwilling to take the time, unbending in their belief that their vote can't possibly have an impact on the outcome of an election. How wrong and how wasteful. By voting, a person chooses leaders, endows them with power, and holds them accountable." We are heartened that great corporate executives can have such deep respect for the political power of the average voter.

9   If it is important to persuade persons whose political undertakings are typically limited to trips to the polling places every two or four years that they nonetheless "matter," this might explain why such dubious normative assertions continue to surface.

10   Aristotle agrees. See *Nicomachean Ethics* 1111b 19–30.

11   Bribing a large number of voters may have an appreciable chance of affecting outcomes. If democratic theory is grounded in the desirability of citizens being able to determine how they shall be governed, it ought to rank artful bribers much higher than simple voters.

12   For charitable contributions deductible from one's taxable income, the cost of private transfers is less than the amount transferred.

13   The supposition is admittedly unrealistic because it assumes an electorate composed entirely of net taxpayers with no net tax recipients. It is, however, instructive as an extreme case. One who craves realism may conceive of it as a plebiscite on foreign aid. This general line of reasoning is suggested by Gordon Tullock, "The Charity of the Uncharitable," *Western Economic Journal* 9 (December 1971): 579–92.

14   This argument was suggested to us by a reading of the account of sympathy in Adam Smith's *The Theory of Moral Sentiments,* Glasgow ed. (Indianapolis, Ind.: Liberty Classics, 1982), especially pp. 113–34. A Smithian moral psychology, although extremely congenial to this argument, is not presupposed by it.

15   Since Adam Smith, it has been commonplace among economists to characterize the market as spontaneously generating an order that no one has chosen or intended. If our argument is correct, the same is true of outcomes that emerge from democratic procedures when the number of people involved is large. It does not, of course, follow that the two are equally efficient ways of allocating resources.

16   See Mueller, *Public Choice,* for a useful survey of the public-choice literature.

CHAPTER 3

Evaluating the institutions of liberal democracy

William Nelson

My topic is the evaluation of democracy. By "democracy" I mean representative government of the kind found in most countries in North America and Western Europe. It is not that I think this the only possible or only correct meaning of "democracy." It is a simplifying assumption, a stipulation. I make it simply because I believe that, for many people at least, it is the evaluation of this kind of government that is of interest, whether or not it is, by somebody's definition, *real* democracy, much less the only kind of government properly called "democratic."

When we evaluate democracy, we are evaluating a system of institutionalized authority. The issue is one of institutional design. When we adopt political institutions – a legislative procedure, for example – we run a risk that it will yield bad legislation. This will be true no matter what standard we use for assessing legislation, and it will be true of democratic as well as nondemocratic procedures. There is nothing magic about democratic procedures. This is not to say that democratic procedures have no advantage over others. We simply question what these advantages are and what disadvantages remain. Well worked out answers to these questions, relative to some specific kind of democratic system, should be of interest practically as well as theoretically, for, among other things, they can point the way toward desirable reforms. But it should be stressed that *any* answer presupposes some standard for the assessment of procedures.

60

In what follows, I shall examine some common objections to democracy and then consider some possible arguments in its defense. In each case, I shall focus on the normative assumptions underlying the criticism or defense in question. The normative positions on which I shall concentrate are positions I associate with the public-choice literature and, especially, with the work of James Buchanan (esp. 1975 and Buchanan and Tullock, 1962). This work is marked by a concern both to respect the choices and preferences of individuals and to protect individual rights over person and property. I want to explore how these two concerns bear on the evaluation of democracy as well as how they are related to one another. It might be thought that the three are clearly consistent and even support each other, but I shall argue that the relations among them are far more complicated. For example, there is no guarantee that democratic procedures will respect property rights, and, indeed, they frequently do not. At the same time, however, when contrasted with the ideal of simply respecting the choices or preferences of individuals, both democratic institutions and property rights institutions have a great deal in common.

The question for democratic theory, as for political theory generally, is how these conflicts are to be resolved. In the latter part of this essay, I describe an approach to normative theory and to problems of institutional design that provides, if not an answer to this question, at least a way to think about answering it. This approach embodies a kind of ideal of social and political relations, as does, I believe, the concern to respect individual choices and preferences. It differs from the latter in ways that I shall describe, but it does so without abandoning the basic humanistic individualism that seems to underlie it. More important, for my purposes here, it provides a way of characterizing what is good about democracy as well as a way of thinking about the flaws of the system as we know it.

1   Problems with democracy

Taking political institutions in the United States to be democratic, in line with the definition of democracy given at the beginning of this essay, there is much, or so it seems, that can be said in criticism of this form of government. There are, for one thing, both empirical and a priori reasons for thinking that legislation, the paradigmatic output of the political process, cannot be said to represent the will of the electorate. First, no one knows even how to define for any interesting range of cases "what society prefers" as opposed to what this or that person prefers. Moreover, even if we were simply to stipulate that what the people prefer refers to the outcome of the vote when people follow some particular voting procedure – like a majority procedure – the fact is that people frequently do not vote, perhaps because, given fairly innocuous assumptions, it seems that they have little or no reason to do so. Moreover, when they do vote, they may not vote for what they actually prefer, voting, instead, for what they prefer to vote for, which is not necessarily the same (see Chapter 2, this volume).

When we turn from the vagaries of the aggregation of preferences to the outcomes of the political process, there is again much that seems objectionable from one perspective or another. It may be clearly desirable that government adopt efficient programs to prevent "market failures" – to promote the production of external economies and prevent external diseconomies. But no democratic government in fact limits itself to these activities. Instead, as it is sometimes put, governments are widely involved in the "public production of private goods": In some cases, people are compelled to provide others with goods of the kind that involve no significant externalities and could perfectly well be produced and sold in the market. In other cases, people are provided with special benefits (e.g., tariff protection, exclusive licenses) that are available only through government and that have the effect of redistributing income from consumers and unprotected businesses toward those receiving special protection. People invest substantial resources in an effort to secure special protections, and the net redistributive effects do not necessarily favor the needy (see Buchanan, Tollison, and Tullock, 1980).

This list of criticisms could be extended, but it is not my main purpose to raise specific objections to democracy. My point here is that each of these objections clearly presupposes some general normative assumptions about the proper functions of the state or about what it is that might make democracy a desirable form of government. Indeed, even the decision to investigate certain questions, like the question of whether there is a rational motive for voting, frequently depends on assumptions about the proper operation of democratic government.

What are the normative assumptions underlying the criticisms of democratic institutions I have described? Obviously, there is no unique answer in the case of a hypothetical criticism that includes no explicit normative assumptions. But in the case of someone who objects to a democratic system on the ground that its decisions fail to reflect the preferences of the people, the likely underlying assumption is simply that collective decisions *ought* to reflect these preferences. Legislation ought, in general, to accord with the "will of the people."

The second objection turns not on a failure of democratically chosen laws to reflect, in some sense, the people's preferences, but rather on the redistributive nature of much democratic legislation. Laws, or too many laws, impose burdens on some for the benefit of others. But it is more difficult to identify a plausible and suitably general principle that might underlie this objection. The critics who put it forward do not often propose positive theories of distributive justice.

The law requires each of us to refrain from killing, maiming, or stealing from others. In doing so, it is providing, at public expense, goods that people could purchase for themselves in the market.[1] These goods then lack one of the features that is thought to argue in favor of public provision. Furthermore, some people might prefer to have no such restrictions at all, or at least to have different restrictions. Perhaps they wish to live by theft and want to be free to take revenge on their enemies in their own way. Perhaps they prefer a world in which they can steal with relative impunity, even if their own goods will be less secure from theft. Perhaps they would like some of the benefits of stable arrangements, but not if anyone *else* benefits as well. Of course, in a world without restrictions, the general insecurity would result in low production and therefore in a more meager existence, even for thieves. But perhaps the material wants of these people are few. They are burdened for the sake of others both by being taxed to provide protection for others and by being coercively prevented from living as they wish. Yet many of us, I assume, would think *this* provision of (largely) private goods at public expense, *this* imposition of a burden on some for the benefit of others, to be entirely appropriate. We might, or might not, feel the same way about taxing some to provide welfare payments or education vouchers for the poor; and, of course, each of us can find numerous examples of the public provision of special benefits and subsidies to particular groups that seem to *us* totally without justification.

For someone who shares opinions like these and who also objects to democratic institutions on the ground that they lead to the unjust imposition of burdens on some for the benefit of others, the problem is to provide a plausible, general account of *which* impositions are just and which unjust. One possibility, of course, is to turn directly to moral philosophy, and especially to the natural rights literature, assuming, perhaps, that it is legitimate to enforce natural rights but that otherwise people are to be left free. But it is controversial what natural rights there are, if any. It is controversial whether property rights are included among natural rights, and, even if they are, what their content is. It is controversial, more generally, whether there are "positive" moral rights the state ought to respect along with "negative" rights against interference.[2] Is there a way to avoid getting into these issues of moral rights? Can the issue be resolved on the basis of minimal assumptions that we can all agree upon?

One possibility is to appeal solely to what people *prefer*. But that seems to be what got us into difficulty in the first place. The redistributive policies that seem objectionable are, after all, preferred by those who receive the benefits at the expense of others. But perhaps that simply means we ought to limit ourselves to what people can agree to *unanimously*. However, by that criterion, under the assumptions I have described, it will not be legitimate to enforce either property rights or rights of the person against bodily harm. The people I described who object to these rights are not ordinary free riders: They do not favor protections for everyone while wanting to violate the rules themselves. They want protections for no one, realizing full well that they are giving up protections for themselves in the process. Perhaps it will be said that such people are rare and, in any case, that if there are such people, their opinions should not count in determining public policy.[3] Perhaps so. But notice that, if we say this, we are also raising a question about the principle of popular sovereignty that seemed to underlie the first set of objections to democratic institutions. If some preferences are so idiosyncratic or antisocial that they should play no role in the choice of public policy, it is not a serious problem for modern democratic systems that they fail to legislate in accord with the preferences of the people. (The obvious question, of course, is how we decide in a principled way which preferences to rule out. I believe it is important to note that many contractualist or preference-centered approaches to normative theory do implicitly limit the range of preferences they consider. The contractualist approach I shall suggest later does so explicitly.)

2   Defending democracy

I have discussed some objections to democracy and have raised questions about the normative principles that might be thought to underlie them. The defender of democracy would be in a much stronger position if he were able not only to cast doubt on the premises of its critics but also to give a persuasive account of its virtues. But here the defender might seem to be in no better position than the critics. One apparent virtue of democracy is that it is a system in which people are able to govern themselves in accordance with their own aims and desires. The first objection I considered, however, is that democracy fails to produce self-government; and the second objection is that government in accordance with the de facto desires and preferences of citizens may not be a good thing in any case. But if the point of democracy is not to collect preferences and produce legislation that somehow reflects them, what is its point?

No doubt many people who believe in democracy do so without thinking seriously about it, and, no doubt also, people who continue to support it after some reflection do so for a variety of reasons. Perhaps one reason is that they think democracy tends to protect individual rights and liberties against the overwhelming power of the state. And perhaps this power seems especially dangerous when it is in the hands of self-righteous moralists out to do good or save souls at any cost. For people with this concern, it will seem liberating to insist that what matters is not abstract morality but rather individual interests and desires. This concern about the repressive implications of traditional religion and morality, combined with the influence of a naturalistic world view, is, I suspect, one of the main intellectual roots of nineteenth- and twentieth-century utilitarianism. It has also influenced the modern development of both democratic theory and the natural rights tradition. All three, in a sense, replace religious or metaphysical views of morality with a humanistic view in which people, their choices and desires, play the central role. But they do so in different ways. Whereas those in the utilitarian tradition seek to settle normative issues by appeal to the collective desires or preferences of individuals, defenders of individual rights seek to protect the aims and projects of individuals against interference from others with contrary aims. The utilitarian wants to ensure that everyone's preferences have some (potential) influence on every decision. The believer in rights seeks some areas of conduct in which an individual's preferences are sovereign. The democrat offers yet another conception of how decision-making power can be distributed among people. But, to repeat, these conceptions are very different.

Though I have presented these approaches to normative theory as if they were all responses to a kind of weak moral skepticism, none is, in fact, a skeptical position. Each, instead, is a positive, if somewhat schematic, account of a type of normative theory. But though these ideas have a common inspiration, none follows logically from the rejection of religious or metaphysical views of morality. Each is a distinct response, an interpretation, of a kind of humanistic individualism. They are not clearly consistent with one another, and they differ in kind. Utilitarianism, in many of its forms, is a direct account of right and wrong conduct, of what individuals should do or refrain from. Commitments to individual rights or to democracy are, at least in the first instance, commitments to certain assignments of decision-making authority: Belief in democracy is a belief that decisions are to be made, say, only by a vote of everyone; a belief in rights is the belief that, with regard to those things to which someone has a right, he and no one else is permitted to decide what is done with them.

Now, it might be hoped that certain distributions of decision-making authority would automatically lead to outcomes that are best by some standard of what ought to be done. For example, it might be hoped that some system of property rights would result in the outcomes preferred under some utilitarian standard or that some democratic system would automatically result in decisions to protect some independently valued system of rights. And some of these hopes are maddeningly close to being realized. But not quite. Just as the idea that a democracy must respect property rights can conflict with the idea that it must respect preferences, utilitarian standards, respect for democracy, and respect for property rights sometimes conflict directly with one another. That is one reason that, within a tradition that takes a relatively hardheaded, humanistic, and secular approach to normative theory, there remain issues about the acceptability of the substantive views within the tradition.

To accept any one of the alternatives I have described is, in effect, to reject the others. If each has some plausibility, then each also, just for that reason, lacks plausibility. And none of them is trivial, if only because to accept any one is to take a position not only on what people may do but also on what they may *not* do. Each involves limitations on liberty. Such limitations can be justified, but only if the principles giving rise to them can be justified. Since the alternatives mentioned are not the only responses to the abandonment of religious or metaphysical views of morality, and since none of them can plausibly claim to be the unique best response, none can be justified simply by a decision to give up such views.

The idea that people's de facto preferences should in some way determine what is or is not done is one alternative to traditional views of morality, but it is not the only alternative. I wish to suggest and defend another one, specifically, a form of contractualism.[4] This alternative is not so much a direct account of what is to be done or of how rights and authority ought to be assigned and distributed as an account of how answers to these questions should be assessed or justified. Thus, according to this form of contractualism, it is perfectly possible that people have and ought to have certain personal and property rights and that, in certain matters at least, their de facto preferences actually ought to govern. But within this approach, any such conclusion will be just that, a conclusion.

Contractualism, as I understand it, focuses not merely on what satisfies preferences, but on what can be *justified* – specifically, on what can be justified *to* people. To defend some claim about what ought or ought not to be done, including claims about rights or other institutional specifications of authority, one must justify this claim *to* others or at least show that it could be so justified. And to justify such a claim to someone is to show, at a minimum, that it can be defended by reference to principles that he is prepared to accept freely.

Clearly, there are difficulties with this idea as it stands. Different people will accept different principles, and some will refuse to accept any at all. But the idea admits of refinement. One well-known possibility, of course, is to appeal to a hypothetical contract situation so defined that unanimity is bound to result. There is much to be said for this approach, but it suffers from the difficulty that it obscures the connection between contractualism and the motives we, at least many of us, have to engage in normative inquiry in the first place. We are likely to be concerned, after all, not with what hypothetical people could agree to, but with what *we* can accept; and we are concerned not with what we could justify to hypothetical people, but with what we can justify to our friends, our neighbors, and to people of goodwill generally. Again, however, it is a problem that different people will accept different principles and that some will not accept any. It is in part these concerns, I think, that prompt Scanlon (1982) to offer the following refinement of contractualism: "An act is wrong if its performance under the circumstances would be disallowed by any system of rules for the general regulation of behavior which no one could reasonably reject as a basis for informed, unforced general agreement" (p. 110). He amplifies this on the next page by saying that someone's rejecting a principle would count as reasonable only if it were reasonable "*given* the aim of finding principles which could be the basis of informed, unforced general agreement."

I do not want, and I suspect Scanlon does not want either, to take this specification of contractualism as being necessarily definitive. I am more interested in it as a general approach to moral or normative theorizing and, in particular, as an alternative to views that take the fundamental data of such theorizing to be de facto preferences. Two points seem to me significant here. First, moral justification is conceived as justification *to* others (or to their representatives) in terms of principles they could reasonably accept; but it is not assumed that justification must meet the objections of just anyone, regardless of his attitudes. We are not compelled to take any account of preferences or demands that cannot be reconciled with a fundamental aim of finding mutually agreeable general principles. Second, though it is *possible* that actual preferences are generally harmonious, it is likely that they are not, and so it is likely that agreement on principles will require prior agreement on a conception of the good – of the relative urgency or importance of different preferences (Scanlon, 1982, pp. 117,120; cf. Scanlon, 1975).

Normative reasoning, normative argument, as I conceive it, has a political dimension in the sense in which politics involves not just disputes about how goods are to be divided among people with fixed tastes or values, but disputes about what tastes or values it is reasonable to adopt in the first place – given, of course, *both* an interest in living well (which is not necessarily identical to satisfying de facto preferences) *and* an interest in finding mutually agreeable principles of conduct. Moral reasoning is like politics where politics is concerned with the development of a shared view of the community's purpose. But nothing in this view assumes that the community's purpose will not turn out to be mainly the protection of individual liberty, personal and property rights, and individual opportunity and security. At the same time, what these rights are is as much a matter for moral/political adjudication as is the question of what we should do collectively *given* a fixed system of rights. In this respect, contractualism is undogmatic. It specifies an *approach* to moral reasoning more than a specific outcome. But it is unlike the view that takes unanimity among just any group of people to be necessary or sufficient to determine what is to be done. What people actually agree to and what people of goodwill could not reasonably reject may be different. The outcome of unanimous agreement may not be *justifiable to* each by reference to principles he could not reasonably reject.

One advantage of this view of the nature of fundamental moral or normative reasoning is that it is fully compatible with a naturalistic world view. It involves no controversial religious or metaphysical assumptions. Instead, it views moral thinking as an extension of a natural, though not universal, human activity – the critical evaluation and justification of our own lives and plans and of the lives and plans of others. What it recognizes is that this process does not presuppose independent, preexisting standards, but rather that the standards themselves can evolve from the process.

A second advantage of this view is that it is compatible with a plausible account of moral motivation. Some people believe that, if there is any such thing as morality, everyone will be moved by moral considerations. Moral principles, on this view, correspond to inescapable motives. No one is indifferent to morality. One possible consequence of this assumption about morality is moral skepticism: If morality must be universally compelling, and nothing is in fact so compelling, it follows that there is no morality. In my view, however, the problem is with the initial assumption. Though it is true that most people take at least some interest in morality, it is not true that everyone does. The account of morality as a kind of potential contract among actual people connects it with a motive many people actually have. In general, on this account, morality will be of interest to anyone who wishes to live openly and in good faith with others similarly motivated, who is concerned to be able to justify his conduct when justification is sought but who is also not indifferent to the way others act. Someone with these interests, who does not want to live by force and fraud and who is willing to deal with others by argument and persuasion, will naturally be interested in finding and living by standards he and others can freely accept as the standards to govern their relations.

But, of course, not everyone has these interests, and so, though many have a natural concern for contractualist morality, not everyone does.

What I propose is that we take this conception of normative inquiry as our starting point when evaluating actions, on the one hand, and principles and institutions, on the other. On this view, whether natural rights principles or some form of preference utilitarianism should be accepted depends on whether they can be rationally acceptable to persons with a shared interest in commonly acceptable standards of conduct. Similarly, whether political democracy is a reasonable solution to the problem of the design of political institutions depends on whether it is compatible with principles that could be universally accepted.

3   Designing political institutions

I have offered an abstract account of the nature of normative principles. It is an account of what such principles are *about,* of what purpose they serve. Principles that satisfy the conditions implicit in this account, like most other normative principles, will say how people are to behave. But, again like other normative principles, they will have implications about the proper design of institutions, about the assignment of rights and positions of authority, and about the procedures to be followed in making decisions. One such issue, assuming that we ought to have a system of laws, is whether some form of representative democracy should be adopted as the procedure for making and changing laws.

In the context of most standard views of morality, or most standard normative perspectives, questions of institutional design, including questions about the specification of rights and authority, are problematic. The reason is that normative views tend to be concerned at least in part with what individuals ought to do or refrain from doing and with the attainment of certain outcomes or the avoidance of others. Yet when we assign rights, grant authority, or adopt a procedure, we commit ourselves not to certain decisions or outcomes but rather to the decision's being made by a certain person or in a certain way. These two kinds of concern – the concern with what is done and the concern with who does it or how it is done – almost always generate a tension within a theory. Of course, this tension is avoided if we adopt a simple enough theory: If our *only* principle is that people have certain rights, and if our principles say nothing about how or to what effect they are to be exercised, there is no tension. As far as the theory goes, our only concern is with respect for and perhaps enforcement of rights. Again, if our *only* principle is that, in making decisions, certain procedures are to be followed, we need simply institutionalize those procedures and follow them. There is no further ground for concern about the outcomes. But most people do not, on reflection, hold such simple normative theories.

Nor does it seem very likely that contractualist principles will be so simple. According to contractualism, principles must be acceptable to everyone with an interest in shared standards as the basis for demands they will make on others and as the source of justifications for their own conduct. But what people care about, for the most part, is their capacity to attain their ends, to pursue their projects to a successful conclusion, and, in general, to live well. It does not follow that people would end up endorsing positive rights to things like this, for, given scarcity and conflicting aims, rights like a general right to live well are obviously problematic. At the same time, they would be wary of other, "negative" rights or assignments of authority to individuals or groups, since these operate by *limiting* the authority of others as much as by granting authority to some. They can stand in the way of a person's pursuit of his aims precisely by denying him the authority to do so. A system of property rights granting exclusive authority to individuals in certain matters is, in this respect, much like any alternative assignment of authority, including the assignment implicit in the adoption of a system of democratic voting.

None of this means that people will not accept rights or acquiesce in authority. Though the rights of others restrict our own capacity to pursue our ends, and though the adoption of procedures for making joint decisions limits our own control over the outcomes, we nevertheless have reason to want such specifications of authority. Though the exclusive rights of others limit our own capacity to act, we are better off having *some* range of exclusive authority for ourselves than having no matters over which we exercise exclusive control. And where there is need for collective action, including action establishing or altering systems of rights and authority, there is a need for some decision-making procedure.

The question is, What is a reasonable approach to the problem of assigning rights and establishing procedures? More particularly, what is a reasonable approach for people concerned with their own needs and projects but also seeking standards of conduct they would willingly live by and which others could be expected to accept as well? Broadly speaking, I can see two interesting alternatives. The first I think of as roughly rule-utilitarian, though it also encompasses the kind of theory that Rawls has put forward. Recognizing the need for rights and procedures, but also concerned about their own access to basic goods, people might begin by specifying certain aggregative or distributive goals (or some combination of the two) and then employ these not only directly as a test for what to do but indirectly as a standard governing the design of institutions – the system of personal and property rights as well as the system of political rights and procedures for making collective decisions. The choice of a system of rights and procedures would then be determined by, or constrained by, the goals already selected. The relevant question would be how a given system of rights and procedures would affect the production and distribution of whatever goods people could come to agree on as basic and necessary.

The second alternative is to reason directly from the underlying conception of the function of normative principles to a choice of procedures for making fundamental social decisions, including decisions regarding specific systems of rights and duties. If we think of normative principles as principles that would arise from a kind of search for mutually acceptable principles among well-meaning people, we could adopt institutions that force people to engage in a joint search for solutions to shared problems.

What I called the rule-utilitarian approach to the justification of rights and procedures assumes that contractualism has produced an answer to the question of what principles people could accept, and it assumes that these principles require the attainment of some goal or goals. It evaluates rights and procedures in terms of the likelihood that they will yield those goals. Any such theory is likely to result in only a qualified endorsement of rights or procedures, for it is unlikely that any system of authority will *automatically* yield the desired results. It is well known, for example, that a standard system of property rights does not automatically yield outcomes on the Pareto frontier. It has, of course, been widely hoped that there is some political procedure that, when combined with a fixed system of rights, would automatically move us the rest of the way. But that hope too seems to be vain. Systems powerful enough to eliminate some externalities tend to produce new ones.

The Pareto principle is, of course, only one conception of the goal society should achieve. Rawls (1971) defends an alternative principle requiring the maximization and more or less equal distribution of certain "primary goods" – liberties, opportunities, and income and wealth – and he argues, on the basis of these goals, for a system of constrained property rights and for a democratic legislature. However, by his basic principle, no particular system of property rights can be construed as final, since any system will need revision if an alternative would improve the distribution of primary goods in accordance with his basic principles. Therefore, one function of the democratic legislature must be to correct property institutions as necessary in light of more basic requirements. Now, it may be true that some democratic procedure is as effective as any other for making the appropriate changes and, more generally, is not contrary to the basic principles of justice, but it would take far more argument than Rawls devotes to the problem to show that this is so. And it is hard to imagine a demonstration that any combination of rights, administrative agencies, and legislature will be *guaranteed* always to produce results in line with Rawls's principles.

The second line of argument I described provides a very different, though perhaps complementary, approach to the defense of democracy, both as a procedure for assigning and adjusting rights and as a procedure for coordinating behavior in other ways. According to this approach, procedures are not to be selected with some specific goals or substantive principles in mind. Instead, the choice is based on a conception of the purpose or function of normative principles. Principles are taken to operate as a standard for the evaluation of conduct by reference to which people with a shared interest in being able to justify and defend their actions (as well as an interest in their own individual good) can guide their choices. Thus, they are principles people could not reasonably reject, in light of their own concerns, given that they also have an interest in finding mutually acceptable principles. They are principles that would emerge, if any would, from a process of open discussion among well-meaning persons. But democracy can be viewed as a procedure for decision making in which proposals are subjected to open criticism and adopted only when they can be defended by cogent argument. Thus, democratic procedures correspond roughly to the procedures that would give rise to valid moral or normative principles as I have defined this idea. So in terms of the conception of morality I have described, there is a plausible, direct argument in favor of the institutions of political democracy. But it is not a conclusive argument for any *specific* institutionalization of democracy. Nor can we conclude from this argument, any more than we can on the basis of an argument from the Pareto criterion, from Rawls's principles, or from a natural rights perspective, that the outcome of the democratic process is immune from criticism.

Valid normative principles are principles for the general regulation of conduct that no one can reasonably reject, given an interest in such principles. Ideally, I want to argue, a representative democracy will adopt policies consistent with such principles. It will adopt laws and policies, but only when they can be justified to everyone in terms of principles none can reject. A representative's job, on this view, is to protect the legitimate and rational interests of his constituents by exercising influence over which laws and policies are adopted. A representative stands between his own constituents and the representatives of other voters. He must formulate a conception of the interests he represents and seek to make a case that they are reasonable and legitimate interests. He must also be prepared to argue against the rationality or legitimacy of potentially conflicting claims articulated by others. There is no reason to assume that "judgmental harmony" will arise automatically. When the system operates at its best, political discussion will lead to the *construction* of a generally acceptable conception of rationality and legitimacy (see Scanlon, 1982, p. 117). In terms of such a conception, a representative will be able to justify his decisions both to his own constituents and to the representatives of others.

The aim of democracy, insofar as it can be justified by this kind of argument, is not to meet every demand. It is not even to see to it that legislation reflects every demand to some extent. Logrolling compromises – something for everyone – are not what democracy, any more than morality, is all about. Some demands do not reflect morally legitimate claims; others conflict with more urgent demands; and some, though legitimate in themselves, will be met, and met more efficiently, by nongovernmental means. When one or another of these conditions obtains, it is the job of the legislator to make the case for saying no.

I suggested earlier that this argument for democracy is complementary to the kind of argument I called "rule-utilitarian." One way in which they are complementary is that one could arrive at principles, perhaps like Rawls's, on the basis of a contractualist conception of morality. In that case, the question of which procedure should be selected could take two forms: Which procedure is most likely to legislate in accordance with these substantive principles, *and* which procedure is likely to produce legislation that can be justified to everyone in terms of mutually acceptable principles? Of course, the answers to these two questions might seem to diverge. In the context of the conception of morality developed here, however, any divergence will reflect as much on the substantive principles as on the procedures. The second of these questions is the more basic. Like institutions, substantive principles are derivative and stand in need of justification.

4   Recurring problems

I have proposed, on the basis of a certain assumption about the nature of normative principles, an argument in support of democratic procedures. What I have emphatically not done is to suggest that any specific democratic system is foolproof. I do not believe this any more than I believe that there is some system of rights the exercise of which, under any possible circumstances, will always produce desirable results. The only way to avoid these conclusions, I think, is to abandon the evaluation of institutional outcomes entirely.

My aim has not been to offer necessarily a *stronger* justification of democracy than those offered by others, but to offer a different characterization of what it is about democracy that makes it valuable. One result is that what will count as a valid objection to democracy on my view is not the same as what will count on some others. It will not count as an objection, on my view, that democracy fails to provide protection for certain alleged rights or that it adopts laws or policies altering their scope or content. It will not count as an objection that the legislature adopts policies imposing burdens on some for the sake of others; and it will not count as an objection that the legislature leaves some preferences unsatisfied or that it frustrates others. The case for democracy does not depend on the idea that legislation should accord with the "will of the people," where the latter is understood as some function of the de facto preferences of individuals. Thus, it is no problem for democratic theory that there seems to be no ideal way to define that function. And since democracy is not viewed as a device that simply takes votes, assumed to represent preferences, amalgamates them, and yields a set of policies that reflect collective preferences, the fact that people frequently do not vote does not show that the system is not operating as it should.

None of these things, at least, will *automatically* count as an objection. To argue that the system is not working as it should, because, for example, it imposes limits on rights or benefits, some at the expense of others, one will have to show that the unlimited rights are *justified,* or that the imposition of burdens on some for the sake of others was *unjustified.* To show that it is wrong to limit rights or impose burdens is to show that doing so would violate principles that no one could reasonably reject, given an interest in finding principles of justification mutually acceptable to everyone who is similarly motivated. In a democratic system, of course, this is a case that can be made politically. In a democratic system that is functioning as it should, moreover, the case will be effective. But, then, no system always functions as it should.

Democracies sometimes impose burdens that cannot be justified, or fail to impose burdens that should be imposed. Or so I believe. In light of the conception of justification proposed here, what institutional reforms might be appropriate? One candidate for reform, obviously, is the voting rules. If only a majority is needed for passage of a bill, a stable majority coalition will be free to disregard the interests of a minority and so may impose burdens on them that cannot be justified *to* them in terms of principles they themselves would be willing to accept. Prima facie, then, there is much to be said for moving to a unanimity rule. On this rule, any bill would have to be justified to every representative. Yet there are also good objections to a unanimity rule. I assume that burdens should not be imposed or rights altered if the burdens or alterations cannot be justified to those who have to live with them. But I also assume that there are justifiable burdens and alterations of rights. Given human nature, however, some will resist these burdens even when they are justified. We are notoriously blind to good arguments when our interests are at stake. And so it is risky to adopt a procedure that gives individuals or small groups something akin to veto power.

It could be replied that I am being too cynical in assuming that people would refuse to acquiesce to well-justified limitations on their freedom. But if this is too cynical, it would also seem cynical to assume that a majority would ride roughshod over a minority without any consideration of what could be justified to members of the minority, especially in matters about which the minority had reason to care a great deal. And to the extent that this does happen, it would seem that there must be good reason to worry about the power of the unanimity rule to stand in the way of needed change.

My argument for a representative democracy, making its decisions in the open under the scrutiny of a free press, is that this system will tend to constrain representatives not to adopt policies they cannot justify in terms of principles held by the general populace or at least justifiable to them. But this argument clearly makes assumptions about how people will respond to the opportunities and constraints the system offers them. It depends, for example, on the vigor of the press and of the politically active populace, but it depends even more on the attitudes of the legislators. It assumes they will be responsive to well-justified demands for change and that they will be unwilling to impose burdens on people unless they are prepared to produce plausible justifications. It assumes, if nothing else, that the glare of publicity will embarrass them into acting this way. If I were looking for institutional or procedural reforms, I would seek changes that would increase the pressure for more open and forthright discussion of proposals and alternatives and that would lead to a more thoroughgoing examination of their full implications. Every politician promises too much and demands too little, exaggerates the benefits of his programs while concealing their costs. And because hypocrisy is the tribute vice pays to virtue, they may thereby reveal some lingering concern for their capacity to justify what they do. But I am doubtful that there is much in the way of purely institutional reform that would compel a change.

In my view, the principles we should act on and the standards we should strive to realize in our institutions are those that would come to be accepted by people freely choosing principles with certain goals in mind. Thus, normative standards are defined in terms of a kind of process, a process that is not unlike the democratic process, operating at its best. In spite of the connection between normative principles and processes, however, there is, in my view, no institutionalized procedure, no system of rights or assignment of authority, that will automatically channel us toward the correct outcomes. We do not have a case here of what Rawls (1971) calls "perfect procedural justice" (p. 85). The reason is that normative standards are defined as those that will result from a certain process among rational people *with certain motives*. It is thus no accident that I find myself, in discussing the pathology of democracy, concentrating on questions about the character and attitudes of legislators.

A significant part of political theory has long been dominated by the example of microeconomics – by the idea that there is some system of institutions, some assignment of rights, that must automatically be exercised to good effect. If there were, its establishment and enforcement would be the sole aim of normative political theory. This is certainly part of the dream of constitutionalism. But I believe it is a dream that will not come true. This does not mean that the task of institutional design is unimportant or that it is not something that can be done either well or badly. But this task must always be undertaken against a background of assumptions about how people operating the institutions will behave. By the same token, the question of how people should behave must depend on assumptions about the institutions under which they live (see Nelson, 1985). There is no perfect system of rights, because there is no way to guarantee that people will exercise rights as they should. And there is no system of rights with no discretionary authority that is better than systems that give people substantial discretion. Or so I believe, in any case. It is easy to be dissatisfied both with institutions and with people. It is even easier to forget how much worse off we might be, in both respects, than we are.

Notes

1   Nozick (1974, ch. 2). Nozick imagines agreement among both buyers and sellers of protection as to what rights are to be protected. I believe, however, that, even without this agreement, a monopoly protective agency would arise in his state of nature, and the system of rights *it* accepted would be the system that was enforced. One might object to this on normative grounds, but not on the ground that it will not work.

2   In saying that it is controversial what rights there are, I am not just making the standard point that liberals and conservatives disagree about the scope and extent of property rights. There are also genuinely disputed questions about the rights of fetuses and neonates, for example, and about the corresponding duties of pregnant women, parents, and physicians.

3   People with extreme tastes or people who are thoroughly antisocial pose a problem for the unanimity rule just as "fanatics" pose a problem for R. M. Hare's (1963) account of moral argument in terms of universaliza-

bility (pp. 159–85). As Hare sees it, moral argument simply breaks down in certain cases. His example is an argument with a racist who is genuinely prepared to accept racist values – even if he were to turn out to be a member of the despised race.

But it might be replied that, as a matter of fact, everyone has his price. Everyone can be induced, at *some* price, to agree to a system of property rights. But then that system will reflect the eccentric, antisocial tastes of those who agree. The result of such an agreement is not a result that can reasonably be justified to those who have to live under it. The initial attractiveness of the unanimity criterion is just that it seems to promise results that everyone will find agreeable. But we do not in fact, and I can think of no good reason why we should, allow ourselves to be held hostage to the extreme desires of others. For an alternative view, see Section 2. For more on the derivation of property rights by unanimous agreement see Buchanan (1975, ch. 2, and pp. 59–68) and Gibbard (1976).

4   The idea here is similar to the idea proposed in Nelson (1980, ch. 6). My subsequent thinking has been much influenced by Scanlon (1982), and my presentation here largely follows his.

References

Buchanan, James M., *The Limits of Liberty* (University of Chicago Press, 1975).
Buchanan, James M.; Tollison, Robert; and Tullock, Gordon, eds., *Toward a Theory of the Rent-Seeking Society* (College Station: Texas A & M, 1980).
Buchanan, James M., and Tullock, Gordon, *The Calculus of Consent: Logical Foundations of Constitutional Democracy* (Ann Arbor: University of Michigan Press, 1962).
Gibbard, A., "Natural Property Rights," *Nous*, 10 (1976): 77–86.
Hare, R. M., *Freedom and Reason* (New York: Oxford University Press, 1963).
Nelson, William, *On Justifying Democracy* (London: Routledge & Kegan Paul, 1980).
"Rights, Responsibilities and Redistribution," in Kenneth Kipnis and Diana Meyers, eds., *Economic Justice: Private Rights and Public Responsibilities* (Totowa, N.J.: Rowman & Allenheld, 1985).
Nozick, Robert, *Anarchy, State and Utopia* (New York: Basic Books, 1974).
Rawls, John, *A Theory of Justice* (Cambridge, Mass.: Harvard University Press, 1971).
Scanlon, Thomas, "Preference and Urgency," *Journal of Philosophy,* 72 (November 1975): 655–69.
"Contractualism and Utilitarianism," in A. Sen and B. Williams, eds., *Utilitarianism and Beyond* (Cambridge University Press, 1982).

CHAPTER 4

Democracy: the public choice approach

Dennis C. Mueller

Whether a society composed of individuals with diverse interests can be organized successfully by democratic means has been a major issue of philosophical debate at least since the time of ancient Greek civilization. That an upstart discipline like public choice could resolve in thirty-five years issues that have been debated for twenty-five hundred would seem improbable, and I will not be so presumptuous as to claim that it has. But it has the potential to shed new light on old questions, and may already have succeeded to some extent in doing so. I shall in this essay examine certain parts of the public choice literature to see what it has to offer to this long debate.

The chief assumption delineating the public choice approach is that political man and economic man are one and the same, each acting rationally in pursuit of his self-interest. They differ only with respect to the environments in which they act. Economic man encounters his fellow *man* in the marketplace, where they engage in mutually beneficial exchanges. Political man, either directly or through his representative, meets his fellow *men* in the assembly, where all engage simultaneously in what we call the "democratic process." That the different contexts in which economic and political man act can have important implications concerning the normative properties of the consequences of these acts has been an important part of the public choice literature ever since Buchanan (1954a) first raised the issue some thirty-five years ago, and I shall return to it later.

78

But the main attraction of the *homo economicus* assumption is not usually thought to be the insight it gives into normative questions. Economics has achieved what success it has through the use of this behavioral postulate as a positive science. It is the power to explain and predict actual human behavior by assuming individuals rationally pursue their own ends that has led to the rise of economics as a scientific discipline. So it is with the sister discipline of economics: public choice. Methodologically economics and public choice are one and the same. Hence, it is not surprising that much of the public choice literature is concerned with positive issues and thus has little or no bearing on the question at hand. But an understanding of the way democratic institutions actually function obviously is relevant to some extent in appraising their normative properties. We begin, therefore, by examining certain segments of the public choice literature that are particularly relevant to a normative evaluation of democracy.

1   Why democracy?

An important impetus to the development of public choice in the fifties and sixties was the significant contributions to public finance theory defining the concepts of public goods and externalities and analyzing their characteristics. This literature made crystal clear that there are certain goods whose physical properties are such that market exchange leads to an inefficient allocation of resources. All could be made better off if some institution could be found for providing public goods to all individuals collectively, for inducing individuals to modify the selfish pursuit of their own goals in order to take account of the unintended external effects of their actions on others.

A testable implication of public goods–externality theory is that goods with certain characteristics should be purchased in cooperation with others, and other goods with identifiable characteristics of a private good nature will be left to the realm of individual choice in the market. To my knowledge these predictions of public goods theory have never been put to empirical test, perhaps because the validity of the predictions is obvious from casual observation. Thus, if one were to formulate a null hypothesis, that the probability of a good's being purchased collectively or privately is independent of its physical characteristics, and test it against the predictions of public goods theory using cross-section data from cities, states, and countries, one would reject the null hypothesis by a comfortable margin. Police protection is purchased invariably collectively, cups and saucers privately. Those goods that are provided collectively in some places and privately in others, like housing and education, are precisely

80	**Dennis C. Mueller**

the goods whose characteristics do not match closely the polar definitions of public and private goods, so-called mixed public–private goods, private goods with significant externalities. This seemingly trivial prediction of public goods–externality theory is fundamental to an understanding of democracy's normative properties. Not only does political man meet his fellow citizens in a different institutional setting than the marketplace, but the *objects* of his action, however selfish and private his motivation, are distinctly different in the public arena. But we get ahead of our story.

Implicit in the assertion that all can be made better off through the collective purchase of a public good is the assumption that the costs of implementing the decision, the costs of running the institution that facilitates collective action, are less than the potential gains from obtaining the optimal amount of the public good. One of the contributions of public choice has been to point out the existence of these transaction costs of collective action and to delineate their nature.

Once one recognizes that the institution of collective action involves costs, a natural question to ask, at least for the public choice scholar, is, Which institution minimizes these costs? What are the costs of different institutions? Posed thus, it would seem obvious that the least-cost institution need not be one that fits any generally accepted definition of democracy. A form of democratic institution might emerge as the most efficient mechanism for deciding collective consumption issues, but there is no a priori reason to limit consideration to democratic procedures or to presume that from a full menu of institutions for making collective choices the one(s) chosen will necessarily be the most democratic or even minimally democratic.

Why, then, the almost exclusive attention of the public choice literature on democratic means for obtaining our collective ends? One answer is undoubtedly that we live in a country with democratic institutions, and it is useful to understand their properties even if these institutions should be judged to be nonoptimal by some efficiency criterion. But I think there is more to our preoccupation with democracy than simply its widespread existence in Western developed countries as a means for arriving at collective decisions.

When Paul Samuelson (1954) concluded his article setting out the conditions for a Pareto-optimal allocation of public and private goods, he posed the question of how one can get individuals to volunteer the information about their preferences for the public good that is needed to achieve Pareto optimality. This "challenge" set out by Samuelson has directly or indirectly been the starting point for much research in public choice on the "preference revelation problem." The presumption has been without exception that an institution would be used in which individuals volunteered information on their preferences for the public good in analogy with the way the market elicits information on preferences for private goods. Thus, collective decisions for public goods would be based on the aggregation of information on individual preferences for public goods. From there, it is a quick but important jump to the conclusion that a democratic, that is, voting, procedure would be used to aggregate this information. I think the reason democratic procedures spring so immediately to mind as the appropriate mechanisms for gathering and aggregating information lies in the stronghold individualism has on our way of thinking in the United States and the United Kingdom and to various degrees in other developed Western democracies. Economics was spawned as a separate discipline in the Enlightenment and has been closely associated with the individualistic ideals of the Enlightenment ever since. It is not surprising that in borrowing the methodology of the economist, public choice has also absorbed its philosophic foundation based on individualism. But it must be stressed, as a normative argument in favor of democracy or a particular democratic institution, that individualism lies outside public choice. Being a public choice analyst does not force one to accept individualism as a personal or social philosophy, any more than being an individual necessitates that one adopt the public choice approach to the study of political institutions, however complementary this philosophy and methodology are. If this view is correct, a large fraction of the normative justification for democracy lies outside the realm of public choice theory in the individualist philosophy that has come down to us from the Enlightenment. This observation has two implications. First, the normative case for democracy, if one can be made, cannot rely on theorems and propositions derived within the public choice field alone. Implicit or explicit in the argument will be assumptions that rely on individualist ethics that come from outside the field. Second, and perhaps more important, given the many negative, normative results public choice has produced, the individualist advocate of democracy may base his defense on the individualistic character of at least some forms of democratic procedure, without troubling with or worrying about its efficiency as an aggregating device. (Buchanan [1954b] made an analogous point in his early critique of Arrow's theorem.) Thus, at best public choice can offer but a partial defense and limited critique of the normative properties of democracy. But let us return to the positive public choice literature.

2   Why democratic participation?

The very nature of public goods that makes consumption by all efficient makes participation by any one individual in the democratic process irrational. If all consume, all should participate, but if all participate, any one voter is likely to have a negligible effect on the outcome, making his participation irrational. This point has been made by numerous writers in public choice and is related to Anthony Downs's (1957) rational-ignorance argument. Given that an individual's vote is unlikely to affect the outcome of an election, it is irrational for him to devote time becoming informed about the issues surrounding the election. Thus, public choice tells us that rational voters will not participate in elections when the number of voters is large and will not be well informed even if they do participate.

Since millions of people do participate in elections each year, and millions of copies of newspapers and magazines with heavy coverage of political events are sold each day, as a positive theory of political participation, public choice would appear to be somewhat lacking in explanatory power. Either the fundamental postulate upon which the public choice approach rests – that is, voters do not behave rationally – is wrong, or if voters do behave rationally, something must be included in their utility-maximizing calculus beyond the probability that their well-informed vote will affect the outcome, and their anticipated gain if it does. Not surprisingly, public choice scholars have chosen not to abandon the rationality postulate upon which their discipline rests, but have chosen to assume that voters purchase political information for its entertainment value and participate in the political process out of a sense of civic duty that makes the voter's benefit from participation stem from the act of participation itself, not from the consequence of that act for the outcome of the election. This method of "saving" the individual rationality assumption also makes it nonoperational. An individual who knowingly drives a car with inoperative brakes might be written off as a rational individual with an extreme taste for thrills. But if millions of people drive such cars, we must revise either our assumption that individuals behave rationally or our definition of what self-interested behavior entails. Or all behavior becomes rationally self-interested.

An alternative way of explaining why people vote, despite the low probability of their vote affecting the outcome of the election, is to view voting as one of those acts each of us commits not because we anticipate an immediate reward satisfying our narrowly defined self-interests, but because we have been conditioned to behave in this way, because our voting improves the social welfare. Each of us has been taught from childhood that there are certain acts that, although to our benefit to commit in the short run, are *wrong* in that if everyone committed similar acts we would all be worse off. Every day, each of us routinely acts in ways that are irrational from a short-run, utility-maximizing perspective but help to maintain the social order in the long run (Buchanan, 1975; Taylor,

1976). In a country that cherishes its political institutions, voting is regarded as one of those actions one "ought to do for the social good," even though it comes at some small sacrifice to the individual who votes.

Treating voting as a *conditioned* response of individuals to being in a situation in which behavior beneficial to others in society is expected allows us to reconcile the act of voting with the egoistic portion of the rational-egoism postulate. The process of reward and punishment by which individuals are conditioned to behave in such seemingly unselfish ways as voting relies entirely upon the inherently hedonistic and selfish interests of individuals (Mueller, 1987). This explanation for the act of voting is also consistent with much of the additional evidence we have about voting. When pollsters ask citizens why they vote, they usually mention "civic duty" or some similar reason.[1] These responses certainly suggest that voters do not anticipate some immediate personal gain from voting, but believe they "ought" to vote, just as they ought not to steal, because society is better off. Education levels are highly correlated with voting participation levels. Schools are one of society's most important institutions for social conditioning. The positive correlation between income and voting participation generally observed may also be a result of a positive correlation between income and social conditioning. Successful individuals have learned to live by and succeed within the rules. They do what is expected of them (Mueller, 1987).

Treating voting as a conditioned response to being in a situation in which socially beneficial behavior is expected alters one's view as to the underlying motivation of the individual voter. The importance of voter motivation to the question of democracy's normative foundations has been raised by Brennan and Buchanan (1983) and Brennan and Lomasky (Chapter 2, this volume). Both essays build on the observation that, because the individual's vote has an infinitesimal probability of affecting the outcome of an election, the choice of party in the voting booth is a fundamentally different choice from the choice, say, of a new car in a dealer's showroom. In the latter setting the individual's choice of one model or brand of car over another, of a car over a boat, is decisive in bringing about the outcome. The full costs of the vote for a particular car in terms of forgone alternatives is consciously borne by the individual decision maker. When expressing a preference for a party or candidate at the polls, however, the individual votes without having to weigh the costs, since he knows his vote is not decisive. He reveals a preference to *vote* for candidate A over candidate B, but not necessarily a preference for the benefits of A's taking office at the expense of B's taking office, for the rational individual knows his vote does not result in this outcome. Both essays present examples suggesting that a voter may regard his expected utility from B's being elected as greater than that from A's election, but nevertheless vote for A because of the small satisfaction of expressing a preference to vote for A given that this expression of preference does not cause B's defeat.

The logic of the argument is clear, but its implications for the normative foundations of democracy are not. The implicit assumption appears to be what I shall define as follows:

Democratic participation axiom. The best decision is reached through a democratic process in which each individual votes *as if* he alone determined the social outcome.

This axiom has a definite resonance with populist traditions of democratic rule in this country. But it should be noted that, even if fulfilled, the decision of a polity might be judged morally repugnant by some other ethical norm. To take an example of Brennan and Lomasky, if a majority of citizens is anti-Semitic, the outcome chosen under majority rule can be an anti-Semitic candidate or policy, even though, indeed precisely because, the democratic participation axiom is satisfied. The social choices of a polity that satisfies the democratic participation axiom are as good or bad, as defined by any other criterion, as the people who make up the polity.

If we maintain the democratic participation axiom as a normative benchmark, then in what sense is this axiom likely to be violated as a result of the nondecisive character of an individual's vote? Consider a specific case, a national referendum of the kind the Swiss hold routinely, to consider a special tax to raise revenues to "save the whales" by launching more boats to police international treaties against killing whales. Individual J has a preference for or against this proposal based on his own concern for the whales and his share of the cost of protecting them. Let us say that he is personally against the proposal, caring little about whales. If he alone could decide the issue, he would turn down the proposal. But he alone cannot decide the issue, and upon stepping into the voting booth he knows that his vote is unlikely to affect the outcome. Therefore, as the Brennan–Buchanan–Lomasky argument goes, he may now vote for the proposal, and to the extent that he and other voters do behave in this way the normative foundations of democracy as captured by the democratic participation axiom are undermined. The obvious question is, Why, if he cares so little for the whales that he would not save them if he were free to do so, does he choose to vote for saving them in the secrecy of the voting booth, when he knows his vote will not count?

One possible explanation, which is consistent with the earlier explanation of why the citizen votes in the first place, is that he weighs the impact of the issue's passage not only on himself but on others. A "civic-minded" voter might vote for the proposal, although its passage would make him personally worse off, because he thinks others will be made better off by the proposal's passage. We might formalize this idea by saying that he envisages his having an equal probability of being any other individual in the community, of having that individual's tastes and income, and chooses the outcome that maximizes the expected utility of the community. Voting in this way the voter would be voting in the same way Buchanan and Tullock (1962) described the rational voter behaving at the constitutional stage. An alternative way to describe this behavior is to think of the voter the way Harsanyi (1955) does, as having two sets of preferences: selfish preferences that consider the effect of a decision upon himself alone, and ethical preferences that weigh in the probabilistic way just described the impact of the decision on all members of the community. With these two sets of preferences as possibilities we can consider the following decision matrix for our whale example:

Matrix 1

	Individual's ethical preferences dictate	
	Vote for	Vote against
Individual's selfish preferences dictate	Vote for 1	3
	Vote against 2	4

The first point to be made is that with the exceptions of a vote against the proposal from square 1 and a vote for that from square 4, a vote for or against the proposal might be made by a rational voter who finds himself in any of the four positions and not violate the democratic participation axiom. In particular, a voter with preferences in square 2 might vote in favor of the proposal, even if he knows that he alone can decide the issue. Why? Because he also knows that it is an issue that affects all members of the community and thus might reason that the decision should be made considering its impact on all citizens, and not just upon himself. The possibility that one individual in a democracy would decide for the polity is sufficiently hypothetical that it is difficult to conceptualize this voter's decision calculus. But one might imagine a process in which each year one citizen is selected at random and allowed to make the decisions for the community (perhaps to save decision-making costs). Such a citizen might make decisions using his ethical preferences, because he decides *for* the entire community and because he knows that next year someone else will be making the community's decisions and he wants that person to feel compelled by the same moral imperative as he is to make decisions on everyone's behalf. By a similar process of reasoning a voter might vote in an election with many other voters using his ethical preferences rather than his selfish preferences, because he realizes he is voting on an issue affecting all members of the community and thus feels he ought to employ a different expected utility calculus than he does when buying a car, with the hope that others will do likewise. A vote in conflict with one's selfish preferences need not violate the democratic participation axiom and thus need not undermine the normative foundation for democracy this axiom provides.

The most plausible situations in which an individual's vote may violate the democratic participation axiom are in boxes 2 and 3. An individual might decide against a proposal if it is left to him alone to decide, but vote for the proposal when he knows his vote will not change the outcome, thereby indulging his conscience by voting according to his ethical preferences, because he knows this conscience vote will not actually cost him anything. Some of the Brennan–Buchanan–Lomasky examples suggest this type of situation. But it is difficult to see how, if the democratic participation axiom is violated in this way, it undermines the normative case for democracy. The individual would then be acting *qua* voter in much the same way that Rawls (1971) says individuals *ought* to act behind the veil of ignorance, except that Rawls would not condone the equal probability–expected utility calculation interpretation of this behavior. Everyday voting outcomes would then have the same normative underpinning as Buchanan and Tullock claim for the constitution and Harsanyi claims for his additive social welfare function. If the democratic participation axiom were violated in this way, to my mind the normative case for democracy would be greatly strengthened.

What would be weakened are the methodological foundations of public choice. If voters do vote using something like their ethical preferences, they vote more or less in the way the traditional "public interest" approach presumed voters and politicians acted. But much of the advance public choice claims to have made over the public interest approach is presumed to have come from the replacement of the public interest behavioral postulate by the selfish utility maximization hypothesis.

Violations of the democratic participation axiom from squares 1 and 4 are much more difficult to rationalize. Certainly, if an individual thought that both he personally, and society collectively, would be better off if the proposal passed and would vote for the proposal if he could decide the issue alone, but voted against the proposal because his vote would not have much chance of changing the outcome, then the normative case for democracy based on individual participation is greatly weakened. But what would motivate someone to vote in this perverse way? True it would not cost much, but what would be the gain? I find such perverse voting behavior particularly difficult to fathom, if the reason voters go to the polls is because of the sense of civic duty described earlier in Prisoner's Dilemma, supergame terms. Would an individual who goes to the polls because he thinks everyone *ought* to vote knowingly vote in such a way that he thought both he and his fellow citizens would be made worse off? If the individual who votes out of a sense of civic duty does not vote for what he thinks to be his own selfish interest, I find it much more plausible to believe he votes for what he believes to be the social interest, that is, what Harsanyi called his ethical preferences.[2]

It is possible that an individual votes against a proposal that would make either himself or the community better off because he incorrectly evaluates the consequences of the proposal. Incorrect calculations of this sort are more likely with public decisions than with private ones because of the low probability of an individual's calculated vote affecting the outcome. We have again Downs's rational-ignorance argument. A sense of civic duty may be strong enough to carry the individual to the polls, but it may not induce him to gather much information about the issues upon which he will vote when he gets there.

The rational-ignorance argument does, I think, seriously undercut the normative case for democracy. The fact that individuals vote in accordance with their preferences, selfish or ethical, does not make a very strong case for democratic rule, if these preferences are formed out of misconceptions of the consequences of the alternatives upon which citizens vote. But it is not an argument that says that individuals vote a different way, because of the small probability of their vote being decisive, than they would were this probability 1, *given the information they gathered in formulating their preferences.* Democratic participation makes as good a case for democracy as the quality of the participants, and this quality depends to an important degree on their knowledge of the consequences of the issues they decide.

3   What are the characteristics of the outcomes?

Suppose that none of the difficulties of the preceding section existed. Each voter was fully informed about every alternative. Each voted on the alternatives as if he alone would decide them. What then could we say about the characteristics of the outcomes under democracy?

On this question public choice has had much to say. Starting with

Arrow's (1951) famous essay, a steady stream of theorems has emerged proving that aggregate collective decisions do not satisfy the most rudimentary and innocuous normative axioms one might wish to impose.[3] These theorems are so general that they rule out all democratic procedures as possible candidates for the aggregation procedure.

If this essay had been written fifteen years ago, it would have stopped at this pessimistic evaluation and then would have begun to examine the implications. But today one is able to sketch, if not paint, a much more optimistic picture of the possible normative consequences of at least some democratic aggregation procedures.

It is important when discussing the normative properties of voting procedures to distinguish between committee procedures, that is, voting rules designed to reveal the preferences of those casting the votes as in a direct democracy, and representative democracy voting rules. In recent years several new voting rules have been developed for revealing voters' preferences on the issues to be decided. These demand-revealing processes elicit information about individual preferences for collective outcomes and build in strong incentives for the honest revelation of preferences.[4] The outcomes are efficient in the same sense that competitive markets produce efficient outcomes; that is, they are Pareto optimal and/ or maximize the summation of consumer surpluses over all voters from collective action.

Voting by veto asks each voter to propose a final outcome to the collective decision process and then to remove one proposal from the set containing all proposals plus the status quo. The remaining, winning issue has normative properties similar to those of majority rule, but the procedure is not troubled by cycling as majority rule is.[5]

Point voting (each individual allocates a stock of fungible vote points across a set of issues in direct relation to his intensity of preferences over the issues) leads to social outcomes that maximize a weighted sum of individual utilities under the vote-point aggregation rule proposed by Hylland and Zeckhauser (1979).

Although each of these procedures violates one or more of the Arrow axioms by necessity, the normative loss from discarding the axiom in question seems arguably more than offset by the other attractive properties of these procedures. Thus, these procedures and the growing family of new preference revelation procedures from which they are drawn represent an attractive *theoretical* alternative description of the potential of democracy to that which one obtains from the Arrow-theorem literature. Like the latter, these new procedures presume an informed electorate that participates in the democratic process in spite of the issues discussed in the preceding section. Given that these procedures place greater demands on the voter's time and/or intelligence than simple majority rule, as a normative underpinning for the potential of democratic rule, they represent an even more romantic view of the voter's capacity and motivation than implicit in classical democratic theory, in which majority rule is the presumed voting procedure.

The problem of voter motivation is perhaps less severe if we think of these procedures as being employed not by the citizens themselves but by their representatives. The job of the representative is to be informed about the issues, and the incentive to be reelected might serve to induce responsible voting by representatives. The procedures are not so complicated that one cannot presume that elected representatives could not employ them.

The normative properties of the procedures depend upon the relationship between the outcomes from the voting and the preferences of the citizens. To maintain these normative properties under a system of representative voting, a system of representation would have to be employed in which the preferences of the citizens were accurately mirrored by a committee of representatives. A system of proportional representation would be called for (Mueller, forthcoming, ch. 12).

Proportional representation systems seek to select representatives whose voting will accurately reflect the preferences of the individual citizens in the proportions in which these preferences are found in the population. The goal is an accurate representation of preferences. An alternative interpretation of representative democracy is to view the goal of voting as the election of a *government,* a person or group of persons to govern the polity. Recent analyses of this form of representative government indicate that it too can have some attractive properties.

An important assumption in the Arrow impossibility and cycling literatures is that voting is deterministic in the sense that the voter votes with probability 1 for that proposal or candidate promising the highest utility to him. Coughlin and Nitzan (1981) and Ledyard (1984) have argued that this assumption is unrealistic with respect to voting in a representative democracy, because candidates are unlikely to know with certainty all of the characteristics of each voter's utility function. They have replaced the deterministic voting assumption with a probabilistic voting assumption. The probability that a given voter votes for a particular candidate increases the closer the candidate's proposed platform is to the voter's most preferred platform.

Deterministic voting models assume that voter choices gyrate schizophrenically as candidates move about competing for votes. A slight movement to the left loses voter A's vote, but wins B's and C's. Candidates seek to maximize their expected number of votes, and these in turn are simply the sum of the probabilities that each voter votes for the candidate. Define π_{1i} as the probability that voter i votes for candidate 1, and EV_1 as one's expected vote. Then candidate 1 seeks to maximize

$$EV_1 = \sum_{i=1}^{n} \pi_{1i}. \tag{1}$$

Under deterministic voting π_{1i} and π_{2i} take the following step-function form:

$$(\pi_{1i} = 1) \longleftrightarrow U_{1i} > U_{2i}$$
$$(\pi_{1i} = 0) \longleftrightarrow U_{1i} \leq U_{2i} \tag{2}$$
$$(\pi_{2i} = 1) \longleftrightarrow U_{1i} < U_{2i}$$

where U_{1i} and U_{2i} are i's expected utilities under the platforms of 1 and 2, respectively.

Probabilistic voting models replace (2) with the assumption that the probability functions are continuous in U_{1i} and U_{2i}, that is,

$$\pi_{1i} = f_i(U_{1i}, U_{2i}), \quad \frac{\partial f_i}{\partial_{1i}} > 0, \quad \frac{\partial f_i}{\partial U_{2i}} < 0. \tag{3}$$

One need not have much familiarity with mathematics to know that the task of finding a maximum for equation (1) will be much easier if the π_{1i} are smooth, continuous, concave functions than if they are discontinuous functions. The probabilistic voting assumption makes this substitution, and it lies at the heart of the difference between the two models' characteristics.

The utility functions of each voter can be thought of as mountains with peaks at each voter's ideal point. The probabilistic voting assumption transforms these utility mountains into probability mountains, with the probability of any voter voting for a given candidate reaching a peak when the candidate takes a position at the voter's ideal point.

Equation (1) aggregates these individual probability mountains into a single aggregate probability mountain. The competition for votes among candidates drives them to the peak of this mountain.

That the positioning of the candidates at the peak of this mountain is an equilibrium can be established in a variety of ways. For example, the zero-sum nature of competition for votes, combined with the continuity assumptions on the π_{1i} and π_{2i} (implying the continuity of EV_1 and EV_2), can be relied upon to establish a Nash equilibrium (Coughlin and Nitzan, 1981). If the probability functions are strictly concave, the equilibrium is unique, with both candidates offering the same platforms.

Moreover, the equilibrium social outcome that competition for votes produces is one at which a social welfare function defined over all voter utilities is maximized. In one of Coughlin and Nitzan's models it is the Nash social welfare function:

$$W = U_1 \times U_2 \times \cdots \times U_n. \tag{4}$$

In Ledyard's model it is Bentham's

$$W = U_1 + U_2 + \cdots + U_n. \tag{5}$$

Thus, rational, self-interested behavior on the part of voters and candidates in a competitive political process produces the same kind of social outcome in the public sector as rational self-interest and competition have been shown to yield in the private sector.

The probabilistic voting models tell us that the necessity to compete for votes forces candidates to weigh the possible impact of each policy on the welfare of every citizen and propose those policies that maximize the aggregation of these individual utilities in a very specific sense. A better normative case for a competitive democratic process is, from the utilitarian perspective of public choice, difficult to imagine.

Comforting as these results are, they underscore the importance of the issues raised in the preceding section. Political competition is seen as taking place over a well-defined issue space. Voters know and respond to the policy proposals of candidates; candidates choose policies based on the likelihood of each voter's support. Coughlin, Nitzan, and Ledyard have picked up Downs's model of political competition and written a new final chapter, one that gives the story a happy ending. But they have left rational ignorance out of the plot.

One expects, and casual observation confirms, that candidates behave as Downs's rational-ignorance hypothesis implies. Issues are fuzzed over and debates are avoided; when they occur, the topics are discussed in generalities rather than specifics; candidates avoid taking positions for as long as possible. These predictions of a model of political competition with rational ignorance may be Downs's most lasting contribution to our understanding of the nature of representative democracy.

But given the existence of a substantial amount of rational ignorance in the voting populace, it is not clear how much solace can be derived from the knowledge that candidate competition in platitudes maximizes an aggregation of voter utilities based on their misconceptions of candidate positions. The positive public choice literature is filled with studies showing that public bureaucracies are less efficient at providing services than the private sector when the two compete.[6] Similarly, much government activity redistributes income from one group to another in ways that are difficult to rationalize on the basis of any normative theory of redistribution.[7] Regulation frequently has perverse effects that differ from those claimed for it at the time the original legislation is debated.[8] These and other examples of government waste and inefficiency reveal that many of the actual "outputs" of government are not those promised by candidates as they compete for votes, or envisaged by voters when they cast them. Rational ignorance allows a gigantic wedge to be driven between the winning candidate's platform in a competitive political process and the bundle of publicly provided goods and services that actually ensues.

4   What are the implications?

Throughout its short history, public choice has been plagued by two voting paradoxes: the paradox of why rational, self-interested individuals vote when the probability of their vote affecting the outcome is negligible, and the paradox that the aggregation of votes may lead to no determinate outcome. Recent research has gone a long way toward resolving the second paradox. The first remains.

In my view there is far more empirical support for the nonparticipation prediction of public choice than many seem to think. Voting is but one dimension of political participation. Gathering information, contributing funds to candidates, canvassing door to door, and many other dimensions of participation are open to citizens. Participation rates in these more costly modes are far lower.

The act of voting may be viewed as the conditioned response of an individual to being in a situation in which he feels that the long-run viability of democracy depends on citizen participation. To the extent that the normative case for democracy rests on participation in the democratic process by a large number of voters, a voter's belief that democracy is an institution worth preserving and his sense of political obligation go some distance toward sustaining democracy's normative foundation.

The foreboding that the aggregation of individual preferences leads to outcomes that are less than the sum of the parts, promulgated for so many years by public choice theorists, is finally being dispelled. But even the new theoretical results do not promise that the whole will be any more than the sum of the parts. The question still to be answered is, How meaningful are the votes cast in one of the newly invented preference revelation schemes, or for candidates in a competitive election, as indicators of individual preferences for the outputs of the public sector? On this issue I share the concerns of Brennan, Buchanan, and Lomasky.

Suppose we were to conclude that these votes tell us next to nothing about what an informed voter's preferences over public outputs would be.

Elections tell us which candidates uninformed voters *like,* not what policies informed voters *prefer.* What then would be the implication?

One possible implication is that we should leave fewer collective decisions to government and assign more to the private sector: less social insurance, more private insurance; fewer public tennis courts, more private tennis clubs. Though some movement in this direction is probably desirable, indeed has already begun in this country, there are definite limits to how far one can go toward privatizing the public sector. Privatizing the core of public outputs that one finds in the public sector of almost every country, outputs with significant public good–externality attributes, would simply shift to the private sector the significant preference revelation costs with which the public sector so poorly deals.

The dilemma of democratic participation is that the same characteristics of goods that make collective action necessary weaken an individual's incentive to participate in a democratic process that decides the quantity and quality dimensions of the goods. The greater the number of individuals who are affected by a good's provision, the more potentially there is to gain by providing the good collectively and the less incentive any one voter will have to participate in the collective decision. The commonality of wants that pulls people to the polity weakens the participatory bonds that hold a democracy together.

Rather than discard democracy, one might try to reform it. If the rational ignorance of voters is democracy's major shortcoming, one could lower the costs of gathering information and raise the incentives to do so. The quality of outcomes from the democratic process is as pure a public good as one can imagine, and thus an active role for government in lowering the costs of obtaining information about political alternatives is defensible. In the United States an active role for government in providing political information has been eschewed, most likely out of fear that the government, or certain members thereof, would abuse the opportunity to bias the information on its behalf. In European countries the state owns at least one television network and often regulates the others. Public service broadcasting of political news and news about major social issues can be provided directly. The broadcasting of congressional debates over major issues would not seem to run the danger of the party or persons in office gaining unfair advantage. The Cable-Satellite Public Affairs Network (C-SPAN) has been televising live debates in the House of Representatives and other political activities like state caucuses. Initial viewer response suggests that politics is more interesting than soap operas and baseball for a significant fraction of the population (Reid, 1984). Were C-SPAN and state and local political broadcasting free, rather than shown only on pay television, a large number of voters might become regular followers of political issues. To reduce further the opportunity costs of watching these sorts of programs, one might set aside one night per week, or month, as citizen "participation" night, on which competing entertainment and sports programming would be barred from the other networks. Recourse to such action imposes obvious costs on society, but so does the provision of every other public good. If the quality of democratic decisions would be greatly increased by voters becoming better informed, then the cost of achieving this change would have to be borne in one way or another.

The major disincentive to participation in the democratic process is the small probability that the participation will have an effect. This probability can be raised by decentralizing democratic decision making. In the sixties a neighborhood-government movement was afoot; efforts to strengthen our federalist institutions are pushed from time to time. In conjunction with bringing the decisions of government closer to the voter, one might enrich the voter's means of expression by adopting reforms like proportional representation, the Borda count procedure, or even one of the recently developed preference revelation procedures discussed earlier. These changes have costs and disadvantages also. My objective here is not to prescribe, but merely to indicate that options exist.

Though it is easy to think of even fundamental political reforms and possible, but more difficult, to predict their consequences, it is nearly impossible to envisage how they could ever come about. The rational ignorance and inertia of citizens that lead to the need for reform stand in the way of its achievement. Those in the best position to lead a reform movement, leaders of government and business, have the least to gain from such a movement. Thus, the quality of outcomes under our democratic process seems destined to continue to deteriorate, until a point is eventually reached when a sufficient number of citizens will be sufficiently distressed to set aside their private pursuits long enough to participate in a fundamental restructuring of our political institutions. And, one may hope, a modern Jefferson and Paine, and later a Madison, will step forward to lead and guide the process.

Notes

1   See, e.g., Ashenfelter and Kelley (1975) and references cited therein.
2   Brennan and Lomasky describe voters as following fads and regard this as undermining the normative case for democracy. But I do not accept this argument, any more than I accept that consumers' tendency to follow fads in buying undermines the consumer sovereignty defense of the free market. Following a fad is an expression of preference and is presumably based on the belief that either the faddist or his fellow citi-

zens will be made better off by the fad issue winning. Decision matrix 1 must hold whether we refer to post-fad preferences or pre-fad preferences, and the above arguments apply.

An alternative interpretation of the fad argument is that voters are duped into following fads that will harm them or society, because they do not carefully consider the fad issue. But this is a different argument – indeed, the rational-ignorance argument to which we now turn.

3   For surveys of these results, see Sen (1976, 1977) and Mueller (forthcoming, ch. 20).

4   See Clarke (1971), Groves and Ledyard (1977), and Tideman and Tullock (1976).

5   See Mueller (1978, 1984) and Moulin (1981).

6   For surveys of this literature, see Orzechowski (1977) and Borcherding, Pommerehne, and Schneider (1982).

7   Stigler (1970) and Aranson and Ordeshook (1981).

8   Stigler (1971), Peltzman (1976), and Aranson and Ordeshook (1981).

References

Aranson, P., and Ordeshook, P. "Regulation, Redistribution, and Public Choice," *Public Choice* 37 (1981): 69–100.

Arrow, K. J. *Social Choice and Individual Values.* New York: Wiley, 1951, rev. ed. 1963.

Ashenfelter, O., and Kelley, S., Jr. "Determinants of Participation in Presidential Elections," *Journal of Law and Economics* 18 (December 1975): 695–733.

Borcherding, T. E., Pommerehne, W. W., and Schneider, F. "Comparing the Efficiency of Private and Public Production: The Evidence from Five Countries," *Zeitschrift fur Nationalokonomie* 89 (1982): 127–56.

Brennan, G., and Buchanan, J. M. "The Logic of the Levers," mimeo, George Mason University, July 1983.

Buchanan, J. M. "Social Choice, Democracy, and Free Markets," *Journal of Political Economy* 62 (April 1954a): 114–23.

"Individual Choice in Voting and the Market," *Journal of Political Economy* 62 (August 1954b): 334–43.

The Limits of Liberty: Between Anarchy and Leviathan. University of Chicago Press, 1975.

Buchanan, J. M., and Tullock, Gordon. *The Calculus of Consent: Logical Foundations of Constitutional Democracy.* Ann Arbor: University of Michigan Press, 1962.

Clark, E. H. "Multipart Pricing of Public Goods," *Public Choice* 29 (Spring 1971): 17–33.

Coughlin, P., and Nitzan, S. "Electoral Outcomes with Probabilistic Voting and Nash Social Welfare Maxima," *Journal of Public Economics* 15 (1981): 113–21.

Downs, A. *An Economic Theory of Democracy.* New York: Harper & Row, 1957.

Groves, T., and Ledyard, J. "Optimal Allocation of Public Goods: A Solution to the 'Free Rider' Problem," *Econometrica* 45 (May 1977): 783–809.

Harsanyi, John C. "Cardinal Welfare, Individualistic Ethics, and Interpersonal

96   **Dennis C. Mueller**

Comparisons of Utility," *Journal of Political Economy* 63 (August 1955): 309–21.

Hylland, A., and Zeckhauser, R. "Selecting Public Goods Bundles with Preferences Unknown and Tax System Given," mimeo, Harvard University, 1979.

Ledyard, J. "The Pure Theory of Large Two Candidate Elections," *Public Choice* 41 (1984): 7–41.

Moulin, H. "Prudence and Sophistication in Voting Strategy," *Journal of Economic Theory* 24 (1981): 398–412.

Mueller, D. C. "Voting by Veto," *Journal of Public Economics* 10 (August 1978): 57–75.

"Voting by Veto and Majority Rule," in H. Hanusch, ed., *Public Finance and the Quest for Efficiency,* Detroit, Mich.: Wayne State University Press, 1984, pp. 69–85.

"The Voting Paradox," in C. K. Rowley, ed., *Democracy and Public Choice,* Oxford: Blackwell Publisher, 1987, pp. 77–99.

Public Choice II. Cambridge University Press, forthcoming.

Orzechowski, W. "Economic Models of Bureaucracy: Survey, Extensions and Evidence," in T. E. Borcherding, ed., *Budgets and Bureaucrats,* Durham, N.C.: Duke University Press, 1977, pp. 229–59.

Peltzman, S. "Toward a More General Theory of Regulation," *Journal of Law and Economics* 19 (August 1976): 611–40.

Rawls, J. *A Theory of Justice.* Cambridge, Mass.: Harvard University Press, 1971.

Reid, T. R. "Congress: Best Little Soap Opera on Cable," *Washington Post,* April 29, 1984.

Samuelson, P. A. "The Pure Theory of Public Expenditures," *Review of Economics and Statistics* 36 (November 1954): 386–9.

Sen, A. K. "Liberty, Unanimity and Rights," *Economica* 43 (August 1976): 217–45.

"Social Choice Theory: A Re-examination," *Econometrica* 45 (January 1977): 53–89.

Stigler, G. J. "Director's Law of Public Income Redistribution," *Journal of Law and Economics* 13 (April 1970): 1–10.

"The Theory of Economic Regulation," *Bell Journal of Economics and Management* 2 (Spring 1971): 3–21.

Taylor, M. J. *Anarchy and Cooperation.* New York: Wiley, 1976.

Tideman, J. M., and Tullock, G. "A New and Superior Process for Making Social Choices," *Journal of Political Economy* 84 (December 1976): 1145–59.

CHAPTER 5

The democratic order and public choice

Peter H. Aranson

1   Individual preferences, institutions, and public choice

Before the development of public-choice theory, normative writing about the public sector in general, and about democratic politics in particular, belonged to one of two broad categories. First, many critics defended or decried some particular public policy as advancing or denying the achievement of a just society, as they defined it. Both history and contemporary political life provide ample evidence of this kind of critical writing. For example, in earlier days advocates for and against slavery, the gold standard, progressive taxation, labor-union cartels, economic planning, and international isolationism dominated political discourse. And each advocate framed his argument in terms of fulfilling some vision of justice. Today many of the issues seem different, but as contemporary writers argue for or against a woman's right to have an abortion, a greater or lesser amount of income redistribution, or more or less government regulation of the private sector, the framing of argument in terms of justice, rights, and other deontological goals persists.[1]

Second, other writers attacked or defended not the policies of government, but its structure, its organic laws, and the basis of representation, but again in terms of preconceived notions of justice or rights. Surely, such arguments are as old as the state. Plato's *Republic* proposes a structure of governance in terms of anthropomorphic balance, by casting an

97

analogy between just persons and just polities.[2] John Stuart Mill held that proportional representation perfected the relationship between the elector and his agent, inter alia as a matter of right.[3] In this century the debate continued, with some recapitulating the Millian argument[4] but others regarding proportional representation as a source of political instability.[5] Similar arguments focus on problems from expanding the franchise,[6] reapportionment,[7] and gerrymandering,[8] to judicial review of legislative enactments[9] and legislative delegation to administrative agencies.[10]

This second set of commentaries often resembles the first, in that advocates or opponents of structural change or the status quo frame their arguments (though not exclusively) in terms of justice, rights, and other deontological goals. There are notable exceptions, of course. Hobbes, for example, justified absolute monarchy to avoid "continuall feare, and danger of violent death; and the life of man, solitary, poore, nasty, brutish, and short."[11] Not long ago opponents of malapportionment urged reform because, in their view, it would justifiably increase the material well-being of blacks and urban residents.[12] And today writers such as Michelman, in considering governmental structures, argue against an economic interpretation of rights and for one grounded on goals, inter alia, of maximizing political participation.[13] To cast the goal of the state in other terms, by this view, would deny human beings self-actualization through political participation and self-government, activities that Aristotle thought necessary for a claim to humanity.[14]

Public-choice theory differs in at least four respects from these normative exercises about public policy and public institutions. First, public-choice theory, even in its (conditionally) normative forms, remains largely a positive theory. That is, in borrowing its methodology from microeconomics, it takes people's preferences as given[15] and seeks to explain and predict how people will act (and react) in the domains of politics and government, independent of the researcher's view of justice.

Second, public-choice theory rests on a methodological individualism. This dependence implies, first, that the relevant actors are individual human beings themselves, and not groups, classes, nations, races, or collectivities. It implies, second, that the goals and preferences of individual human beings provide the animus for choice and action. Much public-choice scholarship assumes that the functions that people maximize (the risk-adjusted goals they seek to achieve) involve economic outcomes that engage their narrowly defined self-interest. But this description need not hold true. Models incorporating (or claiming to find) ideological motives[16] or other noneconomic or altruistic goals[17] appear regularly in the professional literature. Yet no matter what the public-choice scholar asserts to be the chooser's preference ordering, the source of that ordering is

the chooser himself, and not some incorporeal concept of justice or goodness, although such concepts might inform the chooser's preferences.
Accordingly, public-choice theory relies on no disembodied standard by
which to judge public policies, the outcomes of political and governmental processes. These outcomes public-choice scholars judge (when they do
so) solely by the degree to which they satisfy the preferences and goals that
individual human beings use to order them.

Third, public-choice theory interprets alternative political and governmental structures as more or less perfect engines for converting individual
preferences into public policies. These institutions need not hold value
apart from the collective actions they partly determine. Of course, people
may attach different values to alternative institutional arrangements,
which are distinguishable from the public-policy outcomes that those
arrangements might imply.[18] And such values often seem to be the stuff
out of which people construct debates about institutional legitimacy. But
more often than not, the proponents of institutional change wish either to
bring about a different set of public-policy outcomes or to select a different set of governors. Still, the possibility remains that judgments about
institutions may seem independent of judgments about the outcomes that
those institutions make possible, just as judgments about the outcomes
themselves may not solely reflect economic considerations alone.

Fourth, public-choice theory assesses institutions according to how
well they satisfy individual (instrumental and noninstrumental) preferences, and not according to how well they satisfy some incorporeal view of
justice or goodness, apart from the values and preferences that people
hold themselves. Public-choice scholars, in their clearest modes of
thought, apply standards such as Pareto optimality or technological efficiency to assess the outcomes of political and governmental institutions,
not because they value these standards in and of themselves, but because
these standards provide clearly defined (if not always unique) measures of
how well a particular institutional arrangement converts individual preferences into public choices.

This final difference between public-choice analysis and other varieties
of writing provides the point of departure for this essay; but more important, it describes public-choice theory's most seminal contributions to
scholarly discourse about the democratic order. To put these contributions in proper perspective requires that we elaborate on the term "institution," on the nature of the comparisons that public-choice, comparative theories of institutions might offer, and on the choice of institutions
themselves.

First, by "institution" we mean the formal and informal, written or
unwritten set of rules under which human interaction in general, and

human exchange of all varieties in particular, might occur. A constitution describes the institution of government, its constituent parts (e.g., legislature, courts, and executive branch), their functions and relations, one to the other(s), the methods of officeholder selection, the qualifications, if any, that officeholders and members of the electorate must satisfy, and the institution's enumerated powers and process and value limitations. A market without a common law, law merchant, or customary law, for example, is also an institution,[19] as is a market governed by common law rules of contract or one governed by overtly political institutions, including legislatures, courts, agencies, and executive-branch offices. In its broadest form, then, an institution – a set of rules – provides for an allocation of rights, which rights may be certain or "probabilistic" in their enforcement and alienable or inalienable with respect to those who enjoy them.

Second, it is not sufficient for the comparative assessment of institutions merely to describe people's preferences and individual actions and then to show how a particular set of institutions might convert those preferences into a public choice. Other aspects of the environment, which inhere in the people or the institutions themselves, may also condition the nature of both individual action and collective choice. For example, Coase shows that, in the absence of transaction costs, a common law rule's assignment of rights and liabilities, so long as such a rule is present and the rights defined by it remain alienable, results in an efficient allocation of resources.[20] But if transaction costs are high, perhaps because of large-number problems, then the rule's assignment of rights and liabilities may matter, and the resulting resource allocation may be inefficient.[21] Hence, the relations and conditions prevailing among potential defendants or potential plaintiffs, say, insofar as they affect the levels and varieties of transaction costs, may affect the allocative consequences that the institution of common law courts might imply. Similarly, Buchanan and Tullock, to describe a second example, show that the level of external costs and decision costs can influence the relative merit of majority rule, as compared, for instance, with a rule of extraordinary majorities or of unanimity.[22]

Third, because alternative institutions differ in the way they convert individual preferences into public choices, and because a single institution may convert individual preferences into different public choices as a function of other aspects of the environment, which themselves may vary, it is not surprising that people hold a variety of preferences defined over institutions and therefore that the institutions themselves may be the object of choice.[23] In short, "institutions are probably best seen as congealed tastes. . . . [I]f . . . an institution is sufficiently distasteful to most participants, it is possible to reconstruct institutions. . . . In that sense rules or institutions are just more alternatives in the policy space and the status quo of one set of rules can be supplanted with another set of rules. . . . In the end, therefore, institutions are no more than rules and rules are themselves the product of social decisions."[24]

Because people *can* choose the institutions under which they will make future decisions, and because institutions, given preferences and environmental aspects, have allocative, distributional, and other consequences for public choice, we expect to find, and do find, that discourse about institutions makes up the grand questions of political philosophy. This essay concerns the manner in which one institution, representative democracy, converts individual preferences into public choices. A focus on preference conversion allows us to concentrate on four problems of representative democracy that may make it difficult for this institution to render public choices that satisfy such basic standards as Pareto optimality. These problems include rational abstention, rational ignorance, disequilibrium, and rent seeking. Section 2 describes these problems in turn and links them to degradations in citizens' welfare, compared with (sometimes) theoretically identifiable, superior public choices. Section 3 takes the analysis one step further, to show that in resolving one or more of these problems, we may exacerbate another. Hence, Section 3 considers the connections between and among these problems. Section 4 examines some suggestions for partial and systemic change. Section 5 concludes the essay by reflecting on certain institutional limitations as "self-denying ordinances."

2   Four problems of representative democracy

Any institution of public or private choice exhibits characteristic allocations of rights, obligations, and welfare. And each institution also manifests costs of operation. The manner in which an institution converts preferences into outcomes, net of these costs, provides one way to judge the institution itself. Here we consider four problems of representative democracy that restrict the ability of that institution to achieve reasonable connections between people's preferences and public policy.

Rational abstention

The first problem is rational abstention. Most analyses of the citizen's decision to vote or to abstain cast that decision as one of decision making under conditions of risk, in which the citizen chooses the alternative (to vote or to abstain) that yields him the greater expected utility. Thus, we may represent the citizen's calculus as

$$R = P(U - V) - C, \tag{1}$$

in which R is the citizen's expected utility from voting (minus that from abstaining), P is the sum of the probabilities that the citizen's vote makes or breaks a tie in favor of his preferred candidate, U and V represent, respectively, the citizen's utilities from the elections of the two candidates ($U > V$), and C is the citizen's cost of voting. If we let $U - V = B$, equation (1) becomes

$$R = PB - C. \tag{2}$$

If R exceeds zero, the citizen votes. Otherwise, he abstains.

Downs[25] and later Tullock[26] point out that, if we impute reasonable values to P, B, and C, it is almost always appropriate for citizens to abstain. For example, suppose that $C = \$1.00$ (a very low estimate) and that P is the probability that the citizen's vote is pivotal in an election with 60 million possible voters, whose intentions appear to be random; so $P = 1/60,000,000$. Under this interpretation B would have to exceed a "dollar equivalent" of $60 million for it to be appropriate for the citizen to vote. Therefore, these authors concluded, abstention remains a rational choice.

Several scholars have sought to develop alternative explanations of equation (2), to make voting rational, and thereby to explain the now-paradoxical observation that many citizens do vote. Some writers maintain the expected utility calculation but reinterpret the terms of equation (2). Riker and Ordeshook, for example, make two changes in the interpretation of the equation. First, they abandon the random-intention hypothesis and reinterpret P to measure a subjectively estimated function of the closeness of the election.[27] Second, they observe that a citizen may gain (noninstrumental) utility independent of the election's outcome. They express this consumption utility as D, interpret it as a "sense of civic duty" fulfilled,[28] and add it to the voting calculus thus:

$$R = PB + D - C. \tag{3}$$

Although the power of Riker and Ordeshook's statistical test from actual voting data is subject to criticism, nevertheless this formulation can explain voting, because D need only exceed C for voting to be appropriate. Other writers have tried to calculate P directly, as a function of the electorate's size and the election's expected closeness.[29] The principal conclusion of this literature is that, for the individual citizen, P is somewhat larger than the a priori, equiprobable (random-intention) likelihood of being the pivotal voter. But its value remains below that which we would expect for modern representative democracies, in which turnout occurs at greater than trivial rates.

A second approach takes as its point of departure Downs's[30] claim of conjectural variation in the voting decision: If all citizens abstain, because R is less than zero, then one citizen alone can control the election outcome by voting ($P = 1.0$); but if all citizens so calculate, then all vote (P becomes approximately zero). The result of this process is an infinite regress of the "they think that I think that they think that . . ." variety. If so, the citizen confronts a decision problem (to vote or to abstain) under conditions of uncertainty, and its appropriate solution must lie in the theory of games, perhaps as a minimax-regret decision criterion[31] or as a Nash equilibrium to the underlying n-person game.[32] Sometimes these formulations predict significant turnout,[33] but more often they do not.[34]

It is patent that the institutional character of a large electorate, implying the presence of a potentially large number of voters, leads to a serious erosion of the instrumental value of voting. Hence, few persons might express their preferences in the political process, leaving those preferences potentially uncounted in the formation of public policy. In this sense the institution of representative democracy differs markedly from that of the market. There, the consumer ignores P and B and merely compares C (his consumption opportunity set, derived from relative prices and income) and D (his indifference curves, derived from his preferences for goods themselves), to arrive at an optimal market basket.[35] But "participate" the consumer does, although the collective consequences of his choices remain epiphenomenal to his decision, yet crucially important to the allocation and distribution of productive assets.

It is unclear exactly why abstention, a feature of citizen-preference revelation, seems so troublesome, absent some value for voting in democratic ideology independent of the instrumental value of voting. After all, if the distribution of abstention (or voting) fails to correlate with the distribution of preferences, then preferences among the prevailing set of voters forms a randomly drawn statistical sample of all citizens. Though some error seems likely in drawing the sample, it surely is less than politicians' and pollsters' measurement errors.[36]

A problem emerges, however, if turnout rates do correlate with preferences. And we know that they do. For example, turnout rates in American national elections correlate with race (whites have higher turnout rates than do blacks) and positively with income and education.[37] These variables, in turn, correlate with political preferences and party identification.[38] So the distribution of voters' preferences may differ markedly from the distribution of preferences in the eligible electorate. To the extent that public policy reflects the first and not the second of these distributions, this imperfection in the conversion of citizens' preferences into public policy may be serious.

We understand only imperfectly why 68 percent of citizens with annual incomes above 50,000 dollars voted in the 1980 American presidential election, for example, whereas only 39 percent of citizens with incomes of less than 5,000 dollars did so.[39] But plainly, the explanation for this difference must be endogenous to the citizen's calculus of voting, as equation (3) or some alternative formulation represents it.[40]

Rational ignorance

The second problem, rational ignorance, derives inexorably from the first, rational abstention. Downs first explored both problems and their near identity.[41] He observed that the citizen's instrumental value for information about the issues in an election is a function of the benefit to be gained from making a correct choice, which better information will make more likely. Were the decision a private one, the value of information in our earlier terms, and net of transaction costs, would be no more than $D - C$. But the citizen discounts the collective consequences of his vote, $B = U - V$, by P, and he must discount it further, because the government may not "listen" to him and because the eventual connection between the policy instruments of government (the form of actual statutes and regulations) and their eventual impact on the citizen and on others whom he cares about may seem obscure.[42] Accordingly, if citizens' information about public issues is random, those elected may enjoy a substantial monopoly over public policy. At the very least, accountability may be less than desired.

That citizens may rationally remain ignorant would thus appear to pose a threat to democratic governance. The U.S. Supreme Court shows some evidence of this belief in the steps it has taken to ensure that public discussion of issues can proceed with little fear of successful libel actions if there is no showing of "actual malice,"[43] even when the statements complained of may be erroneous.

> Authoritative interpretations of the First Amendment guarantees consistently have refused to recognize an exception for any test of truth, whether administered by judges, juries, or administrative officials – and especially not one that puts the burden of proving truth to the speaker. The constitutional protection does not turn upon "the truth, popularity, or social utility of the ideas and beliefs which are offered . . . . [E]rroneous statement is inevitable in free debate, and . . . it must be protected if the

freedoms of expression are to have the 'breathing space' that they 'need . . . to survive.' "[44]

But we may ask the same question about rational ignorance that we asked about rational abstention: As long as some citizens are informed, and if the distribution of ignorance fails to correlate with the preferences that might have emerged had all voters been well informed, why should we worry about rational ignorance? Why, indeed? Provided that an electoral equilibrium exists, the location of that equilibrium would not change in the presence of a partially but randomly ignorant electorate, except, perhaps, if citizens' ignorance were complete and therefore voting became entirely random, thus destroying any electoral public-policy equilibrium.

Our concerns here take precisely the same form that they assumed for rational abstention, with one additional problem. The original problem with rational abstention carries forward to rational ignorance: Ignorance and preferences do correlate. Downs is quite specific on this matter. Citizens enjoy more information in their capacity as producers than in their capacity as consumers.[45] This information asymmetry has two sources. First, producers naturally enjoy a superior advantage, because they can specialize in knowledge about their particular product or service, whereas consumers have to know about several goods or services to overcome producers' informational advantages. Second, concerning the issue at hand, say a regulatory policy or tariff in favor of the producer, the producer is likely to have a larger differential benefit B with respect to that issue than is the consumer.

The additional problem flows from the first. Government, as a monopoly, is a producer. Hence, the agents of government might enjoy information about its policies and their consequences that is superior to that of the consumer-citizen. This advantage might then enhance the monopoly power of government beyond what citizens would prefer were their preferences well informed. Indeed, citizens might have no preferences at all on this issue. This additional problem appears to be the principal concern of the Constitution and the Supreme Court in their attempts to guarantee free press, speech, and assembly against governmental actions to limit these activities.

Scholars have responded in two ways to the information problem. The first emerges in the study of retrospective voting, a process wherein citizens merely consult their welfare under past alternative governments.[46] Retrospective voting does not require the citizen to predict the consequences of various proposed public policies to predict future welfare. Nor need the citizen perform any calculations at all, except to correlate the political "brand names" of past presidents and congresses with his personal well-being in the respective periods. Indeed, to the extent that Knightian or more radical forms of uncertainty prevent the citizen from gaining knowledge about future public-policy issues, retrospective voting may be a rational response to that kind of uncertainty.[47]

The second response, relying on a rational-expectations approach, assumes a partially informed electorate, in which information derives principally from polling data and interest-group endorsements.[48] Sequential polls (and past election results) give the uninformed citizen proxies for information about candidates' public-policy positions, and the uninformed citizen then (in experiments) votes accurately about 80 percent of the time (compared with a 90 percent accuracy rate for the citizen who knows the candidates' actual positions).

Both responses to the rational-ignorance problem – retrospective voting and rational expectations – exhibit obvious merit. But they do not necessarily reduce the problem's severity. For example, suppose that producers, including governments, do enjoy an information advantage over consumers of the sort that Downs identifies. The policy consequences of that advantage would then persist in all previous and present elections. Under a retrospective-voting approach, citizens would consult their prior utility streams under previous governments, but to no avail, since expectations about the future would merely recapitulate history, and present promises, under the theory's terms, would be subject to total discounting.

Under a rational-expectations approach, the theory fully incorporates just the kind of interest-group, information-source problem that Downs identifies, inasmuch as the interest groups seem more likely to be producer than consumer organizations.[49] Hence, rational abstention and rational ignorance, through their effects on the nature of voting, generate a problem concerning both the allocative and distributional consequences of public policy, about which problem itself the electorate is effectively incapable of expressing a preference.

Disequilibrium

The first two problems of representative democracy, rational abstention and rational ignorance, concern the nature of the "input" to public-choice institutions and the manner in which those institutions condition that input. The final two problems, disequilibrium and rent seeking, concern as well the "outputs" of those institutions. Disequilibrium formed one of the earliest concerns of social theorists. Its first recorded appearance is in the work of Condorcet[50] and later in that of the Rev. C. L. Dodgson (Lewis Carroll);[51] in this century the fullest initial development appears in monographs by Duncan Black[52] and Kenneth J. Arrow.[53] It is

Table 1. *Simple example of intransitive social preference*

Voter	First choice	Second choice	Third choice
1	A	B	C
2	B	C	A
3	C	A	B

impossible to review here in any detail the very extensive literature in this field.[54]

A simple example illustrates the essence of disequilibrium. Suppose that an electorate of three voters – 1, 2, and 3 – casts pairwise votes for three motions – A, B, and C – and that the three voters have individual preference orders as depicted in Table 1. In a vote between motions A and B, voters 1 and 3 vote for A over B; voter 2 votes for B; and therefore A defeats B by a vote of 2 to 1. In a vote between B and C, 1 and 2 vote for B; 3 votes for C; so B defeats C by the same margin. But in a vote between A and C, 2 and 3 vote for C; 1 votes for A; so C defeats A by the same margin. Hence, the "social-preference" relation is

$$A > B > C > A \tag{4}$$

where ">" reads "is preferred to."

Scholars have spent the years since the publication of the first edition of Arrow's monograph (1951) investigating the implications of results such as that in (4). These implications tend to fall in one of two areas. First, as does Arrow, many writers try to examine the possibility of an institution that simultaneously satisfies certain properties. These properties ordinarily concern the manner in which the institution must convert individual preferences into a collective choice.

Arrow, for example, develops five criteria that, he believes, any institution should satisfy: (1) universal admissibility – the institution should register any possible (strict) preference ordering over the outcomes; (2) nonperversity – a change in at least one person's preference ordering in favor of a particular alternative should not result in that alternative standing lower in the social-preference relation; (3) independence from irrelevant alternatives – if an individual voter's preference ordering not involving his ordering between motions A and B changes, say, then the social preference over A and B should not change; (4) citizens' sovereignty – this condition would be violated, for example, if all citizens ranked A first in their individual preference orderings, but some other motion stood highest in the social-preference relation; and (5) nondictatorship – no voter exists whose most preferred outcome stands highest in the social-preference relation, no matter what individual preference orderings other voters might hold. Arrow proves an impossibility theorem, showing that no institution can simultaneously satisfy all five conditions and yield a connected and transitive social-preference relation. Stated differently, any institution that satisfies conditions (1) – (3) must yield preference relations that are either imposed or dictatorial. (The connection between Arrow's impossibility theorem and the individual orderings found in Table 1 is that his proof uses such an ordering to show impossibility.)

Several scholars take Arrow's work as a point of departure but modify one or more of the conditions in an attempt to delimit the theorem's domain and implications.[55] All five conditions (and alternatives that later essays propose) exhibit normative implications. For example, universal admissibility, to the extent that group identification may correlate with preferences, "looks like" universal suffrage, and nondictatorship means exactly that. Similarly, nonperversity [condition (2)] is at least necessary for Pareto optimality, a central test of any institution. Hence, Arrow's impossibility theorem and its progeny remain troublesome for theorists of democracy precisely because they call on them to sacrifice at least one condition among several that are normatively attractive. Arrow, of course, failed to accomplish what he set out to do: to construct a reasonable social-welfare function based on individual ordinal preferences.

A second line of research, and one in which we have greater interest here, takes individual preferences, such as those in Table 1, and asks directly, What is the outcome of an election over the alternatives? Plainly, an election with all three motions voted on simultaneously will produce a three-way tie. But suppose that the institution incorporates pairwise majority-rule voting. If so, then we know that the social-preference relation is intransitive, and therefore we cannot attribute rationality, in the sense of coherence (transitivity), to this group-decision process: A defeats B, B defeats C, C defeats A, and so on. Furthermore, we cannot predict, merely from the orderings given, which motion the voting body will choose. For there exists no motion that defeats or ties all other motions. The outcomes selected remain in constant disequilibrium, merely an artifice, inter alia, of when the voting stops. In sum, the institution reveals no "group interest" or "public interest."

But there is more. Notice that if one person, say a chairman, chooses the order in which the citizens vote on the alternatives, he can determine which alternative wins. For example, if he most prefers C, he can set A against B in the first vote, and the winner, A, against C, which then wins by a two-to-one vote in the second vote. More generally, by bringing up his most preferred alternative last, against the winner of the previous vote, he ensures that alternative's victory.[56]

But there is still more. Notice from the orderings in Table 1 that, if voter 1 knows that the agenda will be A against B, winner (A) against C, then he also knows that C, his least preferred alternative, will win. Hence, in the first vote, between A and B, 1 might disguise his true preferences and vote for B over A. Motion B will then win and go on to defeat C in the next vote. By this use of "sophisticated voting," or "strategic voting," 1 guarantees himself B, his second choice, over C, his third.[57]

We have not yet begun to exhaust the possibilities that inhere in Table 1. Obviously, the voting rules that characterize the institution, given individual preferences, may determine the outcome. For example, suppose that any motion chosen must then be paired against the status quo, and suppose that A or B or C might be the status quo. Such a rule would then favor the status quo. Or suppose that a committee reports a motion, say A, to the legislature, in which B is the status quo. If no amendments are allowed, A wins. But if a motion, C, can be offered as an amendment to A, C defeats A, which B, the status quo, defeats in turn.

Plainly, the institutional rules are crucial to public choice. A change of rules can induce equilibrium or destroy it;[58] a change of rules can also induce voters to act in a sophisticated, strategic manner or not to do so; and the interplay of rules and voting strategy can reach high levels of complexity.[59] But why should this be so? Given a set of individual preferences, we should expect a "successful" institution to map those preferences into a unique equilibrium alternative, if it exists, or into a set of alternatives, if "social indifference" prevails. Our growing knowledge about the effects of rules suggests a different result, however, one in which rules, not preferences alone, partly determine the alternative(s) chosen.

Because rules can influence the alternative chosen, as we pointed out earlier,[60] we can often find political argument at an earlier stage of choice, concerning which rules to impose on the collective-choice body. As a consequence, any intransitivity in the social-preference relation will pervade decisions about rules as well as about the public choices that people make under those rules.

The search for electoral equilibrium or disequilibrium, as well as attempts to predict the public choices that actually occur, goes forward in two institutional contexts. The first context is a committee deliberation, in which there is a finite number of voters. The second context is the large electorate, which the researcher can describe as containing an uncountably infinite number of voters, the distribution of whose members' most preferred positions he represents by a density function.

Despite occasional claims that these two contexts impose different sets of constraints on participants (e.g., transaction costs),[61] disequilibrium remains in both institutional settings. Any other differences that do emerge appear to be artifacts of mathematical structure, and not of actual choice. For example, citizens in large electorates can and do engage in a form of sophisticated voting in which they vote strategically for their second choice in order to deny a victory to their third choice in a three-candidate election;[62] we now know that, in proportional representation systems, citizens might even find it instrumentally rational to vote for their third choice;[63] and in placing candidates before the general elector-ate, the nominators partly control the agenda and can select candidates with victory in mind.[64] Most important, general theorems have been developed that show global intransitivity in the social-preference relation for either institutional setting.[65] The possibility of intransitivity has even been identified in voting in the U.S. Supreme Court.[66]

No matter what the institution – committee, legislature, court, or large electorate – and no matter which form it addresses – impossibility theorem, proof of instability and disequilibrium, or rules- and strategy-related effects – this body of research presents a raw challenge to the notion that any institution, in principle, can provide a direct and welfare-regarding mapping from citizens' preferences to public choice. Nor can we easily set this challenge aside, for it bespeaks a fundamental incoher-ence in public-choice processes.

Rent seeking

The final problem that we consider here, the collective provision of pri-vate benefits, has been identified in three robust and growing bodies of research. The first of these, informed by the work of Olson,[67] is largely the product of economists and law professors at the University of Chicago.[68] Its principal concern is the use of regulation to provide benefits to regu-lated firms, often through cartelization, to the detriment of consumers' welfare. As such, this body of theoretical research reflects earlier empirical political-science and historical literature on the administrative process, which first developed the "capture" hypothesis concerning regulatory agencies.[69]

The second body of research, carried on by political scientists and economists, seeks to explore the nature of political demand for and supply of public policy in a variety of institutions and to show the interrelation-ships among these institutions with respect to the incentives faced by those who make them up.[70] Many of the principal architects of this ap-proach received their training in the University of Rochester's political science graduate program and in the California Institute of Technology's social science group.

The third and most recent approach is most closely associated with the "Virginia school" and the Center for Study of Public Choice at George Mason University.[71] This work concentrates on the "rent-seeking" aspects of political demand for private advantage, and as such it builds on the earlier research of Krueger.[72] Though it is the latest addition to the literature, it is expanding more rapidly than the other two branches.

But what is the problem that these three bodies of research address? Like Arrow's approach, this research sets up a set of properties or conditions that political and governmental institutions must satisfy. Then it proceeds to show, both theoretically and empirically, that representative democracy fails to satisfy them. And as in Arrow's approach, the properties or conditions assert a set of desirable connections between citizens' preferences and public choices. But in this literature the conditions emerge specifically and sometimes self-consciously out of the economic theory of welfare. That is, utility interdependencies in *private choice* may create situations in which people in various social or economic capacities do not bear the full costs of their activities or cannot capture enough of their activities' benefits to others to induce them to produce at optimal levels. Possible theoretical results for private choice take the form of too high a level of "public bads" (e.g., pollution),[73] too low a level of "public goods" (e.g., national defense),[74] too much market power (monopoly),[75] crowding of resources available in common (e.g., oil deposits or the radio-frequency spectrum),[76] and inadequate levels of mutually preferred, consensual redistribution.[77]

The structure of welfare theory commends itself to those who regard government as the appropriate agency for overcoming these problems, to achieve *theoretically* identifiable, welfare-improving results: "Government provision of public goods is required precisely because each individual in uncoordinated [*sic*] pursuit of his self-interest must act in a manner designed to frustrate the provision of these items."[78]

We must say at the outset that various writings over the past twenty years have smitten the utility-interdependence justification for public action hip and thigh.[79] Various contracting possibilities delimit the range of external diseconomies that a market otherwise cannot resolve.[80] The generation of public goods can also occur in the private sector, sometimes by internalization, sometimes by appropriate contracting,[81] sometimes by only modest changes in property rights,[82] and sometimes by internal restructuring in private organizations.[83] Little remains of monopoly justifications for public choice except in the natural-monopoly, public-utility field, and even that area finds substantial dispute.[84] The solution to crowding appears to be privatization, as most instances of that phenomenon occur in public-sector service areas, for good and sufficient theoretical reasons related to politicians' and bureaucrats' incentives to maximize political support for these programs by charging below market-clearing prices, thus enlarging the population served as a source of political support.[85] Finally, the redistribution problem, again for good and sufficient theoretical reasons, in practice finds use to justify redistributions upward, to high- and middle-income citizens, and not the other way around.[86]

Plainly, much of the intellectual ground has been taken out from under the structure of welfare justifications for state action. Even so, an occasional economist persists in interpreting the actual pattern of state action as corresponding to the supposed imperatives of welfare theory. Mueller is most insistent in this regard, and therefore we quote from him at length. First, he sets the case for welfare theory:

> An important impetus to the development of public choice in the fifties and sixties was the significant contributions to public finance theory defining the concepts of public goods and externalities and analyzing their characteristics. This literature made crystal clear that there are certain goods whose physical properties are such that market exchange leads to an inefficient allocation of resources. All could be made better off if some institution could be found for providing public goods to all individuals collectively, for inducing individuals to modify the selfish pursuit of their own goals in order to take account of the unintended external effects of their actions on others.[87]

We have just examined this claim and found that the theory, on its own terms, resolves into normative recommendations for a far more limited domain of state action than we find practiced today among Western representative democracies. But then comes the special pleading that the theory seems predictively robust:

> A testable implication of public goods–externality theory is that goods with certain characteristics should be purchased in cooperation with others, and other goods with identifiable characteristics of a private good nature will be left to the realm of individual choice in the market. To my knowledge these predictions of public goods theory have never been put to empirical test, perhaps because the validity of the predictions is obvious from casual observation. Thus, if one were to formulate a null hypothesis, that the probability of a good's being purchased collectively or privately is independent of its physical characteristics, and test it against the predictions of public goods theory using cross-section data from cities, states, and countries, one would reject the null hypothesis by a comfortable margin. Police protection is purchased invariably collectively, cups and saucers privately. Those goods that are provided collectively in some places and

privately in others, like housing and education, are precisely the goods whose characteristics do not match closely the polar definitions of public and private goods, so-called mixed public–private goods, private goods with significant externalities.[88]

I am far from as certain as Mueller, "perhaps because the validity of the predictions is obvious from casual observation," that we could reject the null hypothesis that he proposes at a statistically significant level. For example, the private sector pays for and produces directly every manner of police protection and its substitutes, from actual security guards, squad cars, and private detectives and bodyguards to elaborate internal-security arrangements in firms, theft insurance, and security devices.[89] The elaborate landscaping in the front yards of many American homes and commercial buildings also provides significant external benefits to entire neighborhoods and communities. Charitable giving abounds, as do private schools,[90] art museums, and symphony orchestras. But then, free (unpriced) parking lots flourish, providing significant benefits for stores that do not pay for them. An occasional private road is not unheard of, and the number of other privately created facilities ordinarily associated with the production of external benefits might be greater still, had not government taxed away wealth to provide some of these facilities itself.

The other side of any test of Mueller's hypothesis perforce must contemplate that governments do many things that bear no necessary relationship to "public" welfare, as an economist might define it. That is, governments create private benefits, not public goods, at collective cost. Most of the regulation of private firms at federal, state, and local levels is an example of this phenomenon,[91] and the result is the political creation and maintenance of cartels and monopolies, with the supply of their associated rents. Sometimes government subsidizes private consumption and production directly, the beneficiaries being firms in particular industries, particular congressional districts,[92] or identifiable, separable groups in the population. Any external benefits from these programs almost certainly remain Pareto inferior in their allocative consequences.[93]

But even in those instances when government provides public goods or suppresses the production of public bads or redistributes income in the "correct" direction or controls alleged monopolistic effects or practices, the animating spirit behind the actual policy instruments chosen ordinarily turns out to be the collective provision of private benefits. For example, when government provides national defense, the choices of weapons systems, facility sitings, and levels of remuneration of defense contractors appear to reflect concern for particular congressional districts and private-sector suppliers, not for optimal resource allocations.[94] In suppressing real and alleged external diseconomies, government often serves as an auctioneer, and thus is a party in interest, as various sections of the country[95] or producer (or labor)[96] groups bid for policies that will aid them by imposing disproportionately higher costs on their competitors. In redistributing income, government either redistributes in the "wrong" direction, as noted earlier,[97] or creates rents for members of minority groups who already have succeeded. And in controlling the development and actions of firms with supposed market power, until recently government has benefited weak competitors, at the expense of consumers and more efficient firms.[98]

As we suggest earlier,[99] three overlapping and mutually supporting bodies of research explain and document the problem of the collective provision of private benefits. Here we review briefly the second body of research, the extensive study of interrelated public-sector institutions, not because the other two approaches are in any sense inferior, but because the second approach is the one with which we are most familiar.[100]

The problem with the *public* production of public goods is a complete reflection of the problem with the *private* production of public goods: The public sector, as is claimed of the private sector, enjoys no incentives for getting public consumers (voters and interest groups) and public producers (politicians and bureaucrats) to demand and supply such goods. Hence, "market failure" and "political failure" label the same phenomenon, because it occurs in both groups of institutions and for roughly comparable reasons. Indeed, insofar as government *fails* to resolve private-sector, welfare-related problems by the adjustment of property rights, taxes, regulation, and the like, to that extent any existing market failure surely represents but a special case of political failure.

As with the earlier problems that we described, the explanation for the more general case of political failure begins with citizens' preferences. Those preferences may exist in anomic nonrelation to one another in a partly unorganized electorate, or they may describe citizens who in turn belong to specific organized groups in the population. In forming bargains between anomic voters or members of groups, on the one hand, and politicians, on the other, group members enjoy superior economies of scale and scope in information acquisition and transaction (contracting) costs and in maintaining and enforcing agreements.

Most economic models of elections assume that citizens evaluate candidates for office on one or more dimensions, which measure the levels at which various public goods are produced, or public bads suppressed.[101] Indeed, these models also provide the basis for a search for electoral equilibria, in positing that candidates try to adopt positions in the issue space that will defeat or tie all alternative positions, given certain characteristics of the electorate's turnout response and preference distribution.

But such models assume away the important question of whether political competition takes place over alternative levels of public-goods production or whether it takes place over which private benefits the public sector might provide to particular groups, but at public, collective cost. Considering the political superiority of groups in registering their members' preferences in the political process, this question demands an answer, which Table 2 suggests in its simplest form. The table assumes a simple game between (the leaders of) two interest groups, whose mutually exclusive memberships exhaust the population. Each group faces a budget constraint, allowing it to pursue one and only one program in the legislature. One program would give the group a private, divisible benefit of B, whose cost C each group would share. The other program would create a public good, with an associated benefit B, which the members of both groups would consume, with no crowding effects. That program also would cost C, and the members of both groups would bear the cost collectively.

Table 2 shows the resulting game, which assumes that a group is perfectly effective in getting the program it seeks. If B is less than or equal to $C/2$, there is no political demand for either program. But if B is greater than $C/2$, then each group lobbies for its private-benefit program, thus imposing a total social cost of C.[102] Ordeshook and I have generalized this game to models with n groups, with the possibility that each group can oppose other groups' demands,[103] and to coalitions among groups in three-group models.[104] Our findings do little to change the conclusion that political groups are subject to the same Prisoner's Dilemma structure that supposedly afflicts private-sector producers and consumers in their non-production of public goods. The groups' problem is also analogous to that of the overgrazed commons, because individual groups treat the fisc and access to regulatory protection with a substantially reduced concern for the total costs of their political demands.

Furthermore, if groups' budgets are constrained, their leaders will tend to purchase efficient programs in the private sector (for which $B > C$) but demand inefficient ones in the public sector (for which $C > B > C/2$ in the two-group model). Indeed, under one rendering of this theory, political service actually turns out to be an inferior good.[105]

Governmental institutions – legislatures, elected chief executives, bureaus, and courts – provide little surcease from this problem. A theoretical exploration of legislators' decisions shows that their incentives exactly overlay those of interest-group leaders.[106] Recent empirical research on the U.S. Congress merely reinforces the same conclusion.[107] Models of the electoral process for chief executives show that under very restrictive conditions candidates and incumbent officeholders occasionally might

Table 2. *Policy game between two interest groups*

	Group 2's strategies	
Group 1's strategies	Seek public good	Seek private good
Seek public good	$B - C/2, B - C/2$	$B - C, 2B - C$
Seek private good	$2B - C, B - C$	$B - C, B - C$

Source: Peter H. Aranson, *American Government: Strategy and Choice* (Boston: Little, Brown, 1981), p. 237.

seek to limit growth in the number of private-benefit programs enacted, but more often, under the usual circumstances of incremental choice and imperfect citizen information (rational ignorance or fiscal illusion), they seek to expand that number.[108] Bureaucrats, whether they act in their own interest, and thus become indistinguishable from interest groups,[109] or act as agents of the Congress,[110] in which case they reinforce the private-interest nature of its decisions, create the same kinds of public policies. Finally, the courts appear to be locked in an implicit agreement with the legislature, by which terms they faithfully enforce rent-seeking legislative bargains, and the legislature, in its turn, respects judicial "independence."[111]

This fourth problem, like the first three, strikes directly at the notion that citizens' preferences map directly into sensible, welfare-regarding public policies. Most of the private-benefit programs that governments establish at collective cost are cost–benefit inefficient. They also create rents – payments to people at levels above those necessary to bring forth a given supply of goods or services, which thus have no positive social function – and persons, firms, and interest groups allocate substantial resources to the pursuit of these rents.[112] Hence, these private-benefit programs and even the possibility of their enactment lead to a degradation of citizens' welfare. These models also make no claim that governments never produce public goods. Obviously, they do so. But the motive for that production turns out to be the private pursuit of private goods, supplied at collective cost: rent seeking.

3   Interrelationships

Each of these four problems emerges from the larger problem of interdependence of human choice and welfare. Each seems to be a characteristic of group–public–choice. But each problem also exhibits special and unique characteristics, and therefore, for the most part, scholars have considered each in isolation from the others. Here we link them back together, to see what other insights we can gain from the exercise and to lay the groundwork for considering solutions to each problem.

Rational abstention and ignorance and disequilibrium

We consider rational abstention and ignorance together, because they grow out of the same theory, and we connect them in turn to the problems of disequilibrium and rent seeking. To examine the first of these pairs – rational abstention and ignorance, on one side, and disequilibrium, on the other – we reflect specifically on models of elections in large electorates, as described earlier.

Theorists discovered early in the development of these election models[113] that the limiting case of perfect information – among citizens about candidates' positions and among candidates about their opponents' positions and citizens' preferences – could destroy unique equilibrium outcomes, except where the models impose a high degree of symmetry. In an early article in this literature, for instance, Ordeshook and I tried to deduce unique equilibrium strategies for candidates who first must run in a primary election and then, if they win the primary, in a general election, where the distributions of primary and general-election voters' preferences are known but have different medians.[114] We assumed initially that candidates had perfect information about each others' strategies and that voters had the same information about those strategies. Try as we might, we could find no equilibria until we introduced uncertainty about the candidates' positions on the issues. When we reviewed the literature on nomination (primary) campaigns, we were not surprised to find that candidates in those contests were loath to announce clear statements of their policies.[115] The structure of electoral institutions thus leads candidates to *reduce* citizens' information about them, thereby reducing the value of the B term in equation (3), which perforce increases abstention.

Coughlin and Nitzan[116] and Ledyard[117] address the problem of disequilibrium in large electorates. Although the approaches of both articles are important contributions to the literature, neither resolves both the information and disequilibrium problems satisfactorily. Coughlin and Nitzan's models, for example, by casting abstention and voting intention (for one candidate or the other) probabilistically, and not on fully a rational-choice basis, implicitly incorporate citizen uncertainty and therefore ignorance about candidates' positions. Hence, their models resolve the disequilibrium problem by incorporating the rational-ignorance problem as an institutional feature of elections with large numbers of voters. Ledyard's model assumes that voters play a rational-choice, conjectural-variation game. But at equilibrium no one votes. Hence, his model resolves the disequilibrium problem by incorporating the rational-abstention problem as an institutional feature of such elections. In sum, each model solves one problem – disequilibrium – by relying on another's presence (rational ignorance or rational abstention).

We might have predicted these results had we attended to an important series of earlier articles by Shepsle.[118] This line of research began when Shepsle, reflecting on an earlier essay by Zeckhauser,[119] asked whether there was any way out of the paradox of voting that rested on the preference orderings shown in Table 1. The logic of his discussion is thus. Suppose that one candidate offered these three voters not a platform advocating one of the three public-policy alternatives – A or B or C – but in effect a lottery over all three alternatives, each to be chosen after the election, with equal probability. Now suppose that voter 1's utility for A is 1, for C, 0, and for B, k $(1 > k > 0)$. Voter 1 always will prefer A to this lottery, and he will always prefer this lottery to C. Finally, he will prefer this lottery to B only if $k < \frac{1}{2}$. Shepsle then proves a theorem showing that the lottery so described will defeat any certain alternative if for each voter the utility that he associates with his second-choice alternative is less than the expected utility of the lottery.

Shepsle had effectively expanded Arrow's ordinal opportunity set of pure alternatives to the space of cardinal utility with probabilistic alternatives.[120] Coughlin and Nitzan's model effectively does the same thing by mapping participation into probability space, and uncertainty also prevails at both candidates' and citizens' levels in Ledyard's model. But it was not long before Shepsle came to appreciate the (for candidates) strategic possibilities in "risky strategies" and published more general results in which he developed examples of the "strategy of ambiguity" in actual practice.[121]

The strategy of ambiguity, however, leads candidates to reduce the information they provide to citizens, thus exacerbating the rational-ignorance problem. But it also thereby reduces the information about differences between or among candidates that citizens might receive, thus diminishing the B term in equation (3), which in turn erodes voting turnout and the incentives for citizens to seek further information about the candidates' positions. The candidates' response to electoral disequilibrium, therefore, increases rational abstention and ignorance among citizens.

But do the abstention and ignorance problems thereby induced diminish the severity of the disequilibrium problem? Regrettably, no. First, we have no idea what we mean when we say that the candidate's public-policy position consists of a lottery over a range of possibilities, and perhaps over the entire conceivable range of policy options. In terms of judgments about the institution of elections, that construct leaves us no better off than did the original cyclical alternatives. Second, more recent research indicates that the lotteries themselves can and do cycle among themselves, indicating the full depth of the electoral-disequilibrium problem.[122]

Rational abstention, rational ignorance, and rent seeking

We have already implicitly suggested in our review of Downs[123] the manner in which rational abstention and rational ignorance reinforce rent seeking. Each citizen, in his capacity as a producer or specialized consumer, has more information about how government might increase or diminish his welfare in those activities directly affecting income or utility production than he has about government's effects (higher prices and restricted supply) on him as a generalized consumer of other goods and services. Hence, selective rational ignorance creates an equally selective fiscal illusion among voters, whereby they gain little or no knowledge of the costs of government's actions with respect to other producers or specialized consumers. Selective rational abstention follows directly, as citizens find a motive to vote, if they vote at all, principally in those elections in which the issues contested affect them as producers or specialized consumers.

What remains intriguing, however, is the possibility of a connection between justifications for government actions to "internalize" utility interdependencies, such as public-goods and public-bads problems, and proffered solutions to the rational-abstention problem. The justification for government action is, precisely, that people in their private capacities will not contribute (optimally) to the supply of public goods or to the suppression of public bads. But beginning with Downs, and extending through Riker and Ordeshook and Mueller, various scholars, to explain why people *do* vote, have offered the hypothesis that they do so because their votes contribute to the supply of a public good.

Downs, for example, asserts as a general proposition that "rational men in a democracy are motivated to some extent by a sense of social responsibility relatively independent of their own short-run gains and losses."[124] It follows that

> participation in elections is one of the rules of the game in a democracy, because without it democracy cannot work. Since the consequences of universal failure to vote are both obvious and disastrous, and since the cost of voting is small, at least some

men can rationally be motivated to vote even when their personal gains in the short run are outweighed by their personal costs.[125] Riker and Ordeshook similarly include in the D term of equation (3) such components as "the satisfaction of compliance with the ethic of voting . . . of affirming allegiance to the political system . . . of deciding, going to the polls . . . [and] of affirming one's efficacy in the political system."[126] And Mueller goes one step further, because he believes that an explanation for voting may require more than the hypothesized existence of an "entertainment value."[127] In particular,

> the same prisoners' dilemma game [of participation] is to be repeated again and again. Rational voters may in this prisoners' dilemma super game choose the cooperative strategy of participation. Each of us has been taught from childhood that there are certain acts which, although to our benefit to commit in the short run [e.g., abstention], are wrong in that if everyone committed similar acts we would all be worse off. . . . In a country that cherishes its political institutions voting is one of those, not very costly, sacrifices individuals make for the preservation of the social, or in this case, political order.[128]

Although this explanation for voting has some appeal, it similarly should raise a few questions. For example, if we can explain the act of voting in terms of a desire to produce a public good, the survival of the political system, then why do we require government in the first place? We should not expect, in the sense of Mueller, that people are "rational" by parts. If, on account of reason or socialization, people voluntarily supply one public good, they should be willing to supply others as well.[129]

Plainly, here we are arguing with Mueller by contrasting corner solutions, wherein people allocate an "optimal" level of their resources or none at all to the supply of public goods or to the suppression of public bads, without regard to relative prices. Just as plainly, some of the considerations that Mueller and others raise do inform those who voluntarily vote, pay taxes, clean litter from city streets, enlist in time of war, and engage in civic and other eleemosynary activities. But an attention to revealed preferences (which preferences Mueller's essay seeks to explain), no matter how crabbed it may seem, demands that we ask if those not so socialized or enlightened really benefit from the activities of those so benighted. Do they really want, or prefer to have in existence, this political system or that charitable institution?

A somewhat less stark and bizarre form of this question immediately recommends itself. Perhaps those who "believe in" the voluntary supply of voting and other public goods simultaneously differ from those who do not in the production levels of such goods that they find desirable. If so, and I believe that it is so, then when "voluntarists" or "altruists" vote, they will transmit a biased sample of the demand for public-goods production – including redistribution – to the institutions of government. Probably, they will prefer higher production levels and degrees of redistribution than will others. Hence, the public sector will grow too large, compared with its size if the sample of preferences remained unbiased. This result seems fully consistent with Downs's claim that people in their capacities as (voluntary public-goods) producers will more likely vote and have more information about the relation of government actions to the goods and services they supply than will those who are mere consumers of those goods and services.

Disequilibrium and rent seeking

In discussing the final pair of connections, that between disequilibrium and rent seeking, we enjoy the advantage of the plow having already broken the soil. Riker provided a first but largely unnoticed furrow in a 1982 essay that tried to explain why malapportionment might have no public-policy consequences.[130] Reflecting on the local basis of representation in single-member district election systems and on the instability of elections and public policy, Riker, as have others, commented:

> The American representative system . . . provides for an extremely wide range of beneficiaries. Indeed, any minority that includes some voters can get something out of some level of government. By reason of their own need for loyal future voters, legislators are engaged in a restless search for clients to serve. Therefore, persons and groups in the electorate who want service have only to make themselves available as clients, and they will be served. Even the tiniest minority (beekeepers or barbers, for example) can obtain many benefits. This is what those writers are castigating who complain of the extraordinary influence of interest groups in the American polity.[131]

Then, in the following year, Miller turned over the entire lower forty acres.[132] In his elegantly constructed and highly original essay, he demonstrated that there is a connection between the electoral instability inherent in political pluralism and the disequilibrium of public choice. His essay draws heavily on the notion in pluralist literature of "cross-cutting cleavages," which therefore merits a brief review.

Imagine an electorate whose members are entirely alike, except that some are conservative Catholics who oppose abortion and the rest are liberal Protestants who favor its (continued) legalization. Under majority rule, whichever group is larger will win every public-policy contest in the forseeable future, leading to disaffection and perhaps even to open revolt among members of the minority. But suppose that we can further differentiate the electorate according to its members' occupations, as workers and as capitalists. If all workers, say, are Catholic and all capitalists are Protestants, then the resulting cleavages – Catholics versus Protestants and workers versus capitalists – reinforce each other, and conflict and political instability can only worsen. But if some Catholics are capitalists, and some Protestants are workers, then the cleavages cross-cut. Because Catholic and Protestant workers or capitalists must make common cause with each other, each will moderate his attitudes and actions. In the limit we might imagine thousands of potentially cross-cutting cleavages, which work to restore moderation to political attitudes and actions.[133]

Similarly, in the limit the number of issues and "preference clusters" increases apace, leading precisely to the kinds of redistributive and unstable politics that so characterize the problems of both disequilibrium and rent seeking. Miller draws the immediate conclusion that the conditions that underly the stability of representative democracies, wherein shifting government and electoral coalitions satisfy everyone part of the time (rent seeking), are precisely the conditions that underly the instability (disequilibrium) of public choice, and vice versa. For when the same clear majority always prevails all of the time, cleavages are few and do not cross-cut, leading to political instability but electoral, public-choice, majoritarian stability.

Miller's insight remains an important contribution to our understanding of political and governmental institutions, but his normative characterization of this state of affairs has less to recommend it. He believes that

> on the whole, it seems clear that we should choose political stability, although we must recognize that collective rationality is not merely a technical condition, but one that has important implications, both normative . . . and empirical. . . . [C]yclical majority preference is not merely an otherwise undesirable phenomenon that happens to come along with pluralistic preference patterns and that we must accept as the unavoidable cost of achieving the great benefit of political stability, but that the "generic instability". . . of the pluralist political process is itself an important contributing factor to the stability of pluralist political systems.[134]

The problem with Miller's formulation is that he does not recognize, first, that a pluralist political system often engages in activities that enjoy no apparent welfare-related justification, in terms of converting citizens' actual preferences into public policies, and, second, that as each (small) group receives its benefit in turn, all other groups will suffer. That is, if our description of rent seeking, a feature of pluralist politics, is essentially right, then the pluralist political system gains the support of its citizens and maintains its stability by impoverishing them.[135] Stated differently, Miller not only must balance the costs of public-choice instability against the costs of political instability. He also must add in the scales the cost of losses associated with the public supply of putatively inefficient private goods.

Cast in still other terms, Miller contrasts the desideratum of maintaining the pluralist political system, in which politics comes to resemble a Hobbesian "time of Warre, where every man is Enemy to every man" and in which "the life of man" is "solitary [in his group], poore, nasty, brutish" and long and painful, with a tyranny of the majority, in which life is also short. The notion seems to be that, if some gain rents from government, the best political system is one in which all do so. Plainly, Miller's opportunity set of institutional alternatives requires expansion.

4   Proximate solutions to unresolvable problems

The preceding discussion should make it clear that we cannot by parts "solve," or even reduce the costs of, these four problems. Each relates to the others in largely unanticipated ways. Therefore, any attempt at solution must be systemic rather than partial. Here we examine partial solutions first and then turn to more nearly systemic approaches. In doing so, we associate partial solutions that attack either rational abstention or rational ignorance alone, as these problems affect public-choice inputs. Then we associate systemic solutions that attack disequilibrium and rent seeking, as these problems systemically condition public-choice outputs.

Partial approaches

Solutions to the problems of rational abstention and ignorance come immediately to mind. Any policy that will reduce the cost of voting simultaneously will increase turnout. For example, we could reduce waiting time at polling places, increase the number of such places, and provide for their optimal (and notorious) location. Postcard registration would work in the same direction, as would paying citizens to vote or fining abstainers.

Each of these approaches has problems peculiar to it. Most important, we now understand that members of the most significant but often overlooked interest group – incumbent politicians – largely control election rules and procedures to their own advantage.[136] Similarly, we would have to calculate the value of additional turnout before we allocated further resources to securing it. Finally, a tax on abstainers would impose a social cost whose associated benefit seems far from obvious, unless one values turnout in and of itself or believes that removing the bias from sampling the electorate permits such an approach.

But increased turnout might also have an impact on each of the other problems. First, in the absence of other effects, an increase in the number of voters would increase the probability of an intransitive social-preference relation. That result occurs directly in every study of the frequency of the paradox of voting (disequilibrium) of which I am aware.[137] For any number of motions greater than two, and assuming random assignment of (strict) preference orders to voters, as the number of voters increases, so does the probability that the paradox will occur. For example, with three alternatives and three voters (as in Table 1), the probability of a cycle is 5.6 percent; with nine voters, 7.8 percent; and with an infinite number of voters, 8.8 percent. With seven alternatives the probability of a cycle goes from 23.9 percent with three voters to 36.9 percent with an infinite number of voters.

Both Downs's notion of a bias in ignorance (and turnout)[138] and Miller's vision of pluralist democracy[139] suggest (implicitly in Downs and explicitly in Miller) that as turnout increases so will the number of issues increase. Here the effect of an increase in the number of issues (alternatives) on increases in the probability that an intransitive social-preference relation will occur is even more pronounced than in the number-of-voters calculation. With three voters and three alternatives, as just noted, the paradox probability is 5.6 percent; with seven alternatives it grows to 23.9 percent; and with an infinite number of alternatives it grows to 100 percent. For nine voters and three alternatives, the probability is 7.8 percent; for nine voters and seven alternatives, 34.2 percent; and for an infinite number of voters, it grows from 8.8 and 36.9 to 100 percent for three, seven, and an infinite number of alternatives, respectively. In sum, a policy that increases turnout, ceteris paribus, perforce must simultaneously increase the chances of an intransitive social-preference relation.

Increasing turnout also might exacerbate the problem of rent seeking. We have already discussed one mechanism that might create this increase, namely that which Miller identifies: the registration of more preferences for the production of still further private benefits. A second possibility would operate at the level of information and thresholds of perception through a fiscal-illusion process. As more and more groups demand private benefits, each additional benefit, ceteris paribus, is likely to be commensurately smaller than the previous one and below the threshold of perception. But as the number of voters grows, so does the free-rider problem of providing opposition to private-benefit generation through rent seeking.

This discussion leads naturally to a consideration of rational ignorance. We might imagine a variety of policy instruments to overcome it.
For example, broadcasting of legislative debates and regulatory imposition of television programming to include public-policy forums have
received some academic support.[140] The problems with these proposals,
considered alone, resemble those that we associate with policies to increase turnout. First, incumbent politicians could gain control of and
manipulate the kinds of information coming to viewers.[141] Second, regulatory imposition of programming might result in a substantial misallo-
cation of resources, not to mention the attendant First Amendment problems.[142]

But any solution to the rational-ignorance problem may also reinforce
or extend the other three problems. First, consider rational ignorance and
rational abstention. If a pure-strategy electoral equilibrium prevails and
if, as is usually true, that equilibrium finds the candidates converged to the
same position on the issues (that of the median voter), then informing all
citizens of that convergence will drive the B term in equation (3) to zero,
thereby maximizing abstention. Similarly, if disequilibrium prevails, the
candidates will try to offer policy-position lotteries to the voters. If voters
cannot penetrate the ambiguity, an improvement in their knowledge
about the ambiguity itself, given risk aversion, may lead them to abstain
in greater numbers. But if public-information programs "force" candidates to answer public-policy questions unambiguously, the resulting
electoral instability will only deepen. Finally, if the citizen's improved
information contains a better estimate of P [in equation (3)] than the
League of Women Voters ordinarily provides, then the PB term will fall to
zero or close to zero in any large electorate, leading to a lower voter
turnout. In sum, measures aimed solely at overcoming rational ignorance
well might increase rational abstention.

Second, consider rational ignorance and disequilibrium. As just noted,
the second may produce or enhance the first, by operating on either the P
or B term in the citizen's voting calculus. But can increasing the citizen's
information affect disequilibrium? As just noted, it might do so by pene-
trating the strategy of ambiguity. The effects of more information on
disequilibrium, however, might destabilize public choice, but in a round-
about way.

Recall from our earlier discussion[143] that, in the absence of information about the policy instruments that candidates espouse or of information about how those policy instruments affect their welfare, citizens may
vote retrospectively or may rely on interest-group endorsements and polling data reported for various groups in the population. Under retrospective voting, for instance, citizens simply compare their utility streams
under alternative past regimes. This decision process may lend stability to

election outcomes, as candidates work on past commitments and attend to only a small margin of change.[144] But if additional information pierces the candidates' strategy of ambiguity concerning their real postelection intentions, they may cycle all over the issue space, thus increasing citizens' risk. In short, by reducing for the citizen the attractiveness of evaluating candidates retrospectively, additional information may simultaneously increase the likelihood of disequilibrium.

More complex interactions between rational abstention and disequilibrium are also possible. An effect opposite the one just predicted may occur. As candidates increase their cycling, citizens may rely in desperation on more retrospective evaluations than they did when there was less cycling. More likely, however, candidates will enter races later than they do now, to avoid taking defeatable positions early in the campaign. That is, candidates will adopt an alternative technology for inducing voter ignorance.

Third, consider rational ignorance and rent seeking. Perhaps informing the citizen of the nature of rent seeking and of the costs associated with it will lead to a dismantling of pork-barrel and regulatory systems.[145] Indeed, Ordeshook and I discern that it is precisely a fiscal-illusion process, such as Downs describes, giving better information to concentrated producers (or specialized consumers) than dispersed consumers (or producers) enjoy, that makes the problem manifest.[146] But the additional assumption necessary for this result (a growth in the number of programs from rent seeking) is legislative or electoral incrementalism, whereby officeholders choose to add or to delete private-interest programs one or a few at a time. Under global decision procedures, by contrast, some dismantling of such programs remains possible, depending on the fiscal illusion's mathematical properties.

But if citizens' information about rent seeking becomes perfect, so that perceptions of various programs' costs and benefits encounter no thresholds, the expansion or contraction assumptions about candidates' and officeholders' decision-making processes are reversed. If citizens are perfectly informed and if politicians proceed incrementally, a contraction may occur in the number of private-interest programs. But if politicians proceed globally, that number shows a net expansion. The election itself becomes a very unstable redistributive game, one in constant disequilibrium (it has no core).

The principal question remaining is whether some relationship prevails between perfect or imperfect information among citizens and global or incremental decision procedures among candidates. I believe that such a relationship may exist. Perfect information and global choice appear to occur together, as do imperfect information and incremental choice.

Indeed, one explanation that various scholars offer for incremental choice is absence of information. Of course, here information quality describes citizens' choices, and decision procedures describe politicians' strategies, so my hypothesis remains highly tentative. Nevertheless, citizens' demands for efficiency in government, brought on by superior information, may lead politicians to calculate about public policy in global terms, thus worsening the problems of disequilibrium and rent seeking.

Systemic solutions

Partial solutions attend to the quality of inputs of public choice – abstention and ignorance – whereas systemic solutions attend to the quality of outputs – disequilibrium and rent seeking. Our review of partial solutions suggests their limitations: Each may exacerbate the other three problems. This conclusion, however tentative, leads us to ask if more nearly systemic responses to these problems might work better.

There are any number of such proposals, all of which would operate at the constitutional or near-constitutional level and all of which would seek to alter fundamentally the nature of public choices,[147] in each instance to link them more closely to citizens' preferences. The two proposals that we consider here would not address disequilibrium and rent seeking directly. Instead, they would incorporate structural changes that, in turn, would alter citizens' and politicians' incentives, and so constrain their actions.

The first proposal, which assumes many forms, is a balanced-budget amendment to the Constitution (or to an appropriate organic law), with (or without) spending limits. Those who support this proposal commonly recognize that public-sector deficit financing may find a legitimate place in any polity's collection of fiscal tools.[148] But they also believe that deficit financing has become a legislative instrument for responding more readily to rent-seeking demands. That is, the contemporary purpose of public deficits is to fund current private consumption, not public-capital formation. Indeed, insofar as future – and therefore unorganized and unrepresented – generations pay for today's spending, the concentrated-benefits, dispersed-cost explanation for the success of rent seeking remains intact, except that the resulting transfer, at least in part, becomes intertemporal: Future generations pay today's public deficits.

How might the enactment of such a proposal affect each of the four problems described earlier? We begin with rational abstention and ignorance. If we eliminate deficit spending but allow government to increase taxes, then assuming no exogenous growth of government revenues, any new program will require immediate financing through additional taxes. The cost of such a program consequently seems likely to be less hidden, leading to a higher B term in equation (3), provided that one candidate espouses the expansion but the other opposes it. Hence, turnout and information will increase. But if spending itself is constrained, then adopting a new program perforce will require deleting an existing one, leading to an increase in the B term for affected groups in the electorate. Of course, the levels of all programs may also decline to pay for the new program, and it is difficult to say how this possibility might affect turnout and information. More generally, we cannot consider the effect that such a proposal would have on voter turnout or information alone, because the proposal also affects the other two problems, in complex and interrelated ways.

A balanced-budget requirement with a spending limit may have a decided effect on the disequilibrium problem. For example, a well-known result of public-choice theory is that, if the level of government spending is fixed and if the citizens (or legislators) are voting on how to divide the budget between two programs, then a unique equilibrium ordinarily will occur. But if voting goes forward on the spending level as well, then commonly there will be no unique equilibrium.[149]

This prediction may seem helpful, but it has at least two limitations. First, if people must vote on dividing a budget among three or more programs, disequilibrium reappears. Certainly, the exogenous determination of the total-budget issue reduces the dimensions of choice by one dimension, thereby diminishing the probability of disequilibrium (but not in a pure spatial-election model, with continuous alternatives over more than two dimensions). This effect, however, will not be substantial.

Second, the model so described is for elections in which public-goods production levels are issues. If, as the rent-seeking problem would suggest, the election is over private-goods production levels (or the number of such programs), we would require a different model to make predictions, one drawn from the theory of n-person games. But that theory provides a host of solution concepts, most of which identify as equilibria nonunique outcome sets, and therefore disequilibrium.

A "small" assumption about the rules of legislatures, however, might bring us to a firmer conclusion. Suppose that legislators enjoy perfect information, must balance the budget, and cannot spend more than a fixed percentage of (a constant) national product. Disequilibrium will prevail under majority rule. But institutions such as the U.S. Congress use majority rule in name only. In truth, legislative enactments require something closer to unanimous consent, because the ability to protect the status quo is diffused throughout the House and Senate.[150] Were we to impose unanimous consent (a Polish veto) or assume that it operates, we could predict a different result, namely that public policies might be efficient, and there would be a unique equilibrium. The irony of this result is that the development of effective vetoes in Congress probably occurred to protect gains that particular groups achieved through rent seeking.

We have already anticipated, then, the effect of a balanced-budget, spending-limit requirement on rent seeking. And in truth we could treat the proposal as a partial solution to this problem. Such a requirement would put a limit on the number of private-benefit programs supplied through additional taxes or deficits. Of course, nonbudgetary programs, such as cartel formation through regulation, constitute a prominent feature of rent seeking. Stated differently, regulation and the pork barrel are imperfect substitutes for one another. Hence, legislators might partially offset the effects of a balanced-budget, spending-limit requirement by creating more regulation.[151]

Such a requirement nevertheless would be binding at some point, and to that extent it would limit further growth in the success of rent seeking to expansions in the economy. Two other effects could occur. First, some programs might be assigned to the private sector, to make room for others by getting the privatized programs out of the federal budget. For example, Congress might phase out Social Security but require private employers to assume responsibility for the program while guaranteeing equivalent, price-adjusted benefits.[152] On public-policy grounds this proposal has much to recommend it. But it incorporates forced consumption and supply (as at present), and it substitutes a regulatory regime for direct government supply.

The second effect of such a requirement on rent seeking seems more complex, but it may be equally important. Landes and Posner say of private-interest politics that groups demand, and politicians prefer to supply, benefits over longer than shorter time intervals.[153] Interest groups prefer this strategy because it reduces their transaction costs: They need not annually renegotiate each program. It also gives them a more predictable income stream, by reducing their risk from legislators' postcontractual opportunism. Politicians prefer this strategy because it allows them to capitalize immediately their share of the (net present value of the) rents that the process generates, even for rents that a benefited group receives after the enacting politicians have left the legislature. But a balanced-budget, spending-limit requirement would mean that, if government revenues remain constant, then legislators must finance new programs by reducing spending on all or some existing ones. Legislators will compare the plurality- and other payoff-increasing effects of various programmatic trade-offs and surely will find some existing programs to delete. For interest groups this process will make less attractive the pursuit of some "entitlements" and other programs whose benefits flow over time.

A second set of proposals would decentralize government, restricting public-policy jurisdictions to catchments that utility interdependencies naturally and materially affect, with some degree of divisibility. For example, federal "superfund" legislation to clean up unsafe chemical dumps would become inappropriate under this proposal if particular dumps and any effluents from them individually affected only smaller jurisdictions or a few such jurisdictions, which could contract with each other if that seemed beneficial. National defense would remain a federal responsibility, but decentralization would reassign education, most police protection, health and welfare programs, and mass-transit projects entirely to state or local governments.

It is difficult to say what effects this proposal would have on rational abstention and ignorance. Turnout in state and local elections held without federal contests now falls below that found in federal elections. The P term is probably larger in local elections than in federal ones, because the electorate is smaller. The B term is probably smaller at the local level, though, perhaps because the issues do not seem as important as those involving federal contests, or perhaps because local candidates do not advertise as much as national ones, since local offices are of more limited value.

Devolution, however, would return to state and local governments complete control over several important policy areas. As a consequence, the B term might increase for state and local elections but decline somewhat for national ones. Hence, turnout in state and local elections might increase, as would citizens' information about those contests. Indeed, since most benefits and costs of policy alternatives would fall directly on the jurisdiction that adopts them (a matter that we consider presently), an enhancement of the citizen's search for information might occur.

It is also difficult to discern the effects of decentralization on the disequilibrium problem. Surely, the possible addition of more voters with better information may work to destabilize local elections, in the manner that we described earlier.[154] But a separation of programs, with a clear reassignment of each program to a particular level of government (which may decide not to carry the program out), will also simplify the issue space in each election, inter alia, by reducing the number of issue dimensions. On balance, a reduction in the number of voters from 80 million to 10 million (for larger states) or 100,000 (for smaller states) probably will have some small effect on turnout. Municipal elections, however, probably will have enough increased turnout to destabilize them where they are not already so unstable (in off years for national elections). But at the federal level, the influence of both reduced issue dimensionality and declining turnout probably will add even more stability.

The effects of decentralization on rent seeking will be most pronounced. The game in Table 2 explains not only the process of private-benefit demand but also the operation of cost spreading. If each group had to bear the full cost of its program, it would not lobby for programs that were cost–benefit inefficient. But the ability to spread costs to other groups mutes any particular interest group's incentive to consider a program's cost. The problem of intergenerational cost spreading grows worse, through federal supply, if voters in one location can spread program costs to the children of voters elsewhere. Provided that there is some interest in the welfare of one's progeny, the confining of costs to beneficiaries may dampen interest groups' and jurisdictions' reliance on intertemporal (and interjurisdictional) cost spreading.

Most classic pork-barrel legislation – rivers and harbors bills, Urban Development Action Grants, transit subsidies, and the like – share the characteristic of cost spreading. But under decentralization those jurisdictions benefited will have to bear the full costs of such programs. Some redistribution and cost spreading will persist in smaller jurisdictions, but to a lesser extent than occurs under federal subsidy and production. Local (inefficient) cost spreading will also be detrimental to local consumer, factor, and housing markets, so that asset values in jurisdictions that solve the rent-seeking problem will increase relative to those in jurisdictions that do not.

Cost spreading also assumes the form of federal regulations. The Occupational Safety and Health Administration, for example, represents a form of rent seeking by organized labor, in that its enforcement imposes proportionately greater fixed costs on smaller, nonunion firms than on larger, unionized ones.[155] Decentralization of regulation would devolve responsibility to smaller, more nearly homogeneous jurisdictions, which would bear the costs of regulation in a competitive environment among all such jurisdictions.

5   Preference conversion under self-denying ordinances

Not long ago most economists compared markets with supposed imperfections with the operation of a perfectly working public sector. The conclusion of such a comparison followed easily: that in the matter of utility interdependencies such markets map consumers' preferences only imperfectly into final resource allocations. Therefore, government could provide a desirable corrective, in the forms of regulation and direct and subsidized production.

Our newer understanding of markets indicates that the problem of market imperfections is vastly overstated. More important, however, public-choice theory has demonstrated beyond peradventure that the institutions of representative government share important failures in converting citizens' preferences into final allocations of resources through public policy. Indeed, we may now interpret market failure as merely another form of government, political failure.

But all four problems identified here appear to be interrelated, so that a solution to one may exacerbate another. For this reason a more nearly systemic approach, such as a spending limit or decentralization, may hold greater promise for amelioration. Such approaches recognize that there may be flaws in public-choice institutions, thus implying that we should use such institutions to do less and at a more local level.

These approaches similarly rely on the resemblance between earlier castings of market failure and the more contemporary view of government failure. The solution to both sets of problems well might assume the form of a self-denying ordinance,[156] be it in the form of "taxation" or of "regulation." The drawbacks of such ordinances seem plain enough, for they would limit the domain of public choice.[157] But the same problem prevails in governmental approaches to the perceived failures of markets. Those solutions limit the domain of private choice. Nevertheless, as applied to the public sector, this objection may be inapposite. The real question is whether public-choice institutions operating under such ordinances will fashion a better fit between citizens' preferences and public policy than will those not so constrained.

Nor is the final intellectual test of such ordinances their political acceptability. Citizens will choose to have or not to have such ordinances under the same existing rules that make them desirable. And the institution that these rules describe nurtures rational abstention and ignorance, disequilibrium, and rent seeking.

Prepared from a commentary for a Liberty Fund Conference on Individual Liberty and the Democratic Order, Crystal City, Virginia, June 20–3, 1984. The author thanks Loren Lomasky for his helpful comments on an earlier draft.

Notes

1   Compare Ronald Dworkin, *Taking Rights Seriously* (Cambridge, Mass.: Harvard University Press, 1977), with Tibor R. Machan and M. Bruce Johnson, eds., *Rights and Regulation: Ethical, Political, and Economic Issues* (Cambridge, Mass.: Ballinger, 1983).

2   Plato, *The Republic,* translated with notes and an introduction by Allan Bloom (New York: Basic Books, 1968).

3   John Stuart Mill, *Dissertations and Discussions* (New York: Holt, 1874), vol. 4.

4   Clarence Gilbert Hoag and George Henry Hallet, Jr., *Proportional Representation* (New York: Macmillan, 1926).

5   F. A. Hermens, *Democracy or Anarchy? A Study of Proportional Representation* (Notre Dame, Ind.: Review of Politics, 1941).

6   See, e.g., William H. Riker, *Democracy in America*, 2d ed. (New York: Macmillan, 1965).

7   See, e.g., Robert G. Dixon, Jr., *Democratic Representation: Reapportionment in Law and Politics* (New York: Oxford University Press, 1968), and William H. Riker, "Democracy and Representation: A Reconciliation of *Ball v. James* and *Reynolds v. Sims,*" *Supreme Court Economic Review* 1 (1981): 39–68.

8   See, e.g., Dixon, *Democratic Representation*, chap. 18.

9   See, e.g., Bruce A. Ackerman, "The Storrs Lectures: Discovering the Constitution," *Yale Law Journal* 93 (May 1984): 1013–72; John Hart Ely, *Democracy and Distrust: A Theory of Judicial Review* (Cambridge, Mass.: Harvard University Press, 1980); Alexander Bickel, *The Least Dangerous Branch: The Supreme Court at the Bar of Politics* (Indianapolis, Ind.: Bobbs-Merrill, 1962); and idem, *The Supreme Court and the Idea of Progress* (New York: Harper & Row, 1970). The problem of judicial review has two important aspects, only the second of which concerns us here. First, does the Constitution (or did the Founding Fathers) contemplate judicial review of the political branches' actions? Second, under a given theory of democracy, what place, if any, does an unelected judiciary have in constraining an elected branch's decisions? See Peter H. Aranson, "Procedural and Substantive Constitutional Protection of Economic Liberties," *Cato Journal* 7 (Fall 1987): 345–75.

10   The important problem of delegation often arises in political thought, both as a separation-of-powers problem (see, e.g., Baron de Montesquieu, *The Spirit of the Laws* [Berkeley and Los Angeles: University of California Press, 1977]) and as a concern about the quality of public action that results from delegation (see, e.g., John Locke, *Two Treatises of Government* [Cambridge University Press, 1960], pp. 380–1). See generally Peter H. Aranson, Ernest Gellhorn, and Glen O. Robinson, "A Theory of Legislative Delegation," *Cornell Law Review* 68 (November 1982): 1–67. See also Ely, *Democracy and Distrust*, and Cass R. Sunstein, "Interest Groups in American Public Law," *Stanford Law Review* 38 (November 1985): 28–87.

11   Thomas Hobbes, *Leviathan, or the Matter, Forme and Power of a Commonwealth, Ecclesiasticall and Civill*, edited with an introduction by C. B. MacPherson (Harmondsworth: Penguin, 1968), p. 186.

12   See, e.g., Malcolm Jewell, ed., *The Politics of Reapportionment* (New York: Atherton, 1962).

13   See, e.g., Frank I. Michelman, "Politics and Values or What's Really Wrong with Rationality Review?" *Creighton Law Review* 13 (Winter 1979): 487–511.

14   Aristotle, *The Politics,* translated with an introduction, notes, and appendixes by Ernest Barker (New York: Oxford University Press, 1958). See also Robert A. Dahl, *A Preface to Democratic Theory* (University of Chicago Press, 1956), chap. 3. The fullest recent expression of the deontological view appears in Darrell Dobbs, "Reckless Rationalism and Heroic Reverence in Homer's *Odyssey,"* *American Political Science Review* 81 (June 1987): 491–508.

15   Some recent work in economics and biology also seeks to explain preferences themselves. See, e.g., Chris Paul and Paul Rubin, "An Evolutionary Model of Taste for Risk," *Economic Inquiry* 17 (October 1979): 585–96. Theories of preference formation ordinarily ascribe causation to an evolutionary process. Under specified conditions a group, tribe, or society in which children learn certain values is more likely to survive than is one in which people ignore these values. As conditions change the presence of these values may subsequently prove to be "lethal" to the collectivity's survival as a collectivity. Evolutionary survival of the collectivity thus becomes analogous to goal seeking in private, individual choice. The later works of Hayek provide the fullest development of this process. See, e.g., Friedrich A. Hayek, *New Studies in Philosophy, Politics, Economics, and the History of Ideas* (University of Chicago Press, 1978). See generally J. Maynard Smith, "The Theory of Games and the Evolution of Animal Conflict," *Journal of Theoretical Biology* 47 (September 1974): 209–21, for a theoretical perspective, and R. Peter Terrebonne, "A Strictly Evolutionary Model of Common Law," *Journal of Legal Studies* 10 (June 1981): 397–407, for a specific human application.

16   See, e.g., Joseph P. Kalt and Mark A. Zupan, "Capture and Ideology in the Economic Theory of Politics," *American Economic Review* 74 (June 1984): 279–300, and references cited therein. But see James B. Kau and Paul Rubin, "Self-Interest, Ideology, and Logrolling in Congressional Voting," *Journal of Law and Economics* 22 (October 1979): 365–84; Sam Peltzman, "Constituent Interest and Congressional Voting," ibid., 27 (April 1984): 181–210, and references cited therein; and Douglas Nelson and Eugene Silberberg, "Ideology and Legislator Shirking," *Economic Inquiry* 25 (January 1987): 15–25.

17   See, e.g., Harold D. Hochman and James D. Rogers, "Pareto Optimal Redistribution," *American Economic Review* 59 (September 1969): 542–57. But others find nonaltruistic components to claimed altruistic policies. See Geoffrey Brennan, "Pareto Desirable Redistribution: The Non-altruistic Dimension," *Public Choice* 14 (Spring 1973): 43–67, and Louis De Alessi, "Implications of Property Rights for Government Investment Choices," *American Economic Review* 59 (March 1969): 13–24.

18   See Michelman, "Politics and Values."

19   See, e.g., Gordon Tullock, ed., *Explorations in the Theory of Anarchy* (Blacksburg, Va.: Center for the Study of Public Choice, 1972), and

James M. Buchanan, *The Limits of Liberty: Between Anarchy and Utopia* (University of Chicago Press, 1975).

20   Ronald H. Coase, "The Problem of Social Cost," *Journal of Law and Economics* 3 (October 1960): 1–44. The initial assignment of rights may have distributional consequences for the parties involved, but not allocative ones (provided that income effects are negligible).

21   Harold Demsetz, "When Does the Rule of Liability Matter?" *Journal of Legal Studies* 1 (January 1972): 13–28. In the context of legislative rules, see the important exchange in Richard D. McKelvey and Peter C. Ordeshook, "An Experimental Study of the Effects of Procedural Rules on Committee Behavior," *Journal of Politics* 46 (February 1984): 182–205, and Kenneth A. Shepsle and Barry R. Weingast, "When Do Rules of Procedure Matter?" ibid., 46 (February 1984): 206–21.

22   James M. Buchanan and Gordon Tullock, *The Calculus of Consent: Logical Foundations of Constitutional Democracy* (Ann Arbor: University of Michigan Press, 1962). See also James M. Buchanan, "Positive Economics, Welfare Economics, and Political Economy," *Journal of Law and Economics* 2 (October 1959): 124–38.

23   Hayek forcefully denies that we might gain a rationalization for many of the rules that pervade any civilization, and he argues that they may not be the product of conscious choice. See Friedrich A. Hayek, *Law, Legislation, and Liberty,* 3 vols. (University of Chicago Press, 1973, 1976, 1979), and especially vol. 3 of that series, *The Political Order of a Free People* (1979).

24   William H. Riker, "Implications from the Disequilibrium of Majority Rule for the Study of Institutions," *American Political Science Review* 74 (June 1980): 444–5. For an example of the abandonment of preestablished rules in the context of voting in a private association, see Michael Levine and Charles R. Plott, "Agenda Influence and Its Implications," *Virginia Law Review* 63 (May 1977): 561–604.

25   Anthony Downs, *An Economic Theory of Democracy* (New York: Harper & Row, 1957), pp. 260–76.

26   Gordon Tullock, *Toward a Mathematics of Politics* (Ann Arbor: University of Michigan Press, 1968), chap. 7.

27   William H. Riker and Peter C. Ordeshook, "A Theory of the Calculus of Voting," *American Political Science Review* 62 (March 1968): 25–42. See also Richard D. McKelvey and Peter C. Ordeshook, "A General Theory of the Calculus of Voting," in J. F. Herndon and J. L. Bernd, eds., *Mathematical Applications in Political Science* (Charlottesville: University of Virginia Press, 1972), vol. 6, pp. 32–78.

28   Downs, *Economic Theory,* pp. 267–71, had himself posited the existence of a noninstrumental, consumption utility from voting.

29   See, e.g., Neil Beck, "A Note on the Probability of a Tied Election," *Public Choice* 23 (Fall 1975): 75–80; G. Chamberlin and Michael Rothschild, "A Note on the Probability of Casting a Decisive Vote," *Journal of Economic Theory* 25 (August 1981): 152–62; I. J. Good and

Larry S. Mayer, "Estimating the Efficacy of a Vote," *Behavioral Science* 20 (January 1975): 25–33: and Howard Margolis, "Probability of a Tied Election," *Public Choice* 31 (Fall 1977): 135–8. See also Richard G. Niemi, "Costs of Voting and Nonvoting," *Public Choice* 27 (Fall 1976): 115–19, who denies, inter alia, that *C* has a significant value; and Thomas Schwartz, "Your Vote Counts on Account of the Way It Is Counted: An Institutional Solution to the Paradox of Not Voting," *Public Choice* 54 (1987): 101–21, who argues that, even in large electorates, individual districts may be small enough to make voting partly monitorable by politicians and therefore efficacious.

30   Downs, *Economic Theory,* pp. 266–7.

31   See, e.g., John A. Ferejohn and Morris P. Fiorina, "The Paradox of Not Voting: A Decision Theoretic Analysis," *American Political Science Review* 68 (June 1974): 525–36, and idem, "Closeness Counts Only in Horseshoes and Dancing," ibid., 49 (September 1975): 920–5. But see Nathaniel Beck, "The Paradox of Minimax Regret," ibid., p. 918, and Gordon Tullock, "The Paradox of Not Voting for Oneself," ibid., p. 919.

32   Guillermo Owen and Bernard Grofman, "To Vote or Not to Vote: The Paradox of Nonvoting," *Public Choice* 42 (1984): 311–25; John O. Ledyard, "The Pure Theory of Large Two-Candidate Elections," *Public Choice* 44 (1984): 1–60; and Thomas Palfrey and Howard Rosenthal, "Voter Participation and Strategic Uncertainty," *American Political Science Review* 79 (March 1985): 62–78.

33   Ferejohn and Fiorina, "The Paradox of Not Voting."

34   Owen and Grofman, "To Vote or Not to Vote."

35   See James M. Buchanan, "Individual Choice in Voting and the Market," *Journal of Political Economy* 62 (August 1954): 334–43.

36   Indeed, at least one essay suggests the use of random selection, inter alia, to reduce the cost of elections. See Dennis C. Mueller, Robert D. Tollison, and Thomas D. Willet, "Representative Democracy via Random Selection," *Public Choice* 12 (Spring 1972): 57–68. For a related development concerning direct democracy using home computer terminals, see James C. Miller III, "A Program for Direct and Proxy Voting in the Legislative Process," *Public Choice* 7 (Fall 1969): 107–13.

37   See, e.g., Paul R. Abramson, John H. Aldrich, and David W. Rohde, *Change and Continuity in the 1980 Elections* (Washington, D.C.: Congressional Quarterly Press, 1982), pp. 80–1.

38   Ibid., pp. 98–9.

39   Ibid., pp. 80–1.

40   Present explanations argue that *P, B,* or *C* may (or may not) vary systematically with income. See, e.g., Bruno Frey, "Why Do High Income People Participate More in Politics?" *Public Choice* 11 (Fall 1971): 101–5; Keith R. Russel, "Communication," *Public Choice* 13 (Fall 1971): 113–14; John Fraser, "Communication," ibid., pp. 115–18; Bruno Frey, "Reply," ibid., pp. 119–22; Yoram Barzel and Eugene

Silberberg, "Is the Act of Voting Rational?" *Public Choice* 16 (Fall 1973): 51–8; Robert D. Tollison and Thomas D. Willet, "Some Simple Economics of Voting and Not Voting," ibid., pp. 59–71; and Niemi, "Costs of Voting and Nonvoting."

Another problem may emerge if the citizen's vote has little or no instrumental value. If he need not bear the consequences of his actions, the citizen may vote in an irresponsible manner, or merely to express a preference for a particular candidacy or policy that he knows will fail. If every voter acts in this manner, a few collective but unpleasant surprises may result. This practice doubtless exists in some measure, but I do not know how to assess its real effects. For a more illuminating discussion, see Mueller, Chapter 4, this volume, and Brennan and Lomasky, Chapter 2, this volume.

41   Downs, *Economic Theory*, chaps. 11–13. The earliest statement of either problem of which I am aware is that of G. W. F. Hegel, *The Philosophy of Right*, translated with notes by T. M. Knox, vol. 46 of Great Books of the Western World (Chicago: Encyclopedia Brittanica, 1952), p. 104, as identified in James M. Buchanan, "Hegel on the Calculus of Voting," *Public Choice* 17 (Spring 1974): 99–101.

42   See especially Morris P. Fiorina, *Retrospective Voting in American National Elections* (New Haven, Conn.: Yale University Press, 1981), chap. 1.

43   *New York Times v. Sullivan*, 376 U.S. 255 (1964).

44   Ibid., 271 [citing *NAACP v. Button*, 371 U.S. 415, 445 (1963)].

45   Downs, *Economic Theory*, pp. 255–6. We must add to Downs's analysis the observation that sometimes specialized consumer groups enjoy the same kinds of informational advantage as do groups of producers.

46   See Fiorina, *Retrospective Voting*.

47   See Peter H. Aranson, "Risk, Uncertainty, and Retrospective Voting," paper prepared for the Annual Meeting of the American Political Science Association, New York City, September 1981. For the private-sector analogues to this decision approach, see Armen A. Alchian, "Uncertainty, Evolution, and Economic Theory," *Journal of Political Economy* 58 (June 1950): 211–21; G. L. S. Shackle, *Epistemics and Economics* (Cambridge University Press, 1972); and Israel M. Kirzner, *Competition and Entrepreneurship* (University of Chicago Press, 1973).

48   Richard D. McKelvey and Peter C. Ordeshook, "Elections with Limited Information: A Fulfilled Expectations Model Using Contemporaneous Poll and Endorsement Data as Information Sources," *Journal of Economic Theory* 36 (June 1985): 55–85; idem, "Rational Expectations in Elections: Some Experimental Results Based on a Multidimensional Model," *Public Choice* 44 (1984): 61–102; idem, "Sequential Elections with Limited Information," *American Journal of Political Science* 29 (August 1985): 480–512; and idem, "Information, Electoral Equilibria, and the Democratic Ideal," *Journal of Politics* 48 (November 1986): 909–37.

49   See, e.g., Mancur Olson, *The Logic of Collective Action,* rev. ed. (New York: Schocken, 1971); idem, *The Rise and Decline of Nations: Economic Growth, Stagflation, and Social Rigidities* (New Haven, Conn.: Yale University Press, 1982); and works cited in notes 68–72.

50   Marie Jean Antoine Nicolas Caritat, Marquis de Condorcet, *Essai sur l'application de l'analyse à la probabilité des decisions rendues à la pluralité des voix* (Paris, 1785).

51   C. L. Dodgson, *A Discussion of the Various Methods of Procedure in Conducting Elections* (Oxford: Gardner, Hall, & Stacey, 1873), reprinted in Duncan Black, *The Theory of Committees and Elections* (Cambridge University Press, 1958), pp. 214–34. Black's monograph contains a good history of pre-twentieth century developments.

52   Black, *Theory of Committees.*

53   Kenneth J. Arrow, *Social Choice and Individual Values,* 2d ed. (New York: Wiley, 1963).

54   For reviews of the literature, see ibid.; Black, *Theory of Committees;* Peter C. Fishburn, *The Theory of Social Choice* (Princeton, N.J.: Princeton University Press, 1973); David J. Mayston, *The Idea of Social Choice* (New York: St. Martin's Press, 1974); Peter C. Ordeshook, *Game Theory and Political Theory* (Cambridge University Press, 1986); Peter C. Ordeshook and Kenneth A. Shepsle, eds., *Political Equilibrium: A Delicate Balance, Essays in Honor of William H. Riker* (Boston: Kluwer-Nijhoff, 1982); Prasanta K. Pattanaik, *Voting and Collective Choice* (Cambridge University Press, 1971); Charles R. Plott, "Axiomatic Social Choice: An Overview and Interpretation," *American Journal of Political Science* 20 (August 1976): 511–96; William H. Riker, *Liberalism Against Populism: A Confrontation between the Theory of Democracy and the Theory of Social Choice* (San Francisco: Freeman, 1982); A. K. Sen, *Collective Choice and Social Welfare* (San Francisco: Holden-Day, 1970); and Thomas Schwartz, *The Logic of Collective Choice* (New York: Columbia University Press, 1986).

55   See, e.g., Jerry S. Kelley, *Arrow Impossibility Theorems* (New York: Academic Press, 1978).

56   See generally Richard G. Niemi, Bo Bjurulf, and Gordon Blewis, "The Power of the Chairman," *Public Choice* 40 (1983): 293–305; Robin Farquharson, *Theory of Voting* (New Haven, Conn.: Yale University Press, 1969); and Richard D. McKelvey, "Intransitivities in Multidimensional Voting Models and Some Implications for Agenda Control," *Journal of Economic Theory* 12 (June 1976): 472–82.

57   See, e.g., Mark A. Satterthwaite, "Strategy Proofness and Arrow's Conditions: Existence and Corresponding Theorems for Voting Procedures and Social Choice," *Journal of Economic Theory* 10 (April 1975): 197–218; Allan Gibbard, "Manipulation of Voting Schemes: A General Result," *Econometrica* 41 (July 1973): 587–601; Gerald H. Krammer, "Sophisticated Voting over Multidimensional Choice Spaces," *Journal of Mathematical Sociology* 2 (July 1972): 161–81; Richard D. McKelvey

and Richard G. Niemi, "A Multistage Game Representation of Sophisticated Voting for Binary Procedures," *Journal of Economic Theory* 18 (June 1978): 1–22; and Arthur Denzau, William H. Riker, and Kenneth A. Shepsle, "Farquharson and Fenno: Sophisticated Voting and Home Style," *American Political Science Review* 79 (December 1985): 1117–34.

58   See, e.g., Kenneth A. Shepsle and Barry R. Weingast, "Structure-Induced Equilibrium and Legislative Choice," *Public Choice* 37 (1981): 503–19.

59   See idem, "Uncovered Sets and Sophisticated Voting Outcomes with Implications for Agenda Control," *American Journal of Political Science* 28 (February 1984): 49–74.

60   See the text accompanying note 24.

61   See, e.g., Mueller, Chapter 4, this volume.

62   See, e.g., John H. Aldrich, *Voting in Two Presidential Elections: An Analysis Based on the Spatial Model of Electoral Competition* (Ph.D. dissertation, University of Rochester, Rochester, New York, 1975), p. 37. Such elections violate Arrow's condition 3, independence from irrelevant alternatives.

63   Peter H. Aranson, *A Theory of the Calculus of Voting for Alternative, Three-Contestant Election Systems* (Ph.D. dissertation, University of Rochester, Rochester, New York, 1972). See also Lee E. Dutter, "An Application of the Multicandidate Calculus of Voting to the 1972 and 1976 German Federal Elections," *Public Choice* 47 (1985): 405–24.

64   Peter H. Aranson and Peter C. Ordeshook, "Spatial Strategies for Sequential Elections," in Richard G. Niemi and Herbert F. Weisberg, eds., *Probability Models of Collective Decision Making* (Columbus, Ohio: Merrill, 1972), pp. 298–331, and John H. Aldrich, *Before the Convention: Strategies and Choices in Presidential Nominating Campaigns* (University of Chicago Press, 1980).

65   See Richard D. McKelvey, "General Conditions for Global Intransitivities in Formal Voting Models," *Econometrica* 47 (September 1979): 1085–1111, and Norman Schofield, "Instability of Simple Dynamic Games," *Review of Economic Studies* 45 (October 1978): 575–94.

66   Frank H. Easterbrook, "Ways of Criticizing the Court," *Harvard Law Review* 95 (February 1982): 802–32. But see Walter F. Murphy, *Elements of Judicial Strategy* (University of Chicago Press, 1964).

67   See Olson, references cited in note 49.

68   See, e.g., William M. Landes and Richard A. Posner, "The Independent Judiciary from an Interest-group Perspective," *Journal of Law and Economics* 18 (December 1975): 875–901; Sam Peltzman, "Toward a More General Theory of Regulation," ibid., 19 (August 1976): 211–40; Richard A. Posner, "Taxation by Regulation," *Bell Journal of Economics and Management Science* 2 (Spring 1971): 22–50; idem, "Theories of Economic Regulation," ibid., 5 (Autumn 1974): 335–58; George J. Stigler, "The Theory of Economic Regulation," ibid., 2 (Spring 1971):

3–21; and idem, "Free-Riders and Collective Action: An Appendix to Theories of Economic Regulation," ibid., 5 (Autumn 1974): 359–65.

69   See, e.g., Marver H. Bernstein, *Regulating Business by Independent Commission* (Princeton, N.J.: Princeton University Press, 1955); Ellis W. Hawley, *The New Deal and the Problem of Monopoly* (Princeton, N.J.: Princeton University Press, 1966); Gabriel Kolko, *The Triumph of Conservatism* (Chicago: Quadrangle, 1963); idem, *Railroads and Regulation* (New York: Norton, 1965); Theodore J. Lowi, *The End of Liberalism: The Second Republic of the United States*, 2d ed. (New York: Norton, 1979); Albro Martin, *Enterprise Denied: The Origins of the Decline of American Railroads, 1897–1917* (New York: Columbia University Press, 1972); E. E. Schattschneider, *Politics, Pressures, and the Tariff* (Englewood Cliffs, N.J.: Prentice-Hall, 1935); and David B. Truman, *The Governmental Process: Political Interests and Public Opinion* (New York: Knopf, 1951).

70   See, e.g., Peter H. Aranson, "Public Deficits in Normative Economics and Positive Political Theory," in Laurence H. Meyer, ed., *The Economic Consequences of Government Deficits* (Boston: Kluwer-Nijhoff, 1983), pp. 157–82; Aranson, Gellhorn, and Robinson, "Theory of Legislative Delegation"; Peter H. Aranson and Peter C. Ordeshook, "A Prolegomenon to a Theory of the Failure of Representative Democracy," in Richard D. Auster and Barbara Sears, eds., *American Re-evolution: Papers and Proceedings* (Tucson: University of Arizona, Department of Economics, 1977), pp. 23–46; idem, "Public Interest, Private Interest, and the Democratic Polity," in Roger Benjamin and Stephen Elkin, eds., *The Democratic State* (Lawrence: University Press of Kansas, 1985), pp. 86–177; idem, "The Political Bases of Public Sector Growth in a Representative Democracy," paper prepared for the Annual Meeting of the American Political Science Association, New York City, 1978; idem, "Alternative Theories of the Growth of Government and Their Implications for Constitutional Tax and Spending Limits," in Helen F. Ladd and T. Nicholas Tideman, eds., *Tax and Expenditure Limitations* (Washington, D.C.: Urban Institute Press, 1981), pp. 143–76; idem, "Regulation, Redistribution, and Public Choice," *Public Choice* 37 (1981): 69–100; idem, "Incrementalism, the Fiscal Illusion, and the Growth of Government in Representative Democracies," paper prepared for the Annual Meeting of the Southern Economic Association, New Orleans, 1977; Morris P. Fiorina, *Congress: Keystone of the Washington Establishment* (New Haven, Conn.: Yale University Press, 1977); Kenneth A. Shepsle and Barry R. Weingast, "Political Preferences for the Pork Barrel," *American Journal of Political Science* 25 (February 1981): 96–111; idem, "Political Solutions to Market Problems," *American Political Science Review* 78 (June 1984): 417–34; and Barry R. Weingast, Kenneth A. Shepsle, and Christopher Johnsen, "The Political Economy of Benefits and Costs: A Neoclassical Approach to Distributive Politics," *Journal of Political Economy* 89 (August 1981): 642–64.

71   Much of this work is conveniently collected in James M. Buchanan, Robert D. Tollison, and Gordon Tullock, eds., *The Theory of the Rent-Seeking Society* (College Station: Texas A & M Press, 1980). But earlier work by these and other scholars clearly led to this development. See, e.g., Gordon Tullock, "The Welfare Cost of Tariffs, Monopoly, and Theft," *Western Economic Journal* 5 (June 1967): 224–32.

72   Anne O. Krueger, "The Political Economy of the Rent-Seeking Society," *American Economic Review* 64 (June 1974): 291–303.

73   See, e.g., Allen V. Kneese and Charles L. Schultze, *Pollution, Prices, and Public Policy* (Washington, D.C.: Brookings Institution, 1975).

74   See Paul A. Samuelson, "The Pure Theory of Public Expenditure," *Review of Economics and Statistics* 36 (November 1954): 387–90.

75   See, e.g., Abba P. Lerner, "Conflicting Principles of Public Utility Regulation," *Journal of Law and Economics* 7 (October 1964): 61–70; but see James M. Buchanan, *The Bases of Collective Action* (New York: General Learning Press, 1971).

76   See, e.g., Garrett Hardin, "The Tragedy of the Commons," *Science* 162 (December 1968): 1243–8, and Ronald H. Coase, "The Federal Communications Commission," *Journal of Law and Economics* 2 (October 1959): 1–40.

77   See, e.g., Hochman and Rodgers, "Pareto Optimal Redistribution."

78   William J. Baumol, *Welfare Economics and the Theory of the State*, 2d ed. rev. (Cambridge, Mass.: Harvard University Press, 1965), p. 21.

79   For a review see Aranson and Ordeshook, "Public Interest," pp. 98–106.

80   See Ronald H. Coase, "The Nature of the Firm," *Economica* 4 (November 1937): 386–405, and idem, "Problem of Social Cost." For examples, see Benjamin Klein, Robert G. Crawford, and Armen A. Alchian, "Vertical Integration, Appropriable Rents, and the Competitive Contracting Process," *Journal of Law and Economics* 21 (October 1978): 297–326; Yoram Barzel, "Measurement Cost and the Organization of Markets," ibid., 25 (April 1982): 27–48; and Steven N. S. Cheung, "On the Contractual Nature of the Firm," ibid., 26 (April 1983): 1–21.

81   See, e.g., Steven N. S. Cheung, "The Fable of the Bees: An Economic Investigation," *Journal of Law and Economics* 16 (April 1973): 11–33; David B. Johnson, "Meade, Bees, and Externalities," ibid., pp. 35–52; and J. R. Gould, "Meade on External Economies: Should the Beneficiaries Be Taxed?" ibid., pp. 53–66.

82   See, e.g., Ronald H. Coase, "The Lighthouse in Economics," *Journal of Law and Economics* 17 (October 1974): 357–76.

83   See, e.g., Armen A. Alchian and Harold Demsetz, "Production, Information Costs, and Economic Organization," *American Economic Review* 62 (December 1972): 777–95; Alfred D. Chandler, Jr., *Strategy and Structure: Chapters in the History of Industrial Enterprise* (Cambridge, Mass.: MIT Press, 1962); Coase, "Nature of the Firm"; and Michael C. Jensen and William H. Meckling, "Theory of the Firm: Management Behavior, Agency Costs, and Ownership Structure," *Journal of Financial Economics* 3 (October 1976): 305–60.

84   See, e.g., Harold Demsetz, "Why Regulate Utilities?" *Journal of Law and Economics* 11 (April 1968): 55–65, and George J. Stigler and Claire Friedland, "What Can Regulators Regulate? The Case of Electricity," ibid., pp. 1–16.

85   See, e.g., Cotton Mather Lindsay, "A Theory of Government Enterprise," *Journal of Political Economy* 84 (October 1976): 1061–77, and Fiorina, *Congress.*

86   See, e.g., W. Lee Hansen, "Income Distribution Effects of Higher Education," *American Economic Review* 60 (May 1970): 335–40; W. Lee Hansen and Burton A. Weisbrod, *Benefits, Costs, and Finance of Public Higher Education* (Chicago: Markham, 1969); Brennan, "Pareto Desirable Redistribution"; and George J. Stigler, "Director's Law of Public Income Redistribution," *Journal of Law and Economics* 13 (April 1970): 1–10.

87   Mueller, Chapter 4, this volume.

88   Ibid.

89   The 1984–5 *Atlanta Yellow Pages* shows 72 entries under "Detective Agencies" and 81 entries under "Investigators." There is some duplication of entries. The directory also shows 50 entries under "Security Consultants" and 45 under "Security Control Equipment and Systems." Again, there are some multiple entries between these categories and among the other categories. Similarly, there are listings for 5 firms under "Guard Dogs," 65 under "Guard and Patrol Services," 11 under "Guards – Door and Window," and 76 under "Guns and Gunsmiths." There are 110 listings under "Burglar Alarm Systems" and an additional 5 under "Burglar Alarm Systems – Whol. and Mfrs.," and 22 under "Burglar Bars." I found 10 pages of listings under "Locks and Locksmiths," and 34 pages under the more general heading "Insurance."

90   See, e.g., Edwin G. West, "The Political Economy of American Public School Legislation," *Journal of Law and Economics* 10 (October 1967): 101–28, and idem, "An Economic Analysis of the Law and Politics of Non-Public School 'Aid'," ibid., 19 (April 1976): 79–101.

91   See, e.g., Robert W. Poole, Jr., ed., *Instead of Regulation: Alternatives to Federal Regulatory Agencies* (Lexington, Mass.: Heath, 1983); Aranson and Ordeshook, "Regulation"; Paul B. Downing and Gordon L. Brady, "Constrained Self Interest and the Formation of Public Policy," *Public Choice* 34 (1979): 15–28; William A. Jordan, "Producer Protection, Prior Market Structure, and the Effects of Government Regulation," *Journal of Law and Economics* 15 (April 1972): 151–76; Kolko, *Triumph of Conservatism;* Michael T. Maloney and Robert E. McCormick, "A Positive Theory of Environmental Quality Regulation," *Journal of Law and Economics* 25 (April 1982): 99–123; Jerry L. Mashaw, "Constitutional Deregulation: Notes Toward a Public-Public Law," *Tulane Law Review* 31 (1981): 849–76; Peter B. Pashigian, "Environmental Regulation: Whose Self-Interests Are Being Protected?" *Economic Inquiry* 23 (October 1985): 551–84; Peltzman, "Toward a More General

Theory"; Posner, "Taxation by Regulation"; Stigler, "Theory of Economic Regulation"; and James Q. Wilson, ed., *The Politics of Regulation* (New York: Basic Books, 1980).

92   See, e.g., John A. Ferejohn, *Pork Barrel Politics* (Stanford, Calif.: Stanford University Press, 1974); Fiorina, *Congress;* Shepsle and Weingast, "Political Preferences"; and Weingast, Shepsle, and Johnsen, "Political Economy."

93   See, e.g., West, "Political Economy of American Public School Legislation."

94   Caspar Weinberger, secretary of defense in the Reagan administration, sometimes turned aside congressional demands for defense-spending cuts by presenting the results of previously prepared calculations showing the effects of a particular cut on a particular (critical) senator's or congressman's state or district. For a theoretical perspective, see Kenneth D. Goldin, "Price Externalities Influence Public Policy," *Public Choice* 23 (Fall 1975): 1–10.

95   See, e.g., Maloney and McCormick, "Positive Theory"; Pashigian, "Environmental Regulation"; and Bruce A. Ackerman and William T. Hassler, *Clean Coal/Dirty Air* (New Haven, Conn.: Yale University Press, 1977).

96   See, e.g., James B. Kau and Paul H. Rubin, "Voting on Minimum Wages: A Time-Series Analysis," *Journal of Political Economy* 86 (April 1978): 337–42, and James C. Miller III, "Is Organized Labor Rational in Supporting OSHA?" *Southern Economic Journal* 50 (January 1984): 881–5. See also Harold W. Elder, "An Economic Analysis of Factor Usage and Workplace Regulation," *Southern Economic Journal* 52 (October 1985): 315–31.

97   See references cited in note 86.

98   See, e.g., Robert H. Bork, *The Antitrust Paradox: A Policy at War with Itself* (New York: Basic Books, 1978).

99   See references cited in and text accompanying notes 68–72.

100   For an extensive review of this development through 1984, see Aranson and Ordeshook, "Public Interest." The following discussion draws heavily on this account.

101   See, e.g., Downs, *Economic Theory;* Howard R. Bowen, "The Interpretation of Voting in the Allocation of Economic Resources," *Quarterly Journal of Economics* 58 (November 1943): 27–48; and William H. Riker and Peter C. Ordeshook, *An Introduction to Positive Political Theory* (Englewood Cliffs, N.J.: Prentice-Hall, 1973), chaps. 11 and 12.

102   Actually, this calculation understates the social cost, for if the two groups split lobbying costs for the public-good program, then the difference in costs between the private- and public-benefit programs would be greater. An attention to "lobbying" and related costs of side payments to politicians occupies much of the analysis of rent seeking. See references cited in note 71.

103   Aranson and Ordeshook, "Prolegomenon."

104   Idem, "Political Bases."

105   Idem, "Alternative Theories." This development is fully anticipated in James M. Buchanan, "Notes for an Economic Theory of Socialism," *Public Choice* 8 (Spring 1970): 29–43. Buchanan identifies additional sources of inefficiency in the likelihood that the groups will prefer different levels of a collectively consumed but theoretically divisible private benefit.

106   Aranson and Ordeshook, "Political Bases"; Shepsle and Weingast, "Political Preferences"; and Weingast, Shepsle, and Johnsen, "Political Economy."

107   Fiorina, *Congress,* and David R. Mayhew, *Congress: The Electoral Connection* (New Haven, Conn.: Yale University Press, 1974).

108   Aranson and Ordeshook, "Incrementalism."

109   William A. Niskanen, Jr., *Bureaucracy and Representative Government* (Chicago: Aldine Atherton, 1971). See also William P. Orzechowski, "Economic Models of Bureaucracy: Survey, Extensions, and Evidence," in Thomas E. Borcherding, ed., *Budgets and Bureaucrats: The Sources of Government Growth* (Durham, N.C.: Duke University Press, 1977), pp. 229–59, and De Alessi, "Implications of Property Rights."

110   Barry R. Weingast and Mark J. Moran, "Congress as the Source of Regulatory Decisions: The Case of the Federal Trade Commission," *American Economic Review: Papers and Proceedings* 72 (May 1982): 109–13; Barry R. Weingast, "Regulation, Reregulation, and Deregulation: The Political Foundations of Agency Clientele Relations," *Law and Contemporary Problems* 44 (Winter 1981): 247–77; Barry R. Weingast and Mark J. Moran, "Bureaucratic Discretion or Congressional Control? Regulatory Policymaking by the Federal Trade Commission," *Journal of Political Economy* 91 (October 1983): 765–800; and Barry R. Weingast, "A Principal-Agent Perspective on Congressional-Bureaucratic Relations: Evidence from the Securities and Exchange Commission" (unpublished manuscript, 1983). See also Gregg A. Jarrell, "Change at the Exchange: The Causes and Effects of Deregulation," *Journal of Law and Economics* 27 (October 1984): 273–312.

111   Landes and Posner, "Independent Judiciary"; Peter H. Aranson, "Judicial Control of the Political Branches: Public Purpose and Public Law," *Cato Journal* 4 (Winter 1985): 719–82; and idem, "Economic Liberties."

112   See Tullock, "Welfare Cost."

113   See references cited in and text accompanying note 101.

114   Aranson and Ordeshook, "Spatial Strategies."

115   See, e.g., Nelson A. Polsby and Aaron Wildavsky, *Presidential Elections,* 2d ed. (New York: Scribners, 1968), p. 74.

116   Peter J. Coughlin and Shmuel Nitzan, "Electoral Outcomes with Probabilistic Voting and Nash Social Welfare Maxima," *Journal of Public Economics* 15 (February 1981): 113–21. See also Peter J. Coughlin,

"Elections and Income Redistribution," *Public Choice* 50 (1986): 27–91.

117   Ledyard, "Pure Theory."

118   Kenneth A. Shepsle, "A Note on Zeckhauser's 'Majority Rule with Lotteries on Alternatives': A Case of the Paradox of Voting," *Quarterly Journal of Economics* 84 (November 1970): 705–9; idem, "The Paradox of Voting and Uncertainty," in Richard D. Niemi and Herbert F. Weisberg, eds., *Probability Models of Collective Decision Making* (Columbus, Ohio: Merrill, 1972), pp. 252–70; idem, "Parties, Voters, and the Risk Environment: A Mathematical Treatment of Electoral Competition Under Uncertainty," in ibid., pp. 173–297; and idem, "The Strategy of Ambiguity: Uncertainty and Electoral Competition," *American Political Science Review* 66 (June 1972): 555–68. See also Benjamin I. Page, "The Theory of Political Ambiguity," ibid., 66 (September 1976): 742–52.

119   Richard Zeckhauser, "Majorty Rule with Lotteries on Alternatives," *Quarterly Journal of Economics* 83 (November 1969): 696–703.

120   Shepsle, "On Zeckhauser's 'Majority Rule,'" and idem, "Paradox of Voting and Uncertainty."

121   Idem, "Parties, Voters, and Risk Environment," and idem, "Strategy of Ambiguity."

122   See Fishburn, *Theory of Social Choice*, p. 251 and passim, and Richard D. McKelvey and Jeff Richelson, "Cycles of Risk," *Public Choice* 18 (Summer 1974): 41–66. We omit here a discussion of several related legislative topics, including the elimination or insistence upon roll-call votes and the structuring of legislative agendas to enhance ambiguity or to embarass certain incumbents, and the problem of coalitions of minorities, which again creates an incentive for candidates to remain ambiguous. On coalitions of minorities, see Downs, *Economic Theory*, pp. 55–60.

123   Ibid., pp. 255–6. See also the text accompanying note 45.

124   Ibid., p. 267.

125   Ibid., p. 269.

126   Riker and Ordeshook, "Calculus of Voting," p. 28.

127   Mueller, Chapter 4, this volume. Mueller extends this argument to a set of activities beyond voting in "Rational Egoism *versus* Adaptive Egoism as Fundamental Postulate for a Descriptive Theory of Human Behavior," *Public Choice* 51 (1986): 3–23.

128   Mueller, Chapter 4, this volume.

129   Downs, *Economic Theory*, p. 269, comes very close to this argument in explaining why citizens would vote but would not become well informed.

130   Riker, "Democracy and Representation." See also Riker, *Liberalism Against Populism*, pp. 197–8.

131   Riker, "Democracy and Representation," p. 52 (footnotes omitted). The relationship between logrolling and minority representation in the

presence of complex or simple issue spaces is discussed earlier in Edwin T. Haefele, "Coalitions, Minority Representation, and Vote-Trading Probabilities," *Public Choice* 8 (Spring 1970): 75–90.

132   Nicholas R. Miller, "Pluralism and Social Choice," *American Political Science Review* 77 (September 1983): 734–47.

133   See, e.g., William Kornhauser, *The Politics of Mass Society* (New York: Free Press, 1959); Arendt Lijphart, *Democracy in Plural Societies* (New Haven, Conn.: Yale University Press, 1977); Seymour M. Lipset, *Political Man: The Social Bases of Politics* (New York: Anchor, 1963); E. E. Schattschneider, *Party Government* (New York: Holt, 1942); and Truman, *Governmental Process*.

134   Miller, "Pluralism and Social Choice," p. 742 (citations omitted).

135   The closest that Miller comes to recognizing this problem is in an oblique reference to the political costs of rent-seeking activities: "Of course, since considerable resources are devoted to this competitive treadmill, pluralist politics is somewhat inefficient in economic terms" (ibid., p. 744). Hence, he appears not to recognize the associated welfare loss that attends, say, the restriction on output and increase in price, which are the goals of rent seeking.

136   See, e.g., Peter H. Aranson, *American Government: Strategy and Choice* (Boston: Little, Brown, 1981), pp. 323–9; Peter H. Aranson and Melvin J. Hinich, "Some Aspects of the Political Economy of Election Campaign Contribution Laws," *Public Choice* 34 (1979): 435–61; and Peter H. Aranson and Kenneth A. Shepsle, "The Compensation of Public Officials as a Campaign Issue: An Economic Analysis of *Brown v. Hartlage*," *Supreme Court Economic Review* 2 (1984): 213–76.

137   See, e.g., Richard G. Niemi and Herbert F. Weisberg, "A Mathematical Solution for the Probability of the Paradox of Voting," *Behavioral Science* 13 (July 1968): 317–23; idem, "Probability Calculations for Cyclical Majorities in Congressional Voting," in Niemi and Weisberg, eds., *Probability Models*, pp. 204–31; Frank DeMeyer and Charles R. Plott, "The Probability of a Cyclical Majority," *Econometrica* 38 (March 1970): 345–54; Mark Garman and Morton Kamien, "The Paradox of Voting: Probability Calculations," *Behavioral Science* 13 (July 1968): 306–16; Leon Gleser, "The Paradox of Voting: Some Probabilistic Results," *Public Choice* 7 (1969): 47–64; Colin Campbell and Gordon Tullock, "A Measure of the Importance of Cyclical Majorities," *Economic Journal* 75 (December 1965): 853–7; David Klahr, "A Computer Simulation of the Paradox of Voting," *American Political Science Review* 60 (June 1966): 384–90; and John Pomeranz and Roman Weil, "The Cyclical Majority Problem," *Communications of the ACM* 13 (1970): 251–4.

Changes in the probability of a cycle in large electorates may be small with respect to changes in the number of voters, but they may be larger with respect to changes in the number of issues.

138   Downs, *Economic Theory*, pp. 255–6.

139   Miller, "Pluralism and Social Choice," p. 740. Indeed, Miller there cites much of the relevant literature in note 137.

140   Mueller, Chapter 4, this volume.

141   Milton Friedman reports on Winston Churchill's prewar problems with the BBC in getting that government agency to allow him to air his then-"controversial" anti-German views on the radio. Milton Friedman, *Capitalism and Freedom* (University of Chicago Press, 1962), p. 19. Churchill's problems find their modern counterpart in recent charges that the BBC required clearance of its writers and reporters with MI-5.

142   Recent legislative debates over the "fairness doctrine," requiring radio and television stations to give equal time to opposing candidates, have reflected this problem.

143   See references cited in and text accompanying notes 42–87.

144   This argument receives a more extensive development in Aranson, "Risk, Uncertainty, and Retrospective Voting."

145   Of course, accomplishing this result will require that we overcome the resistance of those politicians who have developed human capital specific to the problem's generation. To the extent that politicians control information, the task becomes more formidable.

146   Aranson and Ordeshook, "Incrementalism."

147   Here we ignore various alternative proposals to change demand-revealing processes. These include approval voting and some newly discovered demand-revealing mechanisms. We omit discussion of these proposals because they are far more difficult to understand than are the electoral mechanisms currently in use (thus exacerbating rational ignorance and abstention) and because they are subject to manipulation (and thus susceptible to instability and "pluralist" rent seeking). On approval voting, see Steven J. Brams and Peter C. Fishburn, "Approval Voting," *American Political Science Review* 72 (September 1978): 831–47. On demand-revealing processes, see T. Nicholas Tideman and Gordon Tullock, "A New and Superior Process for Making Social Choices," *Journal of Political Economy* 84 (December 1976): 1145–59.

148   See, e.g., Aranson, "Public Deficits," and James M. Buchanan, *Public Principles of Public Debt* (Homewood, Ill.: Irwin, 1958).

149   See, e.g., Ordeshook, *Game Theory.*

150   This claim certainly holds true when we calculate the underlying population represented. For example, a filibuster that 41 senators refuse to shut off will sidetrack any bill. If these senators are from the 21 smallest states, they will represent less than 10% of the population.

151   A regulatory analogue to the balanced-budget proposal might reduce this problem. Aranson, Gellhorn, and Robinson, "Theory of Legislative Delegation," suggest such an analogue in the nondelegation doctrine.

152   Barry Weingast suggested this example to me.

153   Landes and Posner, "Independent Judiciary."

154   See text accompanying notes 137–9 and 143–6.

155   See text accompanying and references cited in notes 95–6.
156   The term is from William H. Riker, "Constitutional Limitations as Self-Denying Ordinances," in W. S. Moore and R. G. Penner, eds., *The Constitution and the Budget: Are Constitutional Limits on Tax, Spending, and Budget Powers Desirable at the Federal Level?* (Washington, D.C.: American Enterprise Institute, 1979), pp. 85–90.
157   See, e.g., Roger G. Noll, "The Case Against the Balanced Budget Amendment: Comments on Aranson and Rabushka," in Meyer, ed., *Economic Consequences,* pp. 201–10, and Kenneth A. Shepsle, "Overgrazing the Budgetary Commons: Incentive-Compatible Solutions to the Problem of Deficits," in ibid., pp. 211–19.

CHAPTER 6

Radical federalism: responsiveness, conflict, and efficiency

David Osterfeld

This essay argues that local government is far more responsive than government at the national level. It further argues that exit, or voting with one's feet, is generally a more effective method of ensuring governmental responsiveness than voice, or voting with the ballot. Thus, the conclusion is that local government would be more responsive than national government. However, local government with freedom of exit but no democracy would be more responsive than local government with democracy but no exit. The ideal combination would be local government combined with both exit and democracy, for each would enhance the effectiveness of the other.

1   Introduction: three examples

Appalled by conditions in the English factory system of the early nineteenth century, Parliament enacted various "factory acts" that were intended to limit the number of hours children could work and to force children entirely out of certain occupations deemed too dangerous. The result of this "enforced leisure" of children was a reduction in their earn-

I express my thanks to Loren Lomasky and Larry Eshelman for their valuable comments on an earlier draft of this chapter.

ings and in some cases a loss of employment. This imposed severe economic hardship on children as well as their families. There were numerous reports of children attempting to avoid these laws by drifting to smaller factories and workshops that were able to evade the provisions of the acts. It was precisely in these workplaces, however, that conditions were worse and pay lower. The effects of these reforms are clear. Regardless of how well intended, their enforcement actually aggravated the misery and poverty of the children and their families. Dr. Gaskell, a supporter of many of the reform laws, admitted shortly after their passage that they had only "increased the evils [they] are intended to remedy, and must, of necessity be repealed" (in Hutt 1977, p. 180n). In a revealing comment, economist W. H. Hutt (1977, p. 178) notes:

> The salient fact, and one which most writers fail to stress is that, in so far as the working people then had a "choice of alternative benefits," they chose the conditions which the reformers condemned. Not only did higher wages cause them to prefer factory work to other occupations, but as some of the reformers admitted, when one factory reduced its hours, it would tend to lose its operatives as they would transfer their services to establishments where they could earn more.

The 1840s were a time of massive immigration to the United States. The typical immigrant made the voyage under conditions of crowding, poor sanitation, and bad ventilation. Many – an estimated 10 percent – died en route (Sowell, 1981, p. 56). Observers, particularly those from the upper classes, were appalled by the conditions and worked for reforms. In 1847 the British government passed a law intended to improve voyage conditions for the immigrant. The law went into effect in 1848. What tended to be overlooked was that "improved" conditions entailed higher costs and thus increased fares. The result was that many of the poorest individuals and families in famine-stricken Ireland during the mid-nineteenth century could not afford to pay the higher fares. Immigration declined by about 25 percent, even though that meant nearly certain death by starvation. As Sowell notes (1981, p. 56), "When the government prohibited certain 'bad' conditions that prohibition in no way enlarged the set of options already available to immigrants and shippers. On the contrary, it eliminated some options without creating any new ones."

On September 3, 1965, the minimum wage in the United States went to $1.25 per hour. One result was the closing of nearly all crab-packing plants in North Carolina, since they were unable to pay $1.25 per hour in addition to the transportation costs required to ship their product to the major markets. Eighteen hundred women lost their jobs directly; hundreds of fishermen who supplied the plants lost their jobs indirectly.

Economist Yale Brozen (1968-9, p. 69) comments that minimum-wage legislation restricts freedom of entry into various occupations and promotes monopoly for those businesses in favorable locations.

These three historical incidents illustrate an important point. It is not that these laws were "bad." Bad laws no doubt will always be passed. It is that the range of a law, that is, the number of people affected by it, is directly related to the level of the government passing the law. Although the point may seem painfully obvious, it has important ramifications that are not.

An individual will choose the alternative that he deems "best" from among the choices open to him. The larger the choice set, other things being equal, the higher will be his utility or satisfaction. Force, or the threat of force, restricts the number of options open to an individual. Government is the repository of force in society. Government force may be required to combat the use of force by others. But the fact remains: Force restricts an individual's choice set. Since it is a repository of force, government reduces the options open to individuals.

This is clearly shown by the three examples. The child laborer had the "option" of unemployment before the reform laws were passed. The fact that he did not take it meant that he preferred work under admittedly miserable conditions to leisure with no income. Or perhaps more accurately, it meant that the preference of the child's parents was for the child to work rather than for a portion of the family income to be sacrificed. The reforms simply closed the former option (i.e., work) without creating any new ones. The would-be Irish immigrant already had the options of cheap passage under unsanitary conditions and better conditions at higher prices. The fact that so many émigrés chose the former meant that, all things considered, they regarded it as the best of the options open to them. Government reforms only succeeded in eliminating that option without adding any new ones. And workers in the crabmeat industry already had the option of demanding higher wages. Their actions clearly show they felt that jobs at lower wages were preferable to no jobs at higher wages. Once again, government reforms eliminated the former option but did not create any new ones in its place.

This is not to say that freedom is an absolute good. We are constantly making incremental trade-offs between freedom and other goods, such as security. We constantly *voluntarily* restrict our choice sets in order to increase our enjoyment of other values. The crucial consideration, however, is that, when government acts, our choices are *coercively* rather than voluntarily restricted. Clearly, if individuals choose the option that they believe will provide them with the greatest amount of utility, or the least disutility, it directly follows that "social utility" will be higher the more localized the level of decision making. And conversely, "social utility" will be lower the higher the level of decision making. Again, the point can be illustrated by reference to the three examples.

Fewer children and their families would have been adversely affected by the English factory acts if they had applied only to, say, the city of Birmingham or Liverpool. Many more would have been affected if the same acts had applied not just to England but to all of Europe. Fewer Irish would have been hurt had the reforms been restricted to, say, Dublin. Many more émigrés would have been adversely affected if they had been extended to all of England or even to Europe. Fewer workers would have been hurt if the higher minimum wage had been applied solely to, say, Raleigh; more would have been harmed if it had been applied to all of North America.

But good laws as well as bad laws are passed. Would not a "good law" passed at the national level create more options than the same good law passed at the state or local level? It is obvious that the effects of truly good legislation are greater when applied to, say, a million people than to a hundred. But what must be realized is that there is a critical *asymmetry* between good and bad legislation, on the one hand, and the level of the decision-making unit, on the other. Ignoring, for the moment, such problems as administration and enforcement, good legislation enacted at the national level would entail widespread benefits. But if decision-making authority were radically decentralized, citizen demand would *require* each of the numerous localities to implement similar or identical legislation. So in the case of good legislation it matters little, if at all, whether the regime is centralized or decentralized. But as the three examples clearly show, the situation is radically different with bad legislation. The ill effects of bad legislation enacted at the national level are imposed on everyone in the nation; the ill effects of bad legislation enacted by a local community are limited to those within that community. This essay presents a model designed to show that there are forces operative at the national level, but nearly absent at the local level, that make this asymmetry inevitable, that is, that the locus of decision-making authority is much more than a difference in degree; it is a difference in kind. It will be argued that the difference in politics between decision-making units at the national level and decision-making units at the local level is analogous to the difference in economics between a situation of a coercively protected monopoly and that of competition in the open market. The policy implication is that a drastic localization of decision-making authority, or radical federalism as it is called here, would make government both more responsive and more efficient, thereby increasing "social utility," that is, the utilities of the individual members of the society.

2   The development of the model

Economics is grounded in the proposition that individuals will act rationally so as to satisfy their preferences; that is they will choose from the set of choices they perceive facing them at any given moment the option that they believe will provide them with more utility, or less disutility, than any of the other components of the set. One of the major propositions derived from this assumption is that, when individuals are free to take their business elsewhere, that is, when they are, to use Albert Hirschman's (1970) term, "free to exit," a business can avoid losses only by providing what consumers wish to buy. This means that given the arrangement of free competition, individuals are led, even when they are concerned solely with their own self-interest, to purse the "common good."

By assuming the same behavioral principle but altering the institutional setting from one of open entry and free competition to one of closed entry and monopoly, the results are drastically altered. Individual consumers no longer have the option of taking their business elsewhere. Freed from the threat of competition, the monopoly is able to raise prices and lower quality. Now profits are not earned by serving others; they can be obtained *at the expense of others.*

This standard economic wisdom will be applied to the political realm. It is a common – but usually implicit – assumption that individuals act in their self-interest, or egoistically, in the private realm but altruistically in the public sphere. But there is no reason to believe that individuals actually compartmentalize their lives in this way. Observation shows that individuals are a mix of egoism and altruism, of self- and other-interested behavior, but that egoism is the dominant motive regardless of the sphere. The model will therefore assume self-interest as the principal mode of behavior by both citizens and public officials and will examine its impact on two distinct decision-making levels: the local and the national.

3   The decision-making level and its effect on "social utility"

Responsiveness

Government, according to Max Weber's classic definition, is that agency that exercises a monopoly over the (legitimate) use of force in a society. It follows that the more local the government unit, the smaller is the geographical area over which it exercises control.

This has important consequences in terms of responsiveness of government. In a country of a given size, it directly follows that the number of governmental units must increase in direct proportion to the degree to which the units are localized. Other things begin equal, the larger the number of governmental units, the easier it will be to transfer loyalties. This means that the more local the governmental unit, the more closely the institutional arrangement will resemble that of a competitive market. Assuming, for the moment, that the "consumer-voters," to use Tiebout's term, are fully mobile and fully informed, it follows that those who dislike the services they are receiving from one government are able to "vote with their feet" by moving to another area, that is, by "adopting" or joining another government and its community. Conversely, those governments that alienate their citizens, that is, their customers, by charging high prices, that is, taxes, or by providing shoddy services, will soon find themselves with few customers. In short, each consumer-voter will select the community that comes closest to satisfying his "total preference pattern." The greater the number of communities, that is, the larger his choice set, the higher his level of satisfaction (Tiebout, 1956, p. 419).

Of course, neither mobility nor information is free. This means that individuals will exit only when the prospective benefits of relocation exceed the total costs. The costs of exit or loyalty transfer are positively correlated with the geographical scope of the governmental unit. The larger the territorial unit, other things being equal, the more costly it is to exit. This is so for two reasons. First, normally both information and moving costs are positively associated with the physical distances involved. For the average individual the costs of obtaining information about conditions in an adjacent country would be considerably less than the costs of obtaining the same information about conditions in, say, Belgrade, Yugoslavia. Similarly, the cost of moving from, say, Rensselaer, Indiana, to Hong Kong would be much greater than moving from Rensselaer to DeMotte, a distance of about twenty miles. Second, greater physical distances often entail even greater *psychological* distances, that is, the difficulties of moving to an entirely new culture, such as getting used to new customs and traditions, learning a new language, finding a new job, and the like.

Thus, individuals can rather easily transfer their patronage from one local community to another, much as in the economic sphere customers can transfer their patronage from one firm to another. Since the cost of loyalty transfer is higher at the national level, one would expect the number of transfers to decline as the scope of government jurisdiction expanded. Transfers at the national level and especially at the international level would be expected to occur only under extreme circumstances. In other words, as the cost of exit rises, the demand for it declines.

Two important consequences emerge. First, since the cost of exit rises as the geographical range of the government expands, the incentive for the government to respond to the demands of "its" clients, that is, the citizens, correspondingly declines. Thus, one would expect local governments to be more responsive than state governments and the latter to be more responsive than national governments. Second, although not irrelevant, the type of government (democracy, dictatorship, etc.) is actually much less important than the range of jurisdiction. *Provided that exit is not barred, a large democracy would be less responsive, and therefore provide less utility to its citizens, than a local dictatorship.* This is so because the moment the dictator became oppressive, citizens could transfer loyalties. Enough exits would, quite literally and peacefully, put the dictator "out of business." Since loyalty transfer is much more costly under a national government, regardless of type, exit could not occur as frequently. And therefore the threat of exit would be less credible.

The conclusion that the scope of jurisdiction renders the type of government relatively unimportant may be surprising. Does not a large democracy, after all, retain the exit option, the option of causing the "exit" of the existing government by voting it out of office? This response ignores a fundamental aspect of government: In contrast to the competitive economic sphere, where adjustments are *marginal,* that is, each individual is able to evaluate each transaction separately, adjustments in the political sphere are, by their nature, *holistic. All* individuals residing within the jurisdiction of the same political unit *must* deal with the same agent, namely the government. The important issue is not *how* decisions are made or who is consulted in the decision-making process, but the *scope* of the decision, once it is made. The democratic process must ultimately result in the selection of one alternative from an indeterminant number of possible alternatives and adopt it in the name of, and impose it upon, the entire society. Whether that alternative reflects the interests of an intense minority, an intense majority, or even an apathetic majority is immaterial. Those whose preferences are not incorporated into the government policy cannot, as is generally the situation with the market, satisfy their preferences by taking their business elsewhere. The best the losers can hope for is to exercise enough influence to get the policy changed. But this only means that the old losers are now winners and the old winners losers; it does not change the nature of the game, only the final score.

If the foregoing is correct, then the more closely political institutions resemble the economic institution of the competitive market, the more responsive they will be. And the more restricted the scope of a political decision, that is, the more localized the political unit, the more it will approximate that arrangement. Thus, the level of government tends to be much more important than its type.

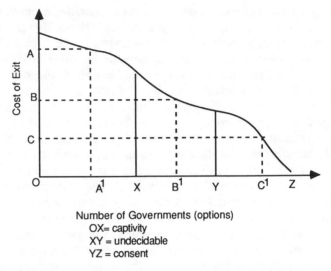

Number of Governments (options)
OX= captivity
XY = undecidable
YZ = consent

Figure 1

This approach enables us to deal with the difficult philosophical problem of consent. Does living under a particular government imply consent? The answer is yes *and* no. If exit is easy, one can interpret residence
as consent. But if exit costs are high, no consent can be inferred. As Joseph
Tussman has observed (in Johnson, 1975–6, p. 17), only if the state is a
voluntary association can one distinguish between "consent" and "captivity." It is a continuum, not a dichotomy. One can distinguish between
black and white, but one cannot tell where on a continuum black ends and
white begins. There is a gray area in between which is neither black nor
white. The same is true of consent. To demand an exact cutoff point is to
demand a false precision.

But if consent is a positive function of ease of exit, and if ease of exit is
correlated with the number of governmental units, it follows that "government by consent" applies to local but not to national governments.
This is shown in Figure 1. Here the cost of exit by individual *A* would be so
high that it would be sensible to construe continued residence as "captivity" rather than "consent." But since the cost of exit is fairly low for
individual *C*, it is reasonable to interpret his continued residence as consent. Finally, given the intermediate costs faced by individual *B*, one
cannot determine whether or not his continued residence implies consent. It would fall into that rather messy gray area labeled "undecidable."

An example ought to make this clear. Before 1962, exit from East to

West Berlin was relatively easy. The mass exits up to that time were a graphic and poignant statement of no consent. The Berlin Wall and other draconian measures instituted in 1962 reduced the number of exits and exit attempts to a trickle. The draconian penalties, including the death penalty, imposed on those caught attempting to escape drastically increased the *cost* of exit. Thus, under the post-1962 conditions, the benefits, however great, of exiting East Berlin were outweighed by the costs, for all but a handful. One can scarcely contend that continued residence under such conditions is an expression of consent. Clearly, the rise in costs made exiting prohibitively expensive.

Amelioration of conflict

The localization of government authority should produce another significant benefit. Just as firms compete by varying their products in order to distinguish them from their competitors' products, one would expect communities and their governments to compete for "members" or "customers" by offering various "package deals" or mixes of services. Such competition not only would help to ensure responsiveness, but also would serve to reduce political conflict. Each individual would be in a position to choose that community offering a mix or package closest to his optimum. This is shown in the two-issue diagram in Figure 2. The optima for individuals *A*, *B*, *C*, *D*, and *E* are shown for both police expenditures on the horizontal axis and the strictness of pollution control on the vertical axis. The particular mix of these two issues is shown for communities *T*, *U*, *V*, and *W*. The circles are indifference planes for each individual. Each individual would join that community whose particular mix was closest to his optimum. Thus, *A* and *B* would join community *W*, *C* would join *V*, *D* would join *U*, and *E* would join *T*.

Given competition by communities for members, one could certainly envision a situation in which an individual, say *E*, was born a resident of community *W*. It would not take long for *E* to discover that other communities and their governments were offering policies closer to his optimum than those of *W*. Provided that the prospective benefits of membership in another community were higher than the cost of exiting, *E* would exit *W* in order to join that community, in this case *T*. It is important to recognize that the ability of any one individual to obtain policies approximating his optimum would not prevent others from obtaining their optima. Thus, there would be no need for an individual, say *E*, who was dissatisfied with the policies of "his" community or its government, say *W*, to attempt the difficult task of moving or bending the policies of *W* in the direction of *E*'s optimum but, in the process, away from the optima of

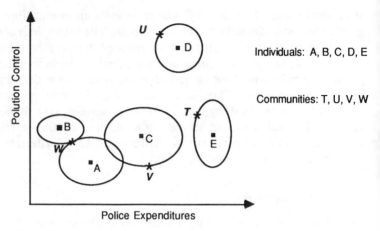

Figure 2

most of the members of *W*. Individual *E* would simply exit *W* and join another community with policies more to his liking. This would leave the satisfied members of *W* free to enjoy their community. Neither side would be forced to undertake political combat in order to enjoy policies closely approximating their values. Neither side would have policies they strenuously objected to imposed upon them.

Once again, the results would *approximate* those of the open market. With a smorgasbord of communities, each could get everything, or nearly everything, he wanted. The greater the number of communities and the larger the variation among them, that is, the larger each individual's choice set, the closer each individual could come to fully achieving his optimum. In such a situation the need for political conflict would be greatly ameliorated.

But although political conflict might be reduced *within* communities, would this not be offset by increased conflict *among* the larger number of more or less autonomous communities? This is certainly a possibility. The question, therefore, is which level of government would be most appropriate for handling this problem? Assuming that any higher level of government could effectively deter or prevent conflicts between any lower level of government, the logical sequence would be as follows:

county governments can prevent conflicts between local governments;
state governments can prevent conflicts between county governments;
national governments can prevent conflicts between state governments;

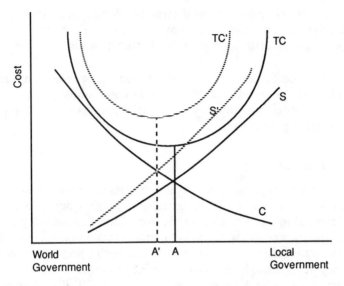

Figure 3

regional governments can prevent conflicts between national governments; and

world government can prevent conflicts between regional governments.

The decision-making calculus is presented in Figure 3. Since the fewer
the individuals involved in the decision-making process the greater the
control each has over the policy adopted, line C, representing control over
security policy, would slope downward to the right. By contrast, security
from external threats would be negatively correlated with localization,
that is, the number of external units. This is represented by line S. The
various "mixes" of control and security, as well as their total cost at any
level of government, are obtained by summing C and S. This is depicted
by line TC. The optimal level of government for handling this particular
function, that is, the level of government that would maximize the degree
of local control over security policy while minimizing the threat of external aggression, would be the lowest point on TC, namely point A. This
optimum would, of course, depend upon circumstances. If at a given time
aggression, or its threat, increased, this would shift line S to S' and thus the
total cost from TC to TC'. A community might then decide (*how* it would
decide is, at this point, irrelevant) to sacrifice some control, or influence,

over security policy for increased security. Hence, under these circumstances the optimal level of government would shift from A to A'. Of course, a reduction in aggression or its threat would have the reverse effect.

In brief, localization would reduce conflict *within* communities. Though it might increase conflict *among* communities, this could be handled by delegating authority for security matters to an appropriate, higher level of government.

Efficiency

Competition among communities (and their governments), which is possible only at local, and to a lesser extent state, levels, would produce both experimentation and a market in the provision of community services. Both of these are absent when decision making takes place at the national level. As is the case in the economic sphere, such competition produces efficiency; its absence breeds waste and inefficiency.

Bureaus, observes Anthony Downs (1967, pp. 29–30), "face no economic markets whatever on the output side. Therefore they have no direct way of evaluating their outputs in relation to the inputs used to make them. This inability is of profound importance in all aspects of bureaucratic behavior." Whereas a private firm operating in an open market has an "objective guide" for determining the efficiency of its operations, namely the ability to earn profits or at least to avoid losses, a bureau does not. Hence, says Downs, "the major yardsticks for decision-making used by private nonbureaucratic firms are *completely unavailable* to men who run bureaus" (emphasis added). Put differently, in the absence of alternatives there is no market. And without a market there is no guidepost against which to measure performance or determine the allocation of inputs. In the absence of any test of efficiency, decisions must be economically arbitrary. Thus, an efficient allocation of a bureau's resources could occur only by chance. This would be a most unlikely outcome and, with changing conditions, a purely temporary one. Hence, bureaucracies are, by their nature, inefficient.

It is likely that the foregoing overstates the case. By definition there is no alternative to, and thus no market for, the output of a *national* bureau. At the local level there are alternatives and thus spatial competition, that is, competition among communities or their governments. The result is at least an *approximation* of a market test for the output of a local bureau. Thus, one would expect local bureaucracies to operate far more efficiently than national ones.

Bureaucratic inefficiency is aggravated by the inherent tendency of

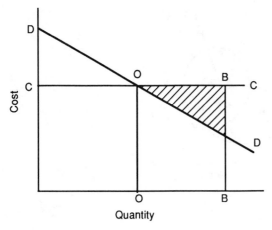

Figure 4

bureaus to expand. Though bureaucrats may *desire* to see their bureaus expand for several reasons, the underlying factors *permitting* expansion is their position as protected monopolies. Being freed from competition enables bureaucrats to use their positions to serve themselves rather than the "public." Bureaus are established to solve particular problems. But if the problem were solved, the bureau could be abolished. Thus, the bureaucrats have a vested interest in perpetuating the very problems they were hired to solve.

It is true that members of any occupation have the same vested interest; doctors have an interest in disease, teachers in ignorance, and auto mechanics in automobiles in need of repair. The difference lies *not in individual motivations but in the institutional arrangement.* It is the presence of alternatives that harmonizes the interests of producer and consumer. The doctor may have an interest in perpetuating disease, but the presence of other doctors prevents him from following that vested interest. The doctor who spread disease rather than cured it would soon lose his customers to other physicians. It is only when individuals or groups are freed from the constraint of serving others that they are in a position to pursue their own vested interests. And only protected monopolies are freed from this constraint.

If the analogy between government bureaus and monopolies is correct, one would expect to find government budgets characterized by socially wasteful expansion. This is shown in Figure 4 (adapted from Tullock, 1976, p. 31). The horizontal line *CC* indicates constant cost. The down-

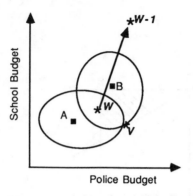

Figure 5

ward-sloping line *DD* represents the demand of the citizens for the service. If the service were supplied competitively on the market, the optimum amount would be at point *O*. The consumer surplus would be represented by the triangle *CDO*. If the service were supplied by a government agency, the normal procedure would be for the agency to receive a budget in return for an agreed-upon output. Its monopolistic position would enable the agency to expand its budget until the entire consumer surplus was eliminated, that is, until the taxpayers were indifferent between the existing level of services at high tax rates and the abolition of the bureau with a corresponding reduction in taxes. Short of this point, which is indicated by line *B*, the monopolistic agency would be failing to exploit profit opportunities open to it; beyond that point, taxpayers would be better off without the service at all.

It is worth noting that this result does not require purely self-interested behavior. Even the other-interested, public-spirited bureaucrat desires to see "his" budget increased. He is aware that the larger budget permits his agency to provide additional benefits to the public. Thus, both self-interested and other-interested bureaucrats desire to see their bureau's budget expand.

If the analogy between localism and free competition, on the one hand, and nationalism and monopolistic control, on the other, is valid and if the foregoing argument regarding the inherent tendency of government bureaus to expand is correct, one would expect bureaus at the national level to be far less efficient than those at the local level. As a local government agency expanded its budget beyond point *O*, it would begin to lose "consumer-voters" to competing communities. This is illustrated in Figure 5. If the government in community *W* expanded its budget to point *W* − 1, individuals A and B would transfer their membership to community V, since this would now be closer to their optima than W after its slide to $W - 1$. The ever-present threat of transferring loyalties would put strict limits on the ability of local government bureaus to exploit their "monopolistic" positions for their own gain. Like a business without income, a government without a tax base could not survive.

The evidence appears to support the theory. Throughout the twentieth century there has been a clear trend from local to national control of government services. In 1900, state and local expenditures were double national expenditures. By 1980 the positions had reversed themselves, with expenditures at the national level now about double total local and state spending. What is startling, however, is the magnitude of the recent national budget increases, especially when one considers that much of it has come under a conservative "budget cutter" like President Reagan. National expenditures in 1960 were $100 billion. By 1970 they had reached $200 billion. In 1976 they were $300 billion. They reached $400 billion in 1978, $600 billion in 1981, and nearly a trillion dollars in 1985. What these figures seem to indicate is that the nationalization of government services has meant their monopolization and that monopolization has indeed been exploited by the monopolists for their own benefit.

Domestic spending is a case in point. In the thirty-year period from 1950 to 1980 GNP rose by 819 percent. Total personal consumption increased by 768 percent. During the same period, expenditures at the national level for domestic services increased by 1,228 percent, or more than one-half more rapidly. Transfer payments to individuals during this period rose by 1,530 percent, and expenditures at the national level for education increased from $123 million in 1950 to $30.8 billion in 1980, an increase of about 25,000 percent (*U.S. Statistical Abstract,* 1953, 1964, 1982–3)!

The fact that total civilian employment by the national government remained virtually unchanged and actually declined as a percentage of the overall work force (Barger, 1984, pp. 155–6) raises the question of how these increases were used. Did they go to provide additional benefits to the public, or were they channeled as monopoly profits to the government bureaucrats? The latter appears to be the case. In a 1979 *Newsweek* article (pp. 57–9), economist Walter Williams noted that, if one simply divided the total amount of money spent in this country each year to "fight poverty" by the number of families with reported incomes below the poverty line, the figure would be $35,000 per family. (In a recent television interview, Williams stated that the figure currently stood at nearly $45,000 per poor family.) Of course, the poor actually receive very little of this. "Most of it goes instead," Williams observed, "for salaries and overhead to run the growing poverty industry." Despite the controversy it raised, Sowell's remark (in Bauer, 1981 p. 145) seems accurate: "To be blunt, the poor are a gold mine. By the time they are studied, advised, experimented with and administered to, the poor have helped many a middle-class liberal to attain affluence with government money."

In a 1977 report, even the Civil Service Commission, hardly one of the bureaucracy's severest critics, acknowledged that at least 150,000 government workers were "overgraded." The commission estimated that the cost to the government was at least $780 million per year in overpaid salaries. But given automatic "merit raises" and the mechanics of the "comparability formula," many observers believe that this is an extremely modest estimate (see Peters, 1983, pp. 44–5). This phenomenon has been aptly, if sarcastically, referred to by Peter Bauer (1981, p. 144) as "Adam Smith's invisible hand in reverse": "Those who sought the public good achieve what was no part of their intentions, namely personal wealth."

Briefly put, national agencies are turning out shoddy services at increasingly exorbitant costs. This is in line with the model. The bureaucrats are using their positions to acquire "monopoly profits" (see Laband, 1983, pp. 311–14).

4   Exit, voice, and the levels of government

In *Exit, Voice and Loyalty,* Albert Hirschman (1970) presented two distinct options or mechanisms for inducing efficiency and responsiveness in organizations: exit and voice. Exit, of course, is the severance of ties with an organization, that is, taking one's business elsewhere; voice is the verbal expression of preferences, or what is commonly known as democracy.

Significantly, the higher the level of government, the *less* effective are both exit and voice. It has already been shown that the greater costs associated with exiting higher levels of government reduce the effectiveness of this option. And higher levels of government likewise impede the effectiveness of the voice option. This is due to the sheer numbers involved. The odds of one vote affecting the outcome of an election at the national level are about 10 million to one (Tullock, 1972, p. 110). The more local the election, the better are the odds. Similarly, the odds against a single individual, say, affecting the policy of the United States toward the Soviet Union or altering the policies of the EPA or the FDA are immense. The odds that an individual will get a small-town city council to install a traffic light at an intersection or change the hours the local park is open to the public are immeasurably better. Thus, the effectiveness of both exit and voice are positively correlated with the localization of decision-making authority.

In his famous "Federalist 10" (Madison et al., 1982, p. 48), James Madison advanced the argument that "the smaller the society" the "smaller the number of individuals composing a majority and the smaller the compass within which they are placed." Hence, "the more easily will they concert and execute their plans of oppression." Madison's "cure" is to enlarge the range of government so as to include a multitude of factions, thereby making the acquisition of power by a tyrannical faction less likely. Thus, in contrast to the thesis of this essay, that decision making at the local level is preferable to decision making at higher levels, Madison's position is that higher decision-making units are preferable to local ones. How can we account for this difference?

Madison's concern is with preventing a powerful majority from abusing the rights of a hapless and helpless minority. He advances "two methods of curing the mischiefs of faction: the one, by removing its causes; the other by controlling its effects." The "causes of faction," he says, can be eliminated in two ways: (1) by "destroying the liberty which is essential to its existence" and (2) by "giving to every citizen the same opinions, the same passions, and the same interests." The former is rejected as "worse than the disease," the latter as contrary to "the nature of man." Since the *causes* of faction cannot be removed, Madison concludes (p. 446) that

> a pure democracy, by which I mean a society consisting of a small number of citizens who assemble and administer the government in person, can admit of no cure for the mischief of faction. A common passion or interest will, in almost every case, be felt by a majority of the whole; a communication and concert results from the form of government itself; and there is nothing to check the inducements to sacrifice the weaker party or an obnoxious individual.

The solution, then, is to control the effects of faction. This, he argues, is accomplished by expanding the range of the decision-making unit (p. 48):

> Extend the sphere and you take in a greater variety of parties and interests; you make it less probable that a majority of the whole will have a common motive to invade the rights of other citizens; or if such a common motive exists, it will be more difficult for all who feel it to discover their own strength and to act in unison with each other.

What is noteworthy about Madison's analysis is that he implicitly assumes that the population is given. *The exit option is ignored.* This omission has serious consequences for the entire Madisonian argument.

Madison is no doubt correct in stating that differences of opinion are part of human nature. And he is probably correct in arguing that, other things being equal, violations of minority rights by overbearing majorities are more likely to occur at local levels, which encompass fewer people and thus contain fewer factions or divisions, than at higher levels encompassing more people and thus more differences of opinion. Thus, Madison's conclusion that large democracies are preferable to local democracies *follows logically from the options, or choice set, he presents.*

But is it really true, as Madison believes, that "the diversity in the faculties of men" presents "an insuperable obstacle to the uniformity of interests" within a given decision-making unit? Yes, but only so long as exit is excluded. The exit option introduces a filtering device or self-selection process in which citizens leave communities they dislike to join others more to their liking. Thus, Madison's entire argument hinges on his (implicit) assumption of an immobile population. Once this arbitrary restriction is lifted and exit is permitted, the entire Madisonian argument is, literally, turned on its head. Exit permits the emergence of precisely that "uniformity of interests" within a community that Madison thought impossible. Moreover, since exit is far more effective at local than national levels, it follows that the "cure for the mischief of factions" lies in the exact opposite direction from that which Madison prescribed: increased rather than reduced localization.

The foregoing is seen in the numerous sectarian communities and religious orders. The Amish, Mennonites, and Quakers, for example, live in communities that many, probably most, would consider oppressive. Yet this "uniformity of interest" within the community actually makes this environment desirable for its members. Those for whom the environment becomes oppressive are free to exit, thereby preserving the uniformity. Moreover, the growing number of exits in recent years by members of various religious orders of priests and nuns highlights another important aspect of exit. In order to stem the growing tide of exits, as well as to attract new members, reforms have been introduced in many orders in an effort to make life more palatable to existing and prospective members. In this way exit and the threat of exit render voice much more effective.

In brief, exit is a key consideration. Unfortunately, it was ignored by Madison. The consequences were serious. Localization, which appeared oppressive and undesirable to Madison, becomes quite attractive and liberating once exit is introduced into the analysis. And conversely, nationalization, which appeared to Madison to be the antidote or cure for local oppression, is revealed as inefficient and unattractive.

A final aspect of voice and exit should be considered. Exit enables everyone, majorities as well as minorities, to pursue their preferences. But regardless of the decision-making rule chosen (majority rule, plurality, two-thirds rule, proportional representation, etc.), voice or democracy can enable only a particular majority to obtain its preferences, and this can be accomplished only by coercing the minorities into actions contrary to their preferences (Osterfeld, 1986, pp. 260–3). As economist James Buchanan (1954, p. 153) has written, "The consistency of market choice," or exit, or "taking one's business elsewhere, is achieved without the overruling of minority values as would be the case if ordinary political voting were made consistent. Therefore, in a very real sense, market decisions are comparable to political decisions only when unanimity is present."

In short, if the foregoing is correct, it is clear that both exit and voice as mechanisms for inducing governmental efficiency and responsiveness are far more effective at the local than the national level. It is also clear that exit is more fundamental than voice since (1) at least at the local level, it is an effective instrument for controlling government regardless of the particular decision-making rule in use, that is, dictatorship or some form of democracy, and (2) exit enhances the effectiveness of the voice option.

5   Policy implication: radical federalism

The policy implication is clear: drastic localization of government decision-making authority. This raises three questions: (1) How far should localization proceed? (2) What should be localized? (3) How much exit can be expected after localization?

How far should localization go?

Thus far we have said only that the more things are localized the better. Unless some counterbalancing factors are identified, this leads logically to the conclusion that "social utility" would be maximized by "making each person his own municipal government" (Tiebout, 1956, p. 421). This conclusion is obviously incorrect. People are not hermits; they derive very great economic, psychological, and other benefits from human interaction. How far, then, should localization go?

Tullock (1969, pp. 19–29) examined two factors that have often been advanced as means to determine the optimum size of government: internalization of externalities or "local border effects" and economies of scale. The problem with the former is that, if a governmental unit is to be large enough to internalize completely all of the effects of a given activity, even "such a minor matter as street cleaning might require a continental or even a world-wide governmental unit." Since the externality principle provides no stopping point short of world government, it is as lopsidedly inadequate as the "infinite communities" assumption, which, as we have seen, would make each person his own municipal government.

Nor does the "economies of scale" principle provide an adequate basis for determining the optimal size of government. Economies of scale are relevant, says Tullock, only if the governmental unit itself must produce a particular service. But

> if it can purchase it from a specialized producer, then the econo-
> mies of scale cease to have relevance to the decision as to the size
> of the governmental unit. . . . Only conservatism and organiza-
> tional rigidities prevent wide-spread purchase of services by gov-
> ernmental units of any size from organizations large enough to
> obtain the full benefit of any economies of scale which may exist.

Thus, he concludes, "the 'optimal size' of the government as producer of services can be dropped" from consideration.

The optimal size of a governmental unit, suggests Tullock, would be one that provided the maximum amount of both efficiency *and* respon-siveness, or control, at the lowest total cost. He reasons as follows. At one extreme one can envision a situation in which all government services are provided at the national level. Clearly, the larger the bundle of services and the greater the number of individuals involved in the decision-mak-ing process, the greater will be the "costs inflicted on the voter through poor control." The costs of control decline as the size of the governmental unit declines. But as his control over the unit increases, so do the informa-tion demands on the individual. Eventually government will become so dispersed or localized that it will all but cease to exist, and each individual will be forced to make numerous decisions in areas in which he has little or no expertise. It is at this point, says Tullock, that the suppliers of "govern-ment services" become "quite uncontrolled" and the costs of control begin to rise. This is depicted by line C in Figure 6.

Line E is "the cost that will be imposed through grouping governmen-tal units in nonoptimum ways." For purposes of analysis it is assumed that government is reduced in size only if it increases efficiency. Hence, "the curve falls monotonically from left to right and eventually reaches a point of zero." The total cost (TC) for a government of any size is ob-tained by summing C and E. The optimal size of government is the lowest point on TC.

The foregoing raises a very interesting question that Tullock seems at least obliquely aware of but does not pursue. In our daily economic life, he says (p. 26), we often encounter

> situations in which the individual cannot hope to make rational
> decisions for himself. I do not make even the slightest effort to

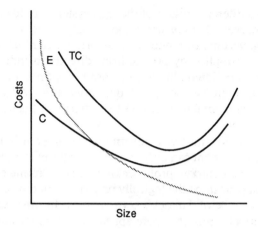

Figure 6

decide the detailed specifications of the automobile that I buy; I leave that to other people and choose among the alternative packages of characteristics that are presented to me. In some cases I hire the services of a specialized consultant, a doctor, for example. . . . Clearly, the same method would be suitable when purchasing government services.

Thus, Tullock proposes to extend the method of normal or rational behavior into the realm of "purchasing government services." But this raises a correlative issue: If the method of "rational economic behavior" should be used in the *purchase* of government services, why should it not be equally desirable in the *provision* of such services? As information costs began to rise with the localization of government functions, would not one expect to see free-market firms emerge in response to the demand for reduced information costs? These firms could offer various package deals or "mixes" of what are traditionally thought of as "government services." Either these services could be contracted out to communities as a whole with payment made via community tax receipts, or their purchase could be left entirely up to the individual. The traditional criticism of this position is that government services are public or collective. They cannot be broken down into marginal units and therefore cannot, or at least cannot efficiently, be sold on the market. But some (see, e.g., Osterfeld, 1986) have maintained that the "collectiveness" of such goods is a product not of the goods and services themselves but of the legal system within which they are offered. That is to say, such goods and services as roads, police and fire protection, and pollution control are not *inherently* but *legally* collective. If so, then a revision of the legal system would permit the extension of the market into those areas traditionally thought to be the natural province of government. Under such an arrangement *all* goods and services would be supplied by private firms directly to individual purchasers, with each individual able to purchase his optimal quantity and quality of "government" services, including none at all. And since this would permit governmental third parties to be bypassed, the need for taxes would be eliminated.

The conclusion is significant. Since government is inherently inefficient and even local government can only approximate the efficiency and responsiveness of the open market, profit-seeking firms operating on the open market would appear to be the logically preferred outcome of "actual economic life," that is, of Tullock's own analysis. In other words, given the logic of Tullock's analysis there appears to be no reason that private firms not only could not supply individuals with "wholesale clusters of activities" but could not supply them better than governments, local or national.

This is not meant to suggest that all government should be abolished. It is meant only to illustrate the range of options that emerge under the type of radical federalism proposed here. Those desiring a thoroughly socialist society in which all property was "collectivized," or a society with extensive social service programs and thus an active government and high taxes, would be free to pool their resources and establish such communities. Those preferring an individualist or free-market anarchism with neither government nor taxes would be free to institute such communities. And the possible mixes between these economic extremes are innumerable. Similarly, those preferring to live in communities with socially strict norms would be free to establish them, and those desiring social permissiveness would likewise be free to institute such communities. Once again, there are myriad possibilities between these social extremes.

Once it is established which kinds of service, if any, a community wants its government(s) to provide, Tullock's criteria can be utilized to help ascertain the size of the community as well as the size and level of its government(s).

The point to be stressed here is that a political framework of radical federalism creates a situation in which, like that of the economic framework of the free market, one individual's ability to obtain his optimal preferences in no way prevents any other individual from achieving his optimal preference pattern. Put differently, the higher the level of decision making, the more the political outcome is zero sum; the lower the level, the more it becomes positive sum.

What should be localized?

What should be decentralized and to what extent are empirical questions. However, my guess is that *all* of the functions of the national government, with the exception of national defense, could be better handled at the state or local level.

One reason I think that it would be better to err on the side of overlocalization is that history seems to indicate that it is much easier for several smaller governmental units to establish a larger governmental entity than for a large government to subdivide itself into several smaller entities. Hence, a reasonable approach would be to decentralize as much and as far as possible. When and if necessary, one could always recentralize.

How much exit?

How much exit or migration should one expect under radical federalism? After justifying the right of revolution, John Locke attempts to quiet the fear that "this Hypothesis lays a ferment for frequent Rebellion." "Revolutions happen," he says (1963, p. 463), "not upon every little mismanagement of publick affairs," but only after "a long train of Abuses, Prevarications and Artifices."

The same would apply to exit. Regardless of the level of government, exit entails cost, not only economically but, perhaps even more importantly, psychologically. Normally, an individual feels an attachment to or part of the community in which he is born and raised. It is where his friends are. He identifies with it. It is "his" community. He is a member of it and feels loyalty to it. It is where his "roots" are. It is "home." Thus, exit, like revolution, will not occur "upon every little mismanagement of publick affairs" or disagreement over public policy.

Moreover, by reducing cost, radical federalism *permits* exit; it does not *require* it. In fact, by rendering exit less costly, radical federalism, as we have seen, would force governments to be more responsive; that is, it would increase the effectiveness of voice. In doing so it would actually reduce the need for exit.

Thus, there is little basis for the fear that radical federalism would destabilize society by encouraging excessive migration or exit for relatively trivial or frivolous reasons.

6   Conclusion

Throughout the twentieth century much of the vitality and variety of local communities have been eliminated by the growing number of rules and regulations of the national government. As the national government has taken an ever-increasing percentage of the average individual's income in taxes, local and state governments have found it more difficult to finance needed projects by raising their own money and have come to rely ever more heavily on "federal aid" programs, complete with national standards and guidelines.

If the argument presented in this chapter has merit, a drastic devolution of decision-making authority would make government both more responsive and more efficient. It would also permit an increase in the variety of local communities. All of this would increase "social utility." The possibilities are eloquently expressed in the following passage from philosopher Robert Nozick (1974, pp. 310–12):

> Utopian authors, each very confident of the virtues of his own vision and of its singular correctness, have differed among themselves . . . in the institutions and kinds of life they present for emulation. Though the picture of an ideal society that each person presents is much too simple . . . we should take the fact of the difference seriously. No utopian author has everyone in his society leading the same life, allocating exactly the same amount of time to exactly the same activities. *Why not?* Don't the reasons also count against just one kind of community?
>
> The conclusion to draw is that there will not be *one* kind of community existing and one kind of life led in utopia. Utopia will consist of utopias, of many different and divergent communities in which people lead different kinds of lives under different conditions. Some kinds of communities will be more attractive to most than others: communities will wax and wane. People will leave some for others or spend their whole lives in one. Utopia is a framework for utopias, a place where people are at liberty to join together voluntarily to pursue and attempt to realize their own vision of the good life in the ideal community but where no one can impose his own utopian vision upon others. . . .
>
> Different communities, each with a slightly different mix, will provide a range from which each individual can choose that community which best approximates *his* balance among competing values.

References

Barger, Harold. *The Impossible Presidency.* Glenville, Ill.: Scott, Foresman, 1984.
Bauer, Peter. *Equality, the Third World and Economic Delusion.* Cambridge, Mass.: Harvard University Press, 1981.

Brozen, Yale. "Is Government the Source of Monopoly?" *Intercollegiate Review* 4 (Winter 1968–9): 67–8.

Buchanan, James. "Social Choice, Democracy and Free Markets," *Journal of Political Economy* 16 (April 1954): 114–23.

Downs, Anthony. *Inside Bureaucracy.* Boston: Little, Brown, 1967.

Hirschman, Albert. *Exit, Voice and Loyalty.* Cambridge, Mass.: Harvard University Press, 1970.

Hutt, W. H. "The Factory System of the Early Nineteenth Century," in *Capitalism and the Historians,* ed. F. A. Hayek. University of Chicago Press, 1977, pp. 156–84.

Johnson, Karen. "Political Obligation and the Voluntary Association Model of the State," *Ethics* 86 (1975–6): 17–29.

Laband, D. N. "Federal Budget Cuts: Bureaucrats Trim the Meat, Not the Fat," *Public Choice* 41, no. 2 (1983): 311–14.

Locke, John. *Two Treatises of Government.* New York: Mentor, 1963.

Madison, James, et al. *The Federalist Papers.* New York: Bantam, 1982.

Nozick, Robert. *Anarchy, State and Utopia.* New York: Basic Books, 1974.

Osterfeld, David. *Freedom, Society and the State.* San Francisco: Cobden Press, 1986.

Peters, Charles. *How Washington Really Works.* Reading, Mass.: Addison-Wesley, 1983.

Sowell, Thomas. *Markets and Minorities.* New York: Basic Books, 1981.

Tiebout, Charles. "A Pure Theory of Local Expenditures," *Journal of Political Economy* 18 (October 1956): 416–24.

Tullock, Gordon. "Federalism: Problems of Scale," *Public Choice* 21 (Spring 1969): 19–29.

  Toward a Mathematics of Politics. Ann Arbor: University of Michigan Press, 1972.

  The Vote Motive. Lansing, England: Institute of Economic Affairs, 1976.

Williams, Walter. "Commentary," *Newsweek* September 24, 1979, pp. 57–9.

U.S. Department of Commerce. *U.S. Statistical Abstract.* Washington, D.C.: U.S. Government Printing Office, various years.

CHAPTER 7

Contractarian presuppositions and democratic governance

James M. Buchanan

1   Introduction

This essay is directed toward clarification of the relationship between contractarianism and majoritarian democracy. Contractarianism does, indeed, presuppose political equality among all members of the politically organized community, both in the operation of the law and in changes in the law, as well as in the determination of collective action within the law. Political equality does not, however, imply majoritarian decision making either in the enforcement of law or in the changing of law; and majoritarian decision making remains only one among several optional means of making collective choices under the range and scope allowed for such action within the law of the constitution.

If politics is to be interpreted in any justificatory or legitimizing sense without the introduction of supraindividual value norms, it must be modeled as a process within which individuals, with separate and potentially different interests and values, interact for the purpose of securing individually valued benefits of cooperative effort. If this presupposition about the nature of politics is accepted, the ultimate model of politics is *contractarian*. There is simply no feasible alternative. This presupposition does not, however, directly yield descriptive implications about the precise structure of political arrangements and hence about "democracy" in the everyday usage of this term. We must acknowledge that, in terms of

174

ordinary language, "nondemocratic" political institutions may be analytically derived from fully consistent contractarian premises.

Hobbes offers, of course, the classic example. Finding themselves in the war of each against all, persons contract with the sovereign; they give up natural liberty for the order and security that the sovereign promises. Decisions made by the sovereign subsequent to this initial contract are not "democratic," in any meaningful sense of the term. Though useful in setting the stage for discussion here, however, the Hobbesian contractual metaphor need not be extended to Hobbes's own gloomy predictions concerning the prospects for limiting the power of the sovereign. The Hobbesian metaphor suggests, nonetheless, that, so long as the sovereign remains within the agreed-on and assigned limits of the initial contract, so long as the sovereign's role remains the maintenance and enforcement of the internal order, "democratic" attributes of the sovereign's decision making would be out of place and, indeed, would be counterproductive.

The principle here may be placed in a more general setting, and it warrants some discussion, because failure to understand the principle has been, and continues to be, a source of widespread confusion. In the most inclusive definitional sense, "politics" embodies all activities within institutions that are coextensive with membership in the collectivity, the organized polity. Politics includes, therefore, the whole structure of legal institutions, the law, as well as political institutions defined in the ordinary sense. It is essential, however, that three quite different stages or levels of collective action be distinguished from one another.

First, there are those activities that involve the enforcement of the law that exists. This classification includes the legitimate activities of the Hobbesian sovereign, those that are included in what I have called the "protective state," which Nozick has called the "minimal state," and which some nineteenth-century philosophers called the "night-watchman state." In the familiar game analogy, the role here is that of the umpire or referee, who is appointed to enforce the rules, to police the playing of the game.

Second, there are those activities that involve collective action within the limits of the law that exists. I have referred to this set of activities as belonging to the "productive state." Hayek refers to "legislation" as distinct from "law." In terms familiar to economists, this set of activities involves the financing, supply, and provision of "public goods and services," those goods and services that may not be supplied efficiently by the activities of individuals and private groups acting within the existing legal rules.

Third, there are those activities that involve changes in the law itself, changes in the set of legal rules that exist. In American usage, this set can perhaps best be described as "constitutional law," although Hayek uses the general term "law" in this context. In the game analogy, the activities here are those that involve changes in the rules of the game that has been and is being played.

In the chaotic intellectual and political setting of the 1980s, we can observe that the three sets of activities are confusedly intermingled. Those agents whose proper role should be confined to the first set feel no compunction whatever (and are encouraged to feel none by their scholastic mentors) in acting within the third set. Modern legal-judicial practice places us all in an ongoing game wherein the umpires themselves continually change the rules and, indeed, openly proclaim this to be their annointed social role. Those representative agents, legislators, whose role properly falls within the second set of activities, do not themselves consciously acknowledge the existence of limits. Modern politicians are encouraged to legitimize any and all extensions of legislative activity so long as "democratic" procedures prevail. Majoritarianism is elevated to a position of a normative ideal. Hence, both judicial and legislative agents invade the territory that the third category describes, and both groups do so under cloaks of claimed legitimacy. It is difficult to imagine a deeper and more widespread confusion than that which now exists, not only among the citizenry but, tragically, among those who might and do exert disproportionate influence on opinion.

We must recognize the intellectual confusion for what it is, and we must studiously avoid the temptation to apply contractarian derivations prematurely to observed institutions that have been warped out of all fit with their proper roles. The derivations must first be applied to meaningful categories. Therefore, within the three-part classification of politics outlined, I shall proceed to examine possible contractarian bases for democratic decision rules, if indeed such bases exist.

2   The enforcement of law

I have already suggested, in earlier reference to Hobbes, that there is no obvious role for "democratic" decision-making procedures in the state's role as law enforcer. In its activities as umpire, the state, through its agents, determines when the existing rules are violated and punishes those who are the violators, again within the rules. In such activity, truth judgments are involved. Was the law violated or was it not violated? Various institutional arrangements may be evaluated in terms of comparative efficacy. The appointed expert judge and the multiperson jury (which may, of course, reach decisions by majority vote or by other rules) may be alternative vehicles for generating desired patterns of results.

To introduce "democratic" decision procedures, with *all* members of the polity equally weighted (ex ante) in collective choices, in the determination of law violations, would be quasi-contradictory to the very meaning of law. To allow a designated plurality, or majority, of all citizens to decide whether a single citizen, or a group, has or has not broken the law would almost directly imply that "law" does not exist independently. Such an institutional arrangement would indeed allow for tyranny by the designated plurality or majority.

It seems evident that these arrangements could never emerge from any contractual agreement that persons enter voluntarily. The first normative principle that emerges from the contractarian perspective is that any agreed-on delegation of authority to the state or its agents be *limited by law*. I will not, in this essay, go through the derivation of this precept. I note only that the principle emerges directly without the necessity of assuming risk aversion in the standard sense.

3 Collective action within the law

The law, inclusively defined, may include a range of collective or state action, a range that is not, in itself, independent of the rules for reaching decisions within the range that is allowed. There may be goods and services that can be, or most effectively be, provided only under the auspices of the collectivity as a unit. There may be "public goods" in modern economists' meaning of this term, and decisions as to how such goods are to be provided may be assigned to the state. The question at issue here involves the possible role for democratic procedures in the making of such decisions. Will individual contractors necessarily adopt majority rule (either among the whole electorate or within a representative legislative assembly) for those political choices that may be confronted within allowable ranges of state action?

The direct answer to this question is clearly negative. Majority rule in the electorate or an assembly may well emerge from contractual agreement entered into by all citizens. But it does so only as one among a set of plausibly acceptable decision rules, any one or all of which might be chosen with equal validity. The removal of the sacrosanct status accorded to majority rule was one of the main purposes of my book written jointly with Gordon Tullock, *The Calculus of Consent* (1962). As the analysis there demonstrated, the rule that emerges from contractual agreement reflects the results of cost–benefit calculations (in some anticipated sense) on the part of the contractors. And because differing sorts of potential collective actions embody differing predicted cost–benefit patterns, there may be scope for the coexistence of several collective decision rules. For many decisions, simple majority voting, both in the selection of political representatives and in the operation of legislative assemblies, may well offer the most effective instruments. For other choices, however, which may be predicted to embody potentially more important consequences in expected costs and benefits, qualified majorities may be required for positive collective action. For still other ranges of state activities, authority may well be delegated to single agents or agencies.

Majority rule, as a uniquely legitimate principle for the making of political decisions, cannot be derived from the contractarian perspective, as such. The perspective is not as empty as it seems, however. It would be difficult, indeed, to derive a delegation of wide-ranging decision-making authority to hereditary monarchy or to a family-defined aristocracy from any contractual process in which all members of the polity participated. Much the same could be said concerning delegation to a self-perpetuating, essentially cooptive ruling elite. Delegation to a selected oligarchy that is regularly rotated through some guaranteed electoral process might possibly emerge in a contract, although the limits within which such an oligarchy might operate would tend to be more tightly drawn than those under more inclusive decision structures.

A critical element in any contractarian perspective, regardless of where the criteria are applied, is *political equality,* especially in the ex ante sense. In an idealized contractual setting, the individual is modeled as making a choice among alternative decision rules without knowing how the operation of particular rules will affect his personal interests or values. In the Rawlsian limit, the person does not know who he will be in the settings where the chosen rule is to be operative. In the somewhat less rarefied Buchanan–Tullock idealization, the person may himself be identified, but there is such uncertainty about the effects of rules on separate individual positions that particular interests cannot be related to particular rules. In either case, the contractual process will tend to exclude from consideration decision rules that explicitly deny some persons or groups ex ante access to the political process. In the Rawlsian logic, the contractor, not knowing whether he will find himself red, white, green, or black, is unlikely to agree on any rule that does not assign equal weights, ex ante, to persons from all groups. In the Buchanan–Tullock logic, the red, white, green, or black person will not agree to assign choices over policies in set X to a rule that fails to incorporate ex ante equal weighting, since he cannot know how choices within the set will influence his own well-being.

Majority rule satisfies the criterion of ex ante political equality, provided that the voting franchise is coextensive with membership in the polity. As previously noted, however, other alternatives also meet this criterion. With all decision rules other than unanimity, however, ex post political equality is violated. The interests and values of those whose choices dominate the outcome are ultimately accorded more weight than those whose choices are ignored. If A is selected by a majority vote of 60 percent, those in the coalition who supported A secure more than those in the 40 percent minority, who supported B.

If, however, ex ante equality is ensured through the open franchise and if political decisions are effectively decentralized over both issues and time, ex post differential weights on particular outcomes may be no cause for concern. Over a whole pattern or sequence of political choices (plays in the ongoing game), the ensured ex ante equality may map into some proximate ex post equality of weights.

4   Changes in law

The preceding section summarizes the argument developed in *The Calculus of Consent* (1962), from almost a quarter of a century's hindsight and with an attempted focus on the topic of this volume. Now, as then, democracy defined as ex ante political equality can be contractually derived, whereas democracy, defined as majority rule, passes muster only under a restricted set of circumstances and is in no sense uniquely related to contractual agreement. As we move to the constitutional stage, where the relevant set of choices comprises those relating to changes in the law, in the rules that constrain both private and public activity, there is no place for majority rule or, indeed, any rule short of unanimity.

It is at this stage, and only at this stage, that the ultimate contract takes place, either in conceptualization or in actuality. And it is here that the basic exchange or cooperative paradigm for politics takes on implications that are dramatically different from those generated by the truth-judgment or the zero-sum paradigm. If politics in the large, defined to encompass the whole structure of governance, is modeled as the cooperative effort of *individuals* to further or advance *their own* interests and values, which only they, as individuals, know, it is evident that all persons must be brought into agreement.

The simple analogy with market exchange illustrates the point. It would seem obvious that both parties to an exchange of apples and oranges must agree on the terms of trade if the reallocation of endowments generated by trade is to qualify as value enhancing for both parties. An enforced "exchange," whether by a third party or by only one of the two traders, cannot satisfy the individualistic value-enhancing criterion.

The complex exchange that describes a change in the constitution (in the rules) is not different in this fundamental respect from a simple exchange between two traders. A change in the rules (the law) that is applicable to all members of the polity can be judged value enhancing only on the expressed agreement of all participants. There is no contractually derivable justification or legitimization for basic structural rules of governance that cannot meet the restricted consensus test. Any justification or legitimization of rule changes that fail the unanimity test must call upon noncontractarian criteria of evaluation, which must be *nonindividualistic* in origin, or at least nonindividualistic in any universalizable sense.

5   From the abstract to the real

As noted, the analysis to this point has been developed with reference to the highly abstract three-stage classification of politics. In this setting, the relationships between contractarianism and democracy can be presented in relatively straightforward fashion. The observed world of politics, however, embodies a confused, and confusing, mixture of the three stages, with law enforcement, legislation, and lawmaking undertaken by almost all political agents. Despite the confusion, however, attempts are made to assign meaningful descriptive attributes such as "democratic" or "nondemocratic" to political arrangements as they are rather than to the idealized models, which do not, have not, and possibly could not exist. In this intensely practical realm of discourse, the relationships cannot be nearly so sharply traced.

Nonetheless, we can isolate and identify critical attributes of observed political process that must be present if any contractarian legitimization is to be advanced. The most important requirement is that law exist, in a meaningful sense of the term. That is to say, both the private and the public activities of individuals must be limited by *constitutional constraints.* State or collective power to operate without limits, *regardless of the particular decision rule,* could never find contractarian justification. I have referred elsewhere to the "electoral fallacy," which has been the source of major misunderstanding, the notion that, so long as "democratic" decision rules are guaranteed, anything goes. Even here, however, there would have to be constitutional prohibitions against changing such rules.

Within the constitutionally or legally authorized exercise of governmental or state power, political arrangements must be characterized by political equality of all those who are included in the polity's membership, at least in some ultimate ex ante sense. This requirement need not, as noted earlier, guarantee that all persons carry equal weight in a defined collective choice. Nor does the requirement guarantee against overt coercion of some persons or group by the collectivity. What is required here is that all persons possess equal access to political influence over a whole pattern or sequence of collective choices. In practical terms, this means that the franchise be open to all, that political agents be rotated on some regular basis, and that gross bundling of separate collective choices be avoided.

Finally, there must exist an observed, and honored, distinction between collective actions carried out within the allowed constitutional constraints, within the law, and collective or group actions that involve changes in the law itself. A polity in which neither practicing politicians nor political-legal scholars distinguish between legislation and law cannot be justified on contractarian grounds. If the distinction here is made, and widely acknowledged, the effective decision rule for changing the basic law must be observed to be more inclusive than the rule for making collective decisions within the law. The abstract contractarian logic need not be pushed to its extreme, which would require that constitutional changes be reached only through unanimous agreement.

To summarize, a political-legal order can broadly be classified as "contractarian" if the following attributes are observed to be present:

(1) Both private and public agents are constrained in their activity by the law, by operative constitutional limits.

(2) Within the law, all members of the polity have equal access to decision-making structures, and all have equal weights in the determination of collective decisions in the appropriately defined ex ante sense.

(3) There is a recognized distinction between collective action within the law and action taken to change the law, with the decision rule for the latter being necessarily more inclusive than the former.

6   Limited and unlimited contractarian application

Note that the criteria for classification listed in the preceding section do *not* include reference to the history of the emergence of existing rules. To say that a political-legal order that satisfies the listed criteria qualifies as "contractarian" is to say something about the *operation* of that order. And there is moral and ethical content in such a statement. But confusion has emerged through a failure to recognize the severely limited scope of such contractarian justification. To say that, given the rules that exist (which must include the distribution of endowments among persons who operate, privately and collectively, within the rules), an observed political-legal order, in its operation, may be conceptually "explained-interpreted-justified-legitimized" by a contractarian-exchange model of interaction is to say nothing whatsoever about the moral and ethical aspects of the distribution of the nominally claimed endowments of persons in some conceptualized "preoperative" stage of politics.

A simple analogy with market exchange may again be helpful here. Suppose that there are two potential traders, each of whom has an endowment of apples and oranges. Mr. A has, before trade, 93 apples and 43 oranges. Mr. B has, before trade, 2 apples and 4 oranges. After trade, Mr. A has 90 apples and 44 oranges; Mr. B has 5 apples and 3 oranges. The limits of the ethical and moral justification of free and nonfraudulent exchange is contained in the argument that *both* parties *gain* in the trading operation. There is no implication that the distribution of endowments, either before or after trade, is justified or made legitimate by the prospects for trade or by its reality.

To extend the contractarian criteria beyond the limited application to the operation of existing political-legal rules, to derive the implied contractarian features of the structure itself, is the task that John Rawls set for himself. There is no call for my judgment here of his success or failure. In my own efforts, I have, perhaps not always consistently, been content with the more limited application. But my sympathy with and affinity for Rawls's effort has been, I hope, evident. At base, we share, along with fellow contractarians of all stripes, an unwillingness normatively to evaluate politics with nonindividualistic standards or positively to interpret politics exclusively as the clash of conflicting interests.

CHAPTER 8

In quest of the social contract

James S. Fishkin

To what extent should we regard the most fundamental principles of a just society as the subject of an agreement, actual or hypothetical? In this essay I look at two famous recent approaches to this question. Then I suggest a more general framework for considering the problem. I begin with brief discussions of the contrasting approaches of James Buchanan and John Rawls.

I would like to focus on a basic issue at the center of both theories: Can a hypothetical choice motivated by self-interest yield unique and significant results and, at the same time, preserve impartiality? By yielding unique and significant results, I mean establishing nonintuitionist first principles (solving the "priority problem") for either the general question of political procedures considered by Buchanan or the even broader question of the distribution of primary goods considered by Rawls.

Both the Buchanan and Tullock constitutional convention and the Rawlsian original position appeal to hypothetical self-interest under fair or impartial conditions. In each case the following problem arises: Can we know enough about our self-interest to choose one and only one first principle and, at the same time, not know so much that the choice has been biased in our own favor? I will claim, on the one hand, that the Buchanan and Tullock contractors, operating from behind a thin veil, know too much and, on the other hand, that the Rawlsian contractors, operating from behind a thick veil, know too little.

Behind the thin veil, there is a basis for varying interpretations of rational self-interest and, hence, contrasting solutions. Behind the thick veil, there is so little basis for interpretations of self-interest that the results are drastically incomplete. The thin veil undermines uniqueness; the thick veil prevents significant, wide-ranging results. In neither case do we get results that are both unique and significant.

In this brief discussion I focus on Buchanan's claims for unanimity and on Rawls's claims for maximin. The difficulty Buchanan faces in establishing unanimity as a unique result and the difficulty Rawls faces in establishing anything so wide ranging and significant as maximin will illustrate the general problem.

1   Buchanan

Buchanan repeats in his essay in this volume (Chapter 7) a point emphasized in his earlier work:

> As we move to the constitutional stage, where the relevant set of choices and those relating to changes in the law, in the rules that constrain both public and private activity, *there is no place for majority rule or,* indeed, *for any rule short of unanimity.* (Emphasis added)

Buchanan's basic position is the same as the one he developed in the *Calculus of Consent*. It finds expression in the famous claim that, as decision rules approach unanimity, external costs go to zero.[1] It is only the decision costs function (which rises precipitously as decision rules approach unanimity) that justifies departure from unanimity as a practical matter.[2]

The rationale behind the special status of unanimity is that "when unanimous agreement is dictated by the decision-making rule, the expected costs on the individual must be zero since he will not willingly allow others to impose external costs on him when he can effectively prevent this from happening."[3]

But is it rational for a hypothetical contractor behind the Buchanan thin veil to make such a calculation? What does he know about himself? In Chapter 7, Buchanan tells us:

> In an idealized contractual setting, the individual is modeled as making a choice among alternative decision rules without knowing how the operation of particular rules will affect his personal interests or values. In the Rawlsian limit, the person does not know who he will be in the setting where the chosen rule will be operative. In the somewhat less rarified Buchanan–Tullock idealization, the person may himself be identified, but there is such uncertainty about the effects of rules on separate individual positions that particular interests cannot be related to particular rules.

However, the Buchanan contractor does know his position in the distribution of income and wealth[4] and presumably his rational capacities and his membership in any ethnic or racial groups that happen to exist in the society. Under these conditions, once he considers the costs of omissions as well as commissions (failures to act, as well as new laws or policies) the unanimity rule loses its special status – precisely because it gives everyone a veto over new policies.

Suppose we are living in a minimal state without any ongoing welfare policies and I am part of a large ghetto underclass. As decision rules become more inclusive, they provide the basis for vetoes over any redistribution – without which I may face starvation, unemployment, and other severe deprivations. At the extreme, the unanimity rule will permit even one person to exercise such a veto. By contrast, if I know my class position and it is privileged, I may calculate that more inclusive rules will function much the way Buchanan hypothesizes: The more inclusive the rule, the more likely it is that I will be able to block government intervention and redistribution that would make me worse off than the status quo. If, however, I know my class position and it is disadvantaged, then the more inclusive the rule, the less likely it is that I will be able to get approval for new policies of redistribution from the privileged that would make me better off than the status quo. Of course, these calculations will vary somewhat with the income distribution. The general point, however, is that the income distribution and one's place in it are known behind the Buchanan thin veil. Hence, the divergence in calculation from the two ends of the income distribution is all we need to establish the claim that the thin veil undermines a unique and significant solution by providing contrasting rational-hypothetical grounds for very different calculations about the self-interest at stake in the choice of a decision rule.

2   Rawls

The problem is quite different for the Rawlsian contractors. For them the question is, Can they know enough to reach any substantial conclusions at all? Behind the Rawlsian thick veil, they know nothing in particular about themselves or about their society. But Rawls argues that there are three chief features that make the choice of maximin rational in this special situation. The first feature is that there are no grounds for calculating probabilities (apart from the principle of insufficient reason). The second feature is that "the person choosing has a conception of the good such that he cares very little, if anything, for what he might gain above the minimum stipend that he can, in fact, be sure of by following the maximin rule." There is, in other words, a satisfactory security level that can be guaranteed by maximin. The third feature is that outcomes below that security level are unacceptable and would be permitted by rival principles. "The rejected alternatives," Rawls concludes, "have outcomes one can hardly accept." [5]

However, this argument does not imply maximin, but only a far weaker conclusion. Let us imagine that there is some amount of primary goods that satisfies the conditions Rawls stipulates in his second and third features – some amount, let us call it X, that has the two characteristics that anything less is disastrous and that compared with the risk of falling below that amount, we are not really concerned about getting more. These assumptions make it rational, in the original position, to require that everyone receive X primary goods. Maximin is only one of several principles that would satisfy the requirement that everyone receive X. We could, for example, give everyone X and then maximize the total. Or we could give everyone X and then increase equality. There is, in other words, a great deal of difference between a guaranteed minimum and a minimum that must continue to rise so far as possible (maximin). The latter principle is too strong a conclusion to draw from the assumptions Rawls permits in the original position. It is too strong because it has important implications that are not required by the argument – implications that distort the entire direction of public policy to produce *additional* gains to the bottom (additional beyond the X level) regardless of the effects on all the other strata.

My basic point is that, so long as we give at least X primary goods to everyone, we have satisfied the security level. It is an open question what we should do after that: increase equality, increase the total, increase the minimum, or whatever. The three features Rawls assumes in the original position imply only a guaranteed minimum and not a maximin. [6]

A guaranteed minimum is a far weaker and less controversial conclusion than a minimum that must be maximized. The latter principle can require great sacrifice from all other strata for the sake of tiny increases at the bottom – increases that might be above an already acceptable threshold. Suppose four primary goods is our definition of such a threshold. Nevertheless, maximin would tell us that B is preferable to A:

A	B
4	4.01
15	4.01
20	4.01
50	4.01

Given the meager information about his self-interest available to an agent in the original position, would it be rational to decide on maximin when another conservative choice strategy – the guaranteed minimum – ensures all that was claimed for maximin (it satisfies the second and third features) without committing itself to a host of additional and disturbing implications?[7] After all, once the veil of ignorance is removed, we might be in one of the higher strata decimated by the choice of *B* rather than *A*. And if we are at the bottom, the tiny increment we get under *B* counts for nothing, by hypothesis, since we are already above the threshold.

Suppose we are right in claiming that Rawls does get a partial substantive conclusion – a guaranteed minimum – from his three features. How much of the priority problem for distributive justice could this settle? I believe Rawls faces the following dilemma: On the one hand, if the threshold defined by the three features is interpreted minimally, a plausible case can be made for uniqueness but at the cost of such radical incompleteness that the resulting principle is nearly trivial in its implications; on the other hand, if the threshold is interpreted ambitiously, it must rest on a controversial theory of the good and the door has been opened to other controversial theories of the good that can provide an equivalent basis for rival principles. If such controversial assumptions about the good are permissible, the basis for a unique solution has been lost.

The minimal interpretation maintains plausibility (but at the cost of radical incompleteness) because it might seem reasonable, if we have no idea of our particular rational life plan, to calculate that the brute "necessaries" (to use Adam Smith's phrase) required for survival and bare membership in the society conform to the "security level" implied by the three features Rawls assumes in the original position. Compared with the risk of falling below such a minimum, we might indeed "care relatively little for what we might gain above" such a level. For example, I would not gamble on winning the jackpot introduced by great inequality if the possibility of such payoffs *introduced* the risk of starvation or other comparable disasters. In this way, Rawls's second and third features can be given plausibility. Not knowing what my rational life plan will be, I must nevertheless secure certain subsistence conditions necessary for my pursuing any rational life plan at all.

But such a minimal safety net is endorsed by virtually every developed country, capitalist or socialist. Giving everyone subsistence leaves almost everything open after that: Should we increase equality, total output, or the minimum level after that? When the security level is set so low that it plausibly corresponds to the three features, it leaves almost everything unsettled.

If, however, we were to set the security level ambitiously – say, two cars and a home of one's own – we would be positing a controversial theory of the good for everyone. The third feature requires that we regard anything less than the threshold as an unacceptable disaster, while the second feature requires that we not be interested in gambling for anything more – relative to the risk of falling below it. Having one car but not two, I can, personally, quite easily imagine a plan of life where I would prefer (1) the *chance* of becoming a millionaire introduced by tolerating inequalities to (2) strict equality but with the guarantee of a second car. The point is that an ambitious threshold corresponding to the second and third features will depend on a controversial theory of the good – one that conforms to some rational life plans but clearly not to others. For such a theory of the good anything less than the second car must be absolutely unacceptable. And compared with the risk of not getting the second car, the prospect of gambling to get Carl Icahn's fortune must mean nothing. I believe the ambitious-threshold approach would require a theory of the good with a particular controversial structure that opened the door to other controversial theories of the good as the basis for competing principles.

A more viable strategy for Rawls would be to interpret the threshold in a minimal way. But then almost all of the significant issues of distributive justice are left open because we can know so very little about our self-interest from behind the veil of ignorance. A thick veil leaves us too much in the dark to get significant wide-ranging results, just as a thin veil gives us too many conflicting perspectives on our self-interest to get unique results. The perplexity at the core of the whole approach remains: How can we choose significant and unique principles out of self-interest and know only so much that we are not biased toward ourselves?

3   Toward reconstruction

If the arguments of Sections 1 and 2 are correct, then the hypothetical stories of both Buchanan and Rawls fail to give us the determinate and ambitious substantive conclusions to which they aspired. However, we might imagine various ways in which the stories could be repaired. The strategies I will mention[8] are instructive, not because they really would succeed, but precisely because, were a theorist to employ them, they would appear, at best, to be desperate attempts to paper over fundamental difficulties.

Buchanan's thin veil permits diverse and conflicting preferences to render the results indeterminate. If my argument is correct, we are reduced to asking an empirical question about imaginary people. Depending on how we characterize their preferences, differing solutions might emerge. But with conflicting class interests and diverse preferences permitted to bear directly on the deliberations, no particular decision rule merits unanimous rational support.

Suppose, however, that the members of the constitutional convention had different preferences. Suppose that all of them were members of a religious sect with uniform and complete devotion to the commands of an all-powerful spiritual leader. If he commanded that they adopt constitution X, they would all be delighted to follow. Conflicting class and other interests would be set aside and the constitution adopted unanimously. Or suppose it were not a religious sect but a political one with a leadership that had effectively brainwashed its followers to defer to its dictated decisions.

Clearly, if we are willing to manipulate the preferences of our hypothetical deliberators, we can get them to agree to almost anything. But then the issue becomes, What moral relevance do the decisions of people with such idiosyncratic preferences have for us? If we are not members of the relevant religious or political sect, or if we have not been exposed to the same brainwashing, their imaginary deliberations have no claim on us. There is no reason that we should be bound by what such people would decide.

Instead of manipulating hypothetical preferences, we could also determine the result by manipulating hypothetical conditions in these choice situations. For example, we could complete the Rawlsian argument so as to endow it with a determinate, ambitious result. If we specified that the contractors would choose in terms of expected utility and would know that they had an equal chance of being anybody after the veil of ignorance was lifted, the gambling argument for average utility would be the theory to come out of the original position.[9] Or if we modeled the conditions of the original position directly on the fair way to cut a cake, we could get an ambitious determinate result, namely maximin (the precise conclusion Rawls proposes to get from his, quite different conditions).[10] If the conditions of choice are sufficiently open to manipulation, a variety of ambitious, substantive results could be generated. But just as in the case of manipulating the preferences of the choosers, such manipulations bring to the fore the question of why we should be bound by the results of that particular hypothetical choice, when rival hypotheticals, also making some plausible claim to fairness or impartiality, yield radically different outcomes.

It may be useful at this point to step back from these two theories and try to place the alternatives within a more general framework. The following chart offers a way of picturing the variety of thought experiments that have been influential in recent liberal theory:

	Situations	
Motivations	Actual	Hypothetical
Brute	I	II
Refined	IV	III

Two kinds of device have been employed to ensure moral relevance or impartiality in the choice of first principles – changes in the situation for choice and changes in the motivation of actors in the hypothesized situation. This fourfold table simply combines the two distinctions.

By "brute" motivations I mean motivations as we find them in actual life when there has been no concerted effort to purge them of bias, indoctrination, or other morally irrelevant factors. By "refined" motivations I mean such efforts to alter or filter motivations (so that only the morally relevant ones bear on the decision) so as to counteract the biases of indoctrination, false consciousness, and other motivations that might distort the choice of first principles. Of course, any particular account of refined preferences will have to offer an explanation of precisely why some preferences are regarded as biased or irrelevant. These are generic categories; they apply to types of theories. Each particular version will face the challenge of justifying its account of the motivations and situation that are held to be morally relevant.

Actual consent theory offers a good example of category I. Motivations and situations are as we find them in real life. If people generally agree to support a regime, it preserves the consent of the governed and maintains a kind of legitimacy. Of course, there are notorious difficulties regarding how many must agree and in what manner, but these issues need not concern us here.[11] Another example of a theory that would fit this category is that proposed by Michael Walzer in *Spheres of Justice,* in which the "shared understandings" current in a society determine the appropriate patterns of distribution.[12] Both actual consent theory and Walzer's variation are vulnerable to the objection that, because they rely on brute preferences, they can legitimate the results of indoctrination and other forms of manipulated preferences that should not be permitted to determine the results. For example, if a successful Orwellian regime were to brainwash its citizens into accepting shared understandings that legitimated its role, then tyranny would have become justice.[13] Precisely because they rely on brute preferences, category I theories have no mechanism for protecting themselves from the challenge that they can wrongly legitimate the results of collective indoctrination.

Category II theories have a partial defense against this problem, but at the cost of vulnerability to another. As in the case of Nozick's theory[14] or of Buchanan's, they must employ preferences as we would realistically find them when there is no mechanism in place for refining them – for purging them of indoctrination or other distorting influences. But category II theories face an additional problem, one that results from their hypothetical character. When we actually agree to something, we can grant the relevance of that agreement because we are the ones who made the agreement. Even if we are concerned that our motivations were biased in some way, there is still the fact to be reckoned with that we actually made that agreement. But in the case of category II theories this fact no longer obtains. The agreement is purely imaginary. Theories of this kind carry the additional burden of establishing the moral relevance of hypothetical events to which we were not actually party. In doing so they become vulnerable to indoctrination problems because they have no mechanism for refining preferences.

Category III theories, such as Rawls's theory of justice, are intended to respond to precisely the latter problem. The thick veil of ignorance rules out all motivations that are biased toward our own interests compared with those of anyone in actual life – because the relevant decision is no longer one that is made in actual life, but is rather one made under carefully controlled, imaginary circumstances.

Precisely because it employs an imaginary choice, theories in category III, like those in category II, face what might be called a *jurisdiction problem*. There are rival hypothetical courts, if you will, each of which would presume to settle our moral issues impartially. Which one has jurisdiction? The claims Rawls makes for the original position are paralleled by claims that could be made for a variety of serious rivals: the variation of the original position that employs the gambling argument for average utility, the perfectly sympathetic spectator of the classical utilitarians, Ackerman's theory of neutral dialogue, which yields a version of initial equality,[15] variations of the cake-cutter analogy, Rae's court of allocation.[16] The list is open-ended. Our fundamental notions of impartiality and fairness can be modeled in a variety of ways. Even slight adjustments in the constraints yield radically different results – as the debate between Rawls and Harsanyi demonstrates very quickly.[17]

Returning to our fourfold table, it should be readily apparent that the *top-row* possibilities, categories I and II, are subject to indoctrination problems because brute preferences have no mechanism for guarding against the biases of distorted preference formation. Furthermore, the *right-column* possibilities, categories II and III, are subject to jurisdiction problems. There remains the theoretical possibility of an approach that might avoid both of these fundamental difficulties, namely any viable variation of category IV. Category IV has the twofold merit that it is protected from indoctrination problems by the fact that preferences are refined and it is protected from jurisdiction problems by the fact that the situation is actual. I mention category IV not to develop a specific version here, but in order to propose a general strategy that might be filled out in various ways. My own attempt to do so will focus on the notion of a self-reflective political culture – one that is significantly self-undermining as a result of unmanipulated debate.[18] Such a system would have instituted liberty of political culture in a demanding sense. The demanding conditions of liberty would provide a refinement mechanism intended to protect against indoctrination problems. Yet the fact that the situation is actual, that it is the culture defining the political understandings of one's actual society – understanding that would have survived the rigorous questioning of a self-reflective political culture – give it an advantage over purely hypothetical situations in claiming jurisdiction. As we saw with Rawls and Buchanan, any number of hypothetical situations can be devised. But if the shared understandings of one's actual society are not decisively undermined by indoctrination problems, they have a way of dealing with jurisdiction problems as well. If such an ongoing system were to be realized, it would be significantly insulated from both of the fundamental problems we found applying to rival theories. If I am right in these speculations, the focus of liberal theory on quadrants I, II, and III has been regrettable. A more adequate theory might well be developed by focusing on category IV.

Notes

1   James Buchanan and Gordon Tullock, *The Calculus of Consent* (Ann Arbor: University of Michigan Press, 1971), p. 65.
2   Ibid., p. 70.
3   Ibid., p. 64.
4   Ibid., p. 46.
5   John Rawls, *A Theory of Justice* (Cambridge, Mass.: Harvard University Press, 1971), p. 154.
6   For graphic representations of these alternative principles compatible with Rawls's three features, see my *Tyranny and Legitimacy* (Baltimore Md.: Johns Hopkins University Press, 1979), app. B.
7   Another bizarre implication of maximin is that it will distribute less in total, less equally. See Douglas Rae, "A Principle of Simple Justice," in Peter Laslett and James Fishkin (eds.), *Philosophy, Politics and Society*, 4th ser. (New Haven, Conn.: Yale University Press, 1979).
8   Some of the ideas in this section are developed in greater detail in my

"Liberal Theory: Strategies of Reconstruction," in A. D'Amico (ed.), *Liberals on Liberalism* (Totowa, N.J.: Rowman & Allanheld, 1986), pp. 54–64.

9   See Rawls, *A Theory of Justice,* p. 165.

10   See my *Tyranny and Legitimacy,* p. 99.

11   For a good discussion, see Hanna Pitkin, "Obligation and Consent," in Peter Laslett, W. G. Runciman, and Quentin Skinner (eds.), *Philosophy, Politics and Society,* 4th ser. (Oxford: Blackwell Publisher, 1972), pp. 45–85.

12   Michael Walzer, *Spheres of Justice* (New York: Basic Books, 1983).

13   For a further statement of this argument see my "Defending Equality: A View from the Cave," *University of Michigan Law Review* 82, no. 4 (February 1984): 755–60.

14   Robert Nozick, *Anarchy, State and Utopia* (New York: Basic Books, 1974). I have in mind the argument from the state of nature to the minimal state in part 1.

15   Bruce Ackerman, *Social Justice in the Liberal State* (New Haven, Conn.: Yale University Press, 1980).

16   Rae, "Simple Justice."

17   See John C. Harsanyi's "Morality and the Theory of Rational Behavior," in Amartya Sen and Bernard Williams (eds.), *Utilitarianism and Beyond* (Cambridge University Press, 1982), pp. 39–62.

18   My current book, entitled *Reconstructing Liberal Theory,* attempts to make this argument in detail.

CHAPTER 9

Rationality and the justification of democracy

Jules Coleman

This is an essay about the justification of democracy in which democracy is understood as a way of making coercively enforceable collective decisions. The problem of justifying democracy arises once a group perceives a need for *collective action,* that is, a need to construct principles specifying the terms of cooperation. One's theory of democracy, then, is likely to depend on one's views about the reasons for collective action. Let us distinguish two such views. In one, collective action is thought necessary to resolve coordination, externality, and Prisoner's Dilemma problems. We might loosely refer to this view as the "market failure theory of collective action."[1] In this account, cooperation is necessary only because markets are imperfectly competitive. Market failure creates a need for individuals to abandon rational self-interested strategies over specifiable domains in favor of compliance with jointly maximizing ones. Over some domains individuals must abandon competition in favor of cooperation; and the question they must ask is, By what rules or principles are the terms of cooperation to be determined?

In the other view of collective action, individuals are already disposed to cooperate with one another on fair terms. Individuals may already share particular conceptions of just cooperation and seek to institutionalize them concretely in political and legal institutions. Or they may share

194

only the ideal of cooperating on fair terms and seek to establish rules for deciding upon particular terms and implementing them.

Whatever motivates schemes of political cooperation, in order to ensure compliance in the joint venture, cooperation must be to each person's advantage, given his conception of good reasons for action. Though cooperation may be rational as against a strategy of widespread noncooperation, it may well be in each person's interest to induce others to cooperate and for himself to defect from the joint strategy, thereby enjoying the fruits of cooperation without incurring the opportunity costs of compliance. This is the essence of the Prisoner's Dilemma, and considerations of this sort have led theorists naturally to think that cooperative or collective decisions must be coercively enforceable. Political solutions to problems of collective action are essentially coercive ones. As Douglas Rae puts it, "Once a political community has decided which of its members are to participate directly in the making of collective policy, an important question remains: 'How many of them must agree before a policy is *imposed* on the community?' " [2] This is essentially the question "By what process are collective decisions to be made?" to which the principle of democratic rule provides an answer.

Answering Rae's question requires a normative framework. We could say that a procedure for making collective decisions is justified if and only if the procedure is one that the parties in the collective – that is, those who will from time to time be required to act contrary to their own preferences – would choose. Let us call this the *contractarian* approach to the justification of collective decision rules. Or we might say that a collective decision-making procedure is justified if and only if following the procedure is likely to promote efficiently the goals of the collective enterprise. Let us call this the *consequentialist* approach to the justification of collective decision. Finally, we might identify a set of ideals with which we believe any collective decision-making procedure ought to comply. We might think of these as procedural ideals, and a process of collective decision making would be more or less justifiable depending on the extent to which it satisfied them. Let us call this the *proceduralist* approach to the justification of collective decision.

As it happens, various theorists have argued for democratic collective decision rules from all three perspectives. Notice, however, that only consequentialists tie the justification of a decision procedure to the outcomes it is likely to produce. For proceduralists, the justification of a decision procedure depends on the procedure's satisfying certain ideals. For contractarians, justification consists in rational acceptance, and though it may be that the effects of reaching decisions in one way rather than another are likely to promote certain collective ends, this causal or statistical relationship is relevant to the justification of decision rules only insofar as it is relevant to a rational person's willingness to assent to a particular decision procedure.

It seems somewhat odd that one could plausibly seek to justify collective decision rules without regard to their likely outcomes. Recall that, in the model I set out, the need for a collective decision rule arises only once a group determines that the solution to certain structural problems of interaction or the pursuit of certain ideals of justice requires collective solutions. How could a procedure of collective decision be justified without regard to its capacity either to solve the relevant structural problems of interaction or to embed the collective sense of justice?

The answer, I think, is that proceduralists and contractarians are concerned primarily with providing an account of legitimacy of political authority or the duty of compliance with law, less so with democracy apart from its connection to these issues. The argument appears to be this: If an individual *chooses* to have collective decisions made by a particular decision procedure, he is bound to comply with the outcomes of the procedure – thus, the relationship between the contractarian approach to collective decision and the duty of compliance. Alternatively, if a decision procedure is a *fair* one, policy is set by a legitimate authority – thus, the connection between the proceduralist approach and the scope of legitimate authority.

Since collective policy is coercively enforceable, one of the central questions collective decision making raises concerns the justification of coercion. The problem of justifying coercion might be resolved either by arguing, as contractarians do, that there is a sense in which the coerced group has agreed to be coerced, or by arguing, as proceduralists do, that in some other way the coercive authority is a legitimate or fair one.

Collective decision making presents at least two normative dimensions relevant to the assessment of alternative decision procedures: one is the instrumental efficacy of the decision procedure, that is, the likelihood that one or another decision procedure will secure the goals of the collective; the other is the coercive enforcement of the proposals or measures adopted in order to secure those ends. The consequentialist framework focuses on the efficacy or means–ends rationality of various decision procedures as the primary basis of assessment. In contrast, the proceduralist and contractarian frameworks see the justification of coercion as the fundamental question in collective (political) decision theory and find in either the satisfaction of certain independent constraints on decision making or the act of giving one's assent to a choice procedure the basis (or bases) for justifying the use of coercion in enforcing social choices or public policies.

All three "pure" approaches to the justification of collective decision face fundamental difficulties. The problem with the consequentialist position is twofold. First, democratic rule may not be the social decision procedure best able to secure the community's collective aims. Second, even if democratic rule is efficient in this sense, there is reason to wonder whether means–ends rationality suffices to justify coercion. One problem with the proceduralist account is that it is doubtful that procedural fairness alone suffices to justify coercively enforcing the outcomes. Fair procedures are compatible with unjust or otherwise undesirable outcomes, and the case for the use of coercion to enforce policy should have something to do with the merits of the policy as well as the procedure that led to its adoption. Second, it is questionable within the framework of collective action I have set forth – where there exist, however abstract, specifiable aims of collective policy – that a procedure for making policy with regard to those aims could ever be justified if no positive correlation between adopted policy and satisfaction of the general aims could be established. If consequentialism can be faulted for its failure to attend to the moral costs of imposing coercive means to secure desired ends, proceduralism can be rightly criticized for failing to incorporate a decision procedure's success as part of the case for its adoption.

If one holds that giving voluntary assent to a policy or rule is binding, one could argue that the contractarian approach might solve the problem of coercion – for one cannot legitimately complain about results to which one has consented. This argument is not convincing, however. First, consenting to a process is not the same thing as consenting to the outcomes of the process. So consenting to having policy made, say democratically, is not tantamount to consenting to the outcomes of the process. Second, if the contractarian position is really the *rational choice* position that individual actors *would have consented* to collective decision by democratic rule because doing so would be in their interest, then the consent argument collapses into an argument from antecedent self-interest. Arguments from consent and those from self-interest have different kinds of normative force. Arguments from hypothetical consent are not consent arguments at all, but are instead arguments of rational choice or ex ante self-interest. This is not to say that arguments from antecedent self-interest are without normative force, or otherwise bad. Rather, because they are arguments from interests and not from autonomous consent, hypothetical consent arguments, unlike actual consent arguments, fall short of justifying coercion on the grounds that the policies enforced against someone are of his own choosing. Finally, actual consent is in fact conceptually distinguishable from self-interested rationality. Because it is, two things follow. First, establishing that actors agree voluntarily to a policy-making procedure is inadequate to establish the means–ends rationality of the procedure – that is, unanimous consent is inadequate to show that the procedure is individually or collectively rational. Second, even if the fact that a person consents to a procedure suffices to undermine any grounds for complaint should collective policy require action contrary to his preferences, it may still fail to establish the *justice* or correctness of the outcomes reached. If I agree to abide by a rule, I *may* have no grounds for complaint should the rule work against my interest; my willingness to abide by the rule, indeed everyone's willingness to do so, is inadequate, however, to make the rule or its outcomes *just* or *correct* – unless, of course, one's theory of morality derives from rational autonomous consent.

In what follows I shall explore in somewhat more detail aspects of both the proceduralist and contractarian approaches to justifying democratic rule. Whereas consequentialists justify democracy in terms of its satisfying the goals of collective action, proceduralists and contractarians seek to justify democracy in the light of its connection to ideals specifiable independent of the ends of cooperative endeavor: In particular, proceduralists appear committed to an equality argument for democracy, contractarians to one rooted in liberty as expressed in the rational consent of each member of the collective. What both the proceduralists and contractarians I discuss have in common is their commitment to a rational choice framework. In the case of proceduralists, various voting rules are to be assessed in light of their rational coherence, that is the rationality of their mappings of individual preferences to social choices. In the case of contractarians, voting rules are to be assessed in terms of whether rational parties would have agreed to them ex ante, that is, in terms (at least) of their individual and collective rationality.

1   Social choice theorists

In the course of this essay I cannot explore all versions of what I am calling the proceduralist view. Instead I want to focus on social choice theory, in particular its leading proponent, William Riker, as representative of a certain kind of rational choice–proceduralist view. I shall develop in detail Riker's position because Riker, perhaps more than others, is himself concerned to explore the relationship of democracy to liberty and equality.

What is the principle of democratic rule? Social choice theorists, like Riker, analyze democracy as a kind of voting rule. All democratic voting institutions, for Riker, share to a greater or lesser extent, commitment to the ideals of equality, liberty, and participation. The commitment to these abstract ideals is what gives rise to the normative constraints imposed on collective decision rules, satisfaction of which suffices to justify a choice procedure.

"The crucial attribute of democracy," Riker writes, "is popular participation in government." [3] Participation, in turn, is analyzed in terms of voting. "Although the institutions of participation have been many and varied, they have always revolved around the simple act of voting." [4] Democracy requires participation. Participation entails voting. But "voting is not equivalent to democracy, only voting that facilitates popular choice is democratic. . . . Or, voting is a necessary, but not a sufficient, condition of democracy. To render them equivalent, voting must be surrounded with numerous institutions like political parties and free speech, which organize voting into genuine choice." [5]

For Riker, the essential normative element in collective decision making is the participation of the collective. Participation is exemplified by voting, and a voting procedure is justifiable provided that it tends to reflect the popular will. Additional normative constraints on voting procedures derive from the requirement that voting meaningfully and fairly reflect the popular will. These normative constraints must then be embodied in the institutional structures that frame the voting procedure. For Riker, the derivative normative elements (though he does not see them necessarily as derivative) are *equality* and *liberty.*

Of the connection between liberty and collective decision making Riker writes, "The historic purpose of . . . fundamental democratic liberties has been *not* to provide freedom as an end in itself, but to render effective both political participation and the process of choice in voting." [6] In the same connection, citing Rousseau, he writes that liberty "resides in participation in government, not in rights distinct from government." [7]

For Riker voting must be *meaningful* and *fair.* These abstract constraints on voting rules derive from the commitment to equality, liberty, and participation. The requirements of meaningfulness (or rational coherence) and fairness are made concrete as follows: In order to be justified, a voting rule must be fair, provide for full and equal participation, and allow for autonomy in the Rousseauean/Kantian sense. However, autonomy in this sense presupposes that the voting rule will produce outcomes that express a collective or general will. This feature of autonomy imposes the meaningfulness criterion, namely that the outcomes of voting must be rationally or conceptually meaningful, that is, coherently connected to individual preference functions. The social choice must be interpretable in terms of individual wills, preferences, or voter profiles. For social choice theorists, the general problem of democratic theory is determining whether a democratic voting procedure can be both meaningful and fair.

Riker believes that no voting rule can be both normatively and analytically meaningful. That is, the outcomes of any democratic voting procedure that is fair in the appropriate sense will be normatively meaningful but not analytically so, and vice versa.

The first part of Riker's argument involves raising doubts about the interpretability or meaningfulness of *all* voting procedures. This argument has two elements. First, cycles in the social choice can arise whenever simple majority voting procedures are applied in pairwise comparisons with more than two alternatives. Such cycles illustrate the well-known paradox of voting. Because simple majority voting in pairwise comparisons involving more than two candidates is potentially paradoxical, outcomes of this sort of voting are not meaningful. Second, given the same initial pattern or profile of preferences, non-simple-majority-voting rules can lead to different social choices. In short, there is no unique way of amalgamating or summarizing preferences. As it stands, this aspect of the argument is insufficient, for it does not follow from the fact that different voting rules produce different social choices from the same initial profiles that the rules are equally defensible – that, in other words, there are no grounds for choosing among them.

To obviate this kind of objection Riker argues as follows: Given a profile of preferences among voters, four methods of amalgamation or summation – the Borda count, cardinal utility comparison, multiplicative cardinal utility comparison, and ordinal pairwise comparison – can result in four different social choices. Each voting procedure satisfies a very general, minimal conception of fairness. Moreover, and this seems to be the important point, there are no a priori grounds for thinking that one rather than any other aggregation procedure represents more accurately the general or popular will.

Riker makes this claim concrete by examining the data displayed in Table 1. It turns out that, among these five alternatives, (a) is the Condorcet or pairwise winner, (b) is the plurality winner, (d) is the sum of cardinal utility method winner, and (e) is the multiplicative cardinal or Nash winner.[8] From this fact alone Riker concludes that, if voting is supposed to represent a general or popular will, then what "will" gets represented by a social choice is as much a function of the method of choice as it is a function of the initial profile from which the choice is derived. For each election, then, there is no way of knowing whether the outcome reflects a popular or collective will since there is always good reason for believing that a different outcome would have been produced by applying a different, equally plausible aggregation procedure. But if a voting procedure, in particular a democratic one, is defensible only if its results meaningfully reflect a public disposition or will, then it is natural to be skeptical about

Table 1. *Imaginary ordinal and cardinal utilities for five alternatives and five persons*

Rank order		Voter 1	Voter 2	Voter 3	Voter 4	Voter 5
Highest	1	a (1.00)	d (1.00)	e (1.00)	b (1.00)	b (1.00)
	2	d (0.90)	a (0.61)	c (0.80)	d (0.90)	e (0.96)
	3	b (0.60)	b (0.60)	a (0.70)	a (0.75)	c (0.70)
	4	c (0.55)	e (0.59)	b (0.55)	e (0.74)	a (0.60)
Lowest	5	e (0.50)	c (0.50)	d (0.50)	c (0.50)	d (0.50)

Note: Cardinal utilities are in parentheses.

the status of voting, for there are apparently no stable equilibria in collective choice situations. This concludes the first part of Riker's argument, the point of which can be summarized as follows: The results of voting over *more than two* alternatives are not in general interpretable; simple majority rule in pairwise comparisons, Borda counting, cardinal utility summation, multiplicative cardinal utility measures, or plurality voting may be employed to reach the social choice. (There are, of course, numerous other but no more obviously plausible alternatives.) If the method of simple majority is used, the social choice may be paradoxical as the paradox of voting demonstrates. If a method other than simple majority is used, the results may not be paradoxical. Nevertheless, they may not be interpretable or meaningful on other grounds. That is, the social choice reflects the choice procedure as much as it reflects the profile of preference to which the procedure is applied. Each procedure is in some ways a fair one, so no procedure is preferable on the grounds that it is uniquely required by our sense of justice. Most important, because each procedure can produce different results from the same profile, it is impossible to identify any one outcome as uniquely reflecting the general or popular will. Each outcome has the same origin: the same profile of individual preferences. The difference results not from the data of choice but from the method of choice, and there exist no grounds that are not question begging for choosing among decision procedures as more or less reflective of the general will.

This brings us to the second part of Riker's argument. The only way around general skepticism about voting is to see if there exists a set of independently justifiable constraints that can be imposed on voting procedures that only one voting procedure satisfies. It is clear from the discussion so far that, if these constraints or conditions are expressed too abstractly – as, for example, minimal fairness – or too narrowly – as, for example, the requirement that the social choice reflect a *unique* general will – or if the procedure applies to three or more alternatives, no voting procedure will emerge as the only one capable of satisfying them. Is there a set of constraints that express a robust conception of procedural fairness and that can be uniquely satisfied by only one voting rule?

It happens that, if we restrict the choice to two alternatives, only the rule of *simple majority* satisfies four conditions of fairness that we might plausibly impose. The argument then is that over two alternatives simple majority alone is both rationally coherent and fair.

The rule of simple majority over two alternatives is as follows: If more people vote for x than for y, x wins; if more vote for y than x, y wins; if x and y receive an equal number of votes, x and y tie. The four constraints on voting that only simple majority satisfies are as follows: (1) For any two alternatives, the rule is *decisive;* it always designates a "winner" (where a tie is a decisive outcome). (2) If after the votes are tabulated, x beats or ties y, then if someone who voted for y switches his vote to x, x beats y. This is the condition of *positive responsiveness or strong monotonicity. Weak monotonicity* is the constraint that an increase in votes for one person will not have perverse results by lowering that person's standing. Strong monotonicity requires that an increase in votes on one's behalf actually strengthen one's position. Simple majority voting is positively responsive or strongly monotonic. (3) *Neutrality* is the requirement that it not matter how the *alternatives* are labeled or named. (4) *Anonymity* is the requirement that the outcome of the voting rule not depend on the labeling of *voters.*

Kenneth May has shown that only simple majority satisfies these four constraints.[9] This uniqueness result solves the problem of choosing among alternative voting rules, however, only if these conditions are themselves related in a significant way to the general aim of social decision making. Recall that for the social choice–proceduralist, a collective choice rule is justifiable if it makes voting meaningful both normatively and conceptually. So the question then becomes, In what ways and to what extent are monotonicity, neutrality, and anonymity connected to the moral and empirical significance of collective choice?

In its most general form, *monotonicity* is the formal property that a social choice reflects individual preferences. If the point of social choice is to summarize preferences in order to reveal the general or popular will, an increase in favorable assessments of an alternative should be counted as such. Monotonicity is *the* condition that must be satisfied for any voting procedure to lay claim to producing outcomes that reflect the general will. Simple majority is strongly monotonic; two-thirds majority, for example, is weakly monotonic. The choice between simple and special majority voting rules, therefore, cannot be made entirely on grounds of monotonicity alone.

If monotonicity is the formal or technical constraint on collective choice minimally necessary for social choice to be empirically significant, neutrality and anonymity are the normative constraints presumably necessary and sufficient for a social choice to be morally significant. Anonymity requires that votes be indistinguishable from one another. Neutrality imposes the same requirements on alternatives.

Both anonymity and neutrality are characterized formally and therefore are, like monotonicity, technical limitations on voting rules. The interesting claim Riker and others make about anonymity and neutrality is that, although both are, strictly speaking, formal constraints, they have normative implications. This feature, among other things, is supposed to distinguish these constraints from monotonicity. It is not clear, however, that compliance or failure to comply with monotonicity is a morally neutral fact about a voting procedure. At the very least, because (1) satisfaction of monotonicity is necessary for a social choice procedure to have any chance of amalgamating individual preferences in a way that reflects a general will, and (2) the production of a general will is necessary for autonomy or liberty in the sense of obedience to laws of one's own making or will, then (3) monotonicity is necessary for autonomy or personal liberty in the Kantian sense. It is very likely a mistake, then, to distinguish between monotonicity, on the one hand, and neutrality and anonymity, on the other, on the grounds that the latter but not the former have "normative" implications or dimensions.

Still, anonymity and neutrality are thought by social choice theorists to have particularly powerful normative implications. A voting procedure that gives more than one vote to a person violates anonymity, as does a procedure that gives each person one vote but that differentiates votes by virtue of the *roles* or *identities* of the voters. For example, a voting procedure that divided the collective into two groups, say A and B, and that required that, in order for a proposal to be adopted, a simple majority of the voters in A and all the voters in B must approve it, would violate anonymity because, although each person would have only one vote, the votes would count differentially; it would matter under this rule whether one were a member of A or of B. Anonymity is violated whenever (1) some persons are able to cast more votes than are others, or (2) persons cast the same number of votes, but the fact that the votes are cast by different persons affects the outcome. The underlying fairness of anonymity has to do, then, with equalizing the *control* or influence of persons on the social choice. Neutrality imposes a "fairness" constraint on alternatives analogous to the fairness constraint anonymity imposes on voters. A voting rule that favors the status quo, for example, by requiring a two-thirds majority for the enactment of new measures violates neutrality.

Though simple majority rule uniquely satisfies anonymity, neutrality, and monotonicity, there is reason to doubt that satisfying these constraints is adequate to justify fully simple majority. Consider monotonicity first. Monotonicity is supposed to guarantee the significance of a social choice by ensuring that the social choice reflects the general will. *At best,* monotonicity is *necessary* for voting to reflect a general will; but it is *not sufficient.* There is first the problem of defining the general will. One can think of the relationship between voting and the general will either *epistemically* or *ontologically.* In the ontological sense a vote of some magnitude or other is *criterial* of (or *defines*) the general will on a particular subject. If some number of positive votes constitutes the general will, the problem is to specify that number. There is a continuum from simple majority through special majorities to unanimity. Simple majority, special majority, and unanimity all satisfy monotonicity. It is controversial where on the continuum one locates the minimum necessary for a popular vote to constitute a popular will. It does not follow from the fact that simple majority rule is monotonic that the outcomes of adhering to simple majority rule constitute expressions of a general will, because monotonicity itself is inadequate to distinguish between simple and special majorities, including unanimity.

One way to avoid this problem is to think of the relationship between voting and the general will as *epistemic.* In this sense, there is a fact of the matter regarding the general will on a particular subject, and voting is merely a device employed to *uncover* what that fact is. Voting may be imperfect, so that even unanimous agreement does *not entail* a convergence between the outcome of the vote and the general will. Rousseau, for one, held what I am calling the epistemic view about the relationship between voting and the general will. The general will, for Rousseau, was the will of an ontologically distinct entity, the polity, distinct from the wills or preferences of its particular members; and so any procedure that amalgamates or summarizes public preferences, that is, a voting procedure, does not *define* a general will, though it might well express a statement of public sentiment. Instead, in Rousseau's view, voting (and he favored simple majority voting) provides members of the community with the instrument for *discovering* the general will or for verifying claims about it.

If one thinks about voting epistemically, monotonicity is neither necessary nor sufficient for voting to reflect the general will in a meaningful way. Indeed, on the epistemic view, monotonicity is irrelevant to determining the general will since the general will transcends opinion and is therefore specifiable independently of voting. If, however, one thinks about voting as criterial of the general will, monotonicity is necessary but not sufficient for a voting procedure to reflect the general will reliably. Monotonicality is either irrelevant to the relationship of simple majority voting to the general will or insufficient to ensure that the outcomes of simple majority voting express the general will.

Because of its alleged connection to the franchise-as-expression-of-the-general-will, monotonicity also figures in one kind of moral defense of democracy, that is, the argument that there is in democracy the possibility of autonomous compliance with laws of one's own creation. The possibility of interpreting democracy (or simple majority) in Kantian terms as providing the opportunity for true liberty in the sense of autonomy underwrites one approach to meeting the anarchist challenge to civil authority. In the anarchist view, an autonomous person could never agree to the formation of coercive political institutions because doing so would require from time to time that he forgo his autonomy. The way to obviate this problem – some have thought – is to conceive of political prescription or legislation as being in some sense of each individual's own making. Such a view presupposes a means of collective decision that will enable social choices to express the general will. The fact that simple majority voting is monotonic is supposed to provide the necessary link between majoritarian social choice and the general will. Once again, it will matter for this response to the anarchist whether one conceives of the relationship between voting and the general will epistemically, like Rousseau, or criterially, like Riker.

In the epistemic interpretation of voting, the general will is specifiable independently of preference or opinion; it is the will of the polity. The general will on any subject is *revealed* by simple majority vote. Each person partakes in the polity in some way. A member of the *minority* on a particular vote is merely learning that he is wrong about what the general will is. The minority does not consist of losers, and the majority winners. Instead, minority members have false beliefs about the general will; members of the majority have true beliefs. So in voting, a member of the minority discovers what *his* general will in some sense really is, and so his compliance, rather than being coerced, is an act expressing his rational autonomous agency. The obvious problem with a position like this is that the notion of a general will specifiable independently of public sentiment but nevertheless revealed reliably by majority voting is very dubious. My aim here, however, is not to offer objections to the epistemic interpretation of voting, but merely to contrast it with the semantic or criterial interpretation of it.

If one views, as Riker does, the relationship between voting and the general will criterially, then a member of the minority on a particular vote really does lose. His sentiments do not coincide with the general will, and so his compliance with an adopted public measure may in fact require coercion or the threat of it. More important, whether compelled or not, his compliance with the law adopted in the face of his opposition to it is not an act of adhering to prescriptions of his own making. In short, one can appeal to democratic theory to meet the anarchist's challenge on its own terms by advancing the metaphysics of a transcendent general will. If, however, one relies on monotonicity, as one does when a certain popular vote is taken to be criterial of that will, one cannot meet the anarchist's challenge on its terms: One cannot say that even a member of that minority complies with laws of his own making and thus that his compliance expresses his autonomy.

Of course, the phrase "legislation of one's own making" is also ambiguous between the claim that the legislator's preference or will is decisive, as it is in Austin's Sovereign, and the very different claim that a voter – whether a winner or a loser with regard to the ultimate outcome – "wills" the law in that he participated fully as a voter in the process of lawmaking. Participation may suffice – as it does for participation theorists – to remove any basis for complaint should a person be required to comply with an outcome he did not favor. It does not suffice, however, to ground the claim that the *reason* a member of the minority is without grounds for complaint is that in fact he chose or willed the outcome or that, in complying with its dictates, he is acting in accord with his will.

Let us move on to the neutrality and anonymity conditions. Since these are expressions of the ideal of formal justice – namely that like cases be treated alike – could not one argue that the fact that simple majority satisfies them counts strongly and uniquely in its favor? On the contrary, one might argue that satisfying both anonymity and neutrality should count decisively in favor of a voting procedure only if one can never imagine circumstances in which influence should be different among voters or in which alternatives should have an advantage. But, of course, we can imagine cases in which it is appropriate to differentiate among voters and/or alternatives. So satisfying anonymity and neutrality is inadequate to justify a voting rule, and we ought not think that simple majority rule is an especially good decision rule simply in virtue of its doing so.

There are several responses to this line of objection. First, one could argue on grounds of economy that, although it would be better to hone more finely our voting rules to their particular domains of application, in the absence of the time and energy to do so, we minimize mistakes or injustices by adopting a rule that in all cases satisfies at least these very general requirements of fairness. Second, one could argue that satisfying anonymity and neutrality guarantees that the outcomes will be *fair*. Tampering with those conditions may produce better, as judged according to other substantive standards, but no fairer outcomes. Anonymity and neutrality are virtues of processes and are to be evaluated independently of the outcomes the process secures. Satisfying them ensures fairness if nothing else; and they are in fact not intended to ensure anything else.

This last response, however, acknowledges that satisfying anonymity and neutrality provides no guarantee that one should like the outcomes of the process that is constrained by them. But then why should one think that procedural fairness, understood as consisting in the satisfaction of these two formal constraints, could ever justify a decision procedure? There are absolutely no grounds for thinking that a decision procedure like simple majority would, *merely in virtue of its satisfying anonymity and neutrality*, produce desirable outcomes or warrant the use of coercion in enforcing the outcomes it produces. To sum up the relationship between monotonicity, neutrality, and anonymity and the moral defense of simply majority rule: Monotonicity by itself is inadequate to ground the liberty or autonomy argument for simple majority rule; and because of their merely formal character, neutrality and anonymity are inadequate to justify simple majority rule as involving the kind of justice that would warrant coercively enforcing its outcomes.

Riker and other social choice theorists appear to accept what I reject – namely the claim that the four constraints that can be satisfied only by simple majority rule suffice to render social choice based on simple majorities meaningful and defensible. This is not to say, however, that Riker himself advances simple majority rule as a social choice procedure. In fact, Riker is a nihilist about voting. His argument can be stated as follows: It is true that only simple majority rule over two alternatives satisfies four independent and independently justifiable constraints on social choice functions. In most cases, however, there are always more than two alternatives. Consequently, the question is whether there are nonarbitrary and otherwise defensible ways of reducing alternatives to two.

Riker denies that there are nonarbitrary ways of reducing alternatives to two. Simple majority voting is the preferred social choice procedure in binary-choice situations. When there are more than two alternatives, simple majority requires that the alternatives be reduced to two. If they are not reduced to two, simple majority is unstable. If they are reduced to two, simple majority is both stable and uniquely defensible. Unfortunately, every procedure for reducing alternatives to two is subject to agenda manipulation, strategic voting, or some other form of manipulation. The net effect of either manipulation or strategic voting is to throw the meaning of the binary choice into doubt. For example, the rational strategy for a voter to adopt when three or more alternatives must be reduced to two may be to vote in such a way as to bring about the weakest possible competition for his preferred alternative in the runoff election. Sometimes this means that, if enough people vote strategically, that is, for choices other than their preferred one, the most preferred choice may be eliminated from the runoff. Riker's nihilism, then, derives from the fact that only the outcomes of simple majority voting in binary-choice situations satisfy his meaningfulness conditions, but that reducing alternatives to two cannot be accomplished without *in every case* raising insurmountable doubts about the content of the social choice. The meaningfulness or rationality of every election, by whatever procedure the outcome is secured, is open to question.

For Riker, three things appear to follow from this general nihilism about voting. First, no purely proceduralist defense of democracy can be sustained, for whatever the virtues of participation or procedural fairness might be, one cannot defend morally what is either paradoxical or otherwise unintelligible. It hardly counts in favor of a procedure that participation is fair, full, and equal if the outcome of every application of the procedure turns out to be paradoxical or unintelligible on other grounds. Second, the argument for autonomy and democracy is undercut since democratic voting procedures do not necessarily yield expressions of the general will, so compliance with measures that result from these procedures is not tantamount to action in compliance with rules of one's own making. Third, radical skepticism about the meaningfulness of voting requires that democracy be defended on *consequentialist* grounds of a special sort having nothing to do with the relationship between democratic collective choice and the aims of collective policy:

> All elections do or have to do is to permit people to get rid of rulers. The people who do this do not themselves need to have a coherent will. . . . The liberal interpretation of voting thus allows elections to be useful and significant even in the presence of cycles, manipulation and other kinds of "errors" in voting. . . . The kind of democracy that thus survives is not, however, popular rule, but rather an intermittent, sometimes random, even perverse, popular veto. . . . Liberal democracy is simply the veto by which it is sometimes possible to restrain official tyranny.[10]

The net effect of democracy is to promote *liberty by veto.* "Suppose freedom is simply the absence of governmental restraint on individual action. Then the chance to engage in vetoing by rejecting officials and the chance that the rejection actually occur are the very essence of this freedom."[11]

In sum, Riker and social choice theorists generally have in mind three ways in which the ideals of democracy and liberty might connect. The first concerns the relationship between voting and those concrete liberties of, say, association and expression that render voting possible and judgments over alternatives informed. The next concerns autonomy or Kantian/ Rousseauean liberty. Here liberty consists entirely in complying with prescriptions of one's own making. The third sort of liberty is negative liberty, or the absence of governmental constraints. In the full theory of the state that ultimately emerges from the social choice theory of democracy, democracy as popular will, as autonomous agency, does not survive. What does survive is a theory of the liberal state in which negative liberty is maximized or ensured through popular elections and in which the liberties necessary for the franchise to be meaningfully exercised are constitutionally guaranteed. It is interesting that a skeletal structure of our conception of liberal constitutional democracy could emerge from so abstract an analysis of the conditions that must be satisfied in order for a social choice procedure to be meaningful. Whether this kind of analysis is rich enough to flesh out the features of constitutional democracies is left for another occasion.

2   Contractarianism

In this last section I explore some of the ways in which the contractarian approach to the justification of democracy connects democratic with liberal ideals. In doing so I discuss in some detail two different contractarian approaches to collective decision making, those of Douglas Rae[12] and of James Buchanan and Gordon Tullock.[13] First I shall make a few very general preliminary remarks about the relationship among the social choice theories of democracy I have just detailed.

Much interesting contemporary contractarian theory locates the basis of political justification in the theory of rational choice – in particular, in rational assent. Political arrangements are justified if and only if they would have been chosen by *rational* persons conceived of and constrained in such and such ways and deciding under such and such conditions. Institutions, especially coercive ones, have to be justified to each person affected by them. This usually requires showing that the institutions in question are in each person's interest and to each person's advantage. This, in turn, is usually taken to mean that justified institutions are individually rational. The collective expression of individually rational action is the social contract – thus, the quite natural connection between justification and rational choice contractarianism.

Social choice theorists, like Riker, are also rational choice theorists, but they apply the methodology of rational choice at a different level. Riker, for one, does not put the question of the justification of collective decision rules in terms of their rational acceptance by those who are to employ them. Rather, as a proceduralist, his main concern is to explore the *structural rationality of various social choice mechanisms;* that is, the extent to which applying various decision rules to profiles of preferences leads to paradoxical or otherwise unintelligible social choices. Riker's concern is the rational coherence of various methods of social choice.

Once the relationship between Riker's methodology and that of the rational choice contractarian is put this way, it is evident that all of Riker's arguments might naturally fit into each rational person's assessment of which voting rule to adopt. That assessment, however, on the traditional rational choice model, will depend on what the individual wants to maximize; and so evidence of cycles or the likelihood of manipulation in certain social choice mechanisms is *adequate* to reject a particular social choice procedure. Since a cyclical individual choice function might well make it impossible for him to choose, a rational person would likely reject a choice principle that led to cycles among his own preferences. But it is another matter entirely whether a rational actor would feel compelled to reject a *social* choice principle that cycled. Cycles may make movement from the status quo impossible or, if not impossible, very costly. Some individuals, heavily invested in the status quo, may prefer to stall movement while at the same time giving the impression of a willingness to go along with the collective will. Consequently, to reject a choice procedure on rational choice–contractarian grounds, one would have to show not just the perverse *social* outcomes of certain voting procedures, but the fact that it would be irrational for individuals to choose such rules.

The contractarian approach to collective choice is to ask which voting rule rational persons would choose. It is important to note that this question is asked at the constitutional level. In other words, the analysis assumes that individuals have found it necessary to engage in collective action and have then decided that rules specifying the scope and limits of political arrangements and institutions must be formulated. Roughly, this is the level of constitutional design. Among the decisions facing the populace at this level is that of determining the procedures by which collective measures are to be adopted. In essence, the constitutional question requires that we already have a procedure in place by which a decision about decision procedures is to be made. The usual solution to this problem is to require unanimity at the constitutional level. Is there a particular collective decision rule that would be rational for *every person?* And would this rule – whatever it might be – constitute some or other form of democratic decision making?

Douglas Rae has argued that rational persons would opt for a simple majority decision rule. The argument can be roughly stated as follows: Sometimes collective choices will fail to coincide with an individual's preference. Because collective policy is coercively enforceable, for every public measure adopted, each individual on the losing side must face the possibility of having imposed on him a decision contrary to the one he prefers. To minimize coercion a rational person therefore wants to maximize the number of times in which the social choice converges with his own preference on the matter, thereby minimizing the number of times he must act contrary to his desires. The rule that maximizes the expected convergence between public choice and personal preference is *simple majority rule*. The rational person, then, will choose to have policy set by a rule of simple majority. Because simple majority rule is democratic rule in all the ways we detailed in the preceding section, Rae's argument constitutes a contractarian defense of simple majority rule.

Rae's argument presumes that rational voters are maximizers and that their maximand is the relative frequency of convergence between social policy and personal preference. Rae's model does not specify or limit in any way the range of issues or the domain over which the social choice function ranges. Certainly, different voters will hold dear different issues, and having one's way over those issues will be more important to each. So it is very likely a mistake to think that for the rational voter all that matters is the relative frequency of convergence between social and personal choice. The numbers count, but so does the matter at risk.

One might try to meet this objection by making the model somewhat more abstract. Imagine that our rational voters are attending a constitutional convention at which they are seeking to determine among other things which social choice rule to adopt. Imagine further that they are in the dark, not necessarily over the social choice procedure's intended scope of application, but over the relative importance of different issues to them. Our voters, in other words, are simply uncertain about their views on various public measures. No voter can then try to impose a rule specifically designed to increase the chances of winning when it matters most, since no one ex ante has the relevant information. Because there is no way of choosing a procedure that will increase the frequency of a voter's winning when he most wants to, the best each can do is to maximize the frequency of wins and minimize the frequency of losses. The rule that accomplishes this from the ex ante perspective is simple majority.

Rae's argument presupposes as well that no voter knows ex ante the frequency with which he casts his vote with the majority. Consequently, no voter can expect to be in the majority any more or less often than the average. If a voter had good reason to believe that he would be in the majority less often than the average, it would be rational for him to prefer special majorities, thereby increasing the frequency with which his choice and the social choice converged.

Compare for a moment Rae's contractarian approach with Riker's. Both Rae and Riker present rationality-based justifications for simple majority decision making. Riker approaches the problem of justifying democracy in terms of the power of simple majorities to put lawmakers at risk, thereby focusing on the rational behavior of the lawmaker hoping to maximize his term of office or to minimize his risk of being removed in an election. Rae focuses on the rational behavior of the voter seeking to maximize the frequency with which his preferences converge with the social choice. Central to both arguments is the existence of shifting (and unstable in that sense) majorities. Were the same majority enduring, a rational voter could determine with greater certainty the likelihood of the convergence of his preferences with those of the majority. Were a majority stable, a lawmaker could confidently cater to its interests without fear of removal by a coalition of dissatisfied constituents. It is the instability of majorities that keeps legislators on their toes and voters in the dark.

The importance of shifting coalitions is not the only or even the most important similarity between Riker's proceduralism and Rae's contractarianism. Both positions seem to suggest the broad outlines of constitutional democracy. Riker's argument goes something like this: For voting to be an effective deterrent to political tyranny, majorities must be shifting and majority voting must be rich and meaningful. Thus, the need arises for constitutional guarantees regarding the liberties that are essentially connected to exercising the franchise – for example, liberty of association and expression. The constitutional guarantees are necessary to render voting meaningful.

On Rae's model, the rational voter wants to maximize the convergence between his preferences and social choices. Certainly, a rational person might believe that his chances for doing so would be improved by providing access to information, through forums or in general by providing the means of free and open debate. In short, each voter might seek the protection of fundamental liberties that would not make these liberties vulnerable to majoritarian will. That is, it would be in the interest of each voter, who might himself fall into the minority, to have the liberties of expression and association protected in a way that did not make them especially vulnerable to majoritarian will and that provided him the opportunity to convince others of the wisdom of his position. Since on Rae's model no voter has any reason to believe that he will be in the majority any more or less often than the average, no voter could sensibly risk leaving such matters up to prevailing public sentiment. Thus, considerations of this sort might suggest the need for constitutional protections of speech and association. One could argue that rational choice models like Rae's and Riker's provide a skeleton of liberal constitutional democracy. In each, public matters are resolved by voting, and simple majorities are decisive. Liberties are of two sorts: constitutional liberties derivable from the need to make voting meaningful (Riker) or from the desire to increase the correspondence between social choice and private "taste" (Rae); and negative liberty, or freedom from coercive rule, derivable either from the rational strategy of officeholders constrained by the next election (Riker) or from shifting majorities (Rae).

Though it is possible to argue from Rae's premises to constitutionally limited government, the fact is that Rae's argument is quite general in the sense that its domain of application is unlimited. Provided that each voter seeks only to maximize the convergence between social and personal preferences, then, no matter which issues are brought up for collective resolution, he will prefer a simple majority decision procedure. But it is not unreasonable to assume that rational voters would not be indifferent over the domain of issues to be resolved by majority voting. In fact, one might argue that a set of constitutional rights or guarantees is the price rational parties would extract from one another as a condition of adopting a rule of simple majority. Where the maximand is convergence between social and personal preferences, rationality endorses simple majority. But rationality, one might suggest, dictates adopting a different maximand, one in which there are domain restrictions on the application of simple majority. The question, then, is whether there is a contractarian defense of simple majority that takes liberty seriously and specifies domain restrictions on the application of majority rule.

In *The Calculus of Consent,* James Buchanan and Gordon Tullock present an argument for a particular kind of democratic rule that specifies a domain of collective action and takes seriously the connection between the justification of democratic rule and the idea of liberty. In the pages that remain I shall outline their general approach and explore the ways in which their account of democracy rests on liberal ideals.

The first difference between Rae and Buchanan and Tullock is that the latter believe that the first problem in the justification of collective decision making is to specify a domain of legitimate collective action. In contrast, Rae's model does not specify a domain of application. In effect, one would secure Rae's result regardless of the domain of collective decision making, so the constraints to be imposed on the scope of majoritarian decision making must be justified in some other way.

The approach Buchanan and Tullock take to defining the scope of collective action is similar to that taken by David Gauthier[14] and myself in other connections.[15] The general model is as follows: The need for collective policy arises because the structure of human interaction is such that each individual, who is out to promote his own interests, may find his efforts frustrated. There are idealized circumstances, however, under which individuals, acting as straightforward utility maximizers, secure optimal equilibria. These are the conditions of perfect competition. In perfectly competitive markets, rational utility-maximizing behavior leads to optimal equilibria. By optimality, we mean that no person's welfare can be enhanced except at another's expense. A perfectly competitive equilibrium is to be contrasted with the suboptimal equilibria of the Prisoner's Dilemma – a game that illustrates the ways in which the structure of human interaction can lead to individuals' being worse off than they would be by acting cooperatively.

Political institutions have, in this model, two roles. Even under the conditions of perfect competition, there must exist an authority to secure the integrity of exchange and to distribute initial property rights. Once this is accomplished, no need for further collective action is required as long as the conditions for perfect competition are satisfied. The perfectly competitive market, however, is like the emperor's new clothes. That is, it just ain't there. Consequently, utility-maximizing behavior is likely to yield suboptimal equilibria. The gap between individual utility maximization and the optimal equilibria of perfect competition represents a "capturable surplus of cooperation," attainable, however, only if individuals forgo acting competitively in favor of pursuing coordinated joint strategies. These joint strategies are aimed at capturing the cooperative surplus. They are collective policies whose purpose is to create and distribute the fruits of cooperation. In the framework we are exploring, here is the second role of political institutions. Collective decisions must be reached in order to capture the cooperative surplus; but by what rule ought collective decisions about such strategies be reached?

The first thing to note about this line of argument is that it specifies a particular domain of collective choice, and it does so by appeal to traditional rational choice–contractarian principles. The domain of collective action is the overcoming of obstacles created by the structure of human interaction. Structural problems make each person worse off than he would be if the conditions of perfect competition were met. Each person stands to be made better off by political action, and so it is in the interest of each to agree on joint strategies for cooperation. It is rational for each person to prefer collective decision making over this domain of activity, but not over others. So, for example, even if there exists a standard according to which we could judge individuals' antecedent holdings as unjust, it would nevertheless be irrational for at least some persons to choose to have collective policy range over the redistribution of prior holdings. In this model, the domain of collective action is coextensive with the realm of mutual advantage. What individuals can secure acting noncooperatively is simply not up for grabs – at least from the point of view of individual rationality.

Notice that this model differs substantially from other contractarian models, like Rawls's in which the domain of collective action is not restricted by initially held property rights. Certain contractarian enterprises may be aimed at settling on the principles of justice that are to govern society, in which case the allocation of property rights legitimately falls within its domain; or the contractarian approach can be directed more narrowly at exploring the contingent rationality of political institutions in the light of principles of mutual advantage. In that case, initial property holdings are at least initially outside the domain of collective decision making, though obviously not beyond the domain of normative assessment. Roughly, in the first model, contractarianism is the instrument of moral justification; in the second, it is the mechanism for uncovering the principles of rational cooperation.

In Buchanan and Tullock's view, the same general considerations that set the scope of collective choice define the collective choice rule. The contingent rationality of political institutions is explored from the contractarian perspective; similarly, the principles of collective decision are derived within the contractarian framework. What this means is that the decision regarding collective policy making takes place at the constitutional level and that only the rule (or rules) that secure unanimous agreement constitute justified decision procedures.

It would be natural at this point to merge the Buchanan–Tullock argument with Rae's. Working within the general contractarian framework, Buchanan and Tullock define a restricted domain of collective policy. Once the domain of its application has been settled, it seems plausible to apply Rae's argument to show that a rational voter at the constitutional convention would prefer simple majority because that rule alone minimizes the frequency of divergence between the social choice and each voter's personal preference. Buchanan and Tullock do not, however, argue for the rationality of simple majority voting as the first-best solution to the problem of social choice. Instead, they argue for the rationality of a unanimity rule – a position they later modify in virtue of considerations pertaining to the costs to each voter of securing consensus. In effect the argument is that, were decision making costless, rational voters would choose a unanimity rule. Because decision making is not costless, simple majority is the "second-best" solution.

Presumably the costs of making decisions or securing a consensus play no role in Rae's argument. That is, whether or not decision making is costless, Rae's voters opt for simple majority. So Rae's position and that of Buchanan and Tullock are fundamentally different. Given that both adopt the contractarian approach to justifying collective choice rules, what explains the difference between them?

The answer, I believe, is that Buchanan and Tullock approach the problem of choosing a voting rule at the constitutional level after having first defined the scope of collective policy within a more general economic-contractarian position, whereas Rae is silent about the domain of collective policy making. This "two-step" aspect of the Buchanan – Tullock approach is such that the solution given at the first stage to the question of the domain of social choice restricts (by the requirements of overall theoretical consistency) the kinds of answers that are plausible at the second stage – that is, the matter of settling on a social choice procedure at the constitutional convention. Recall that, for Buchanan and Tullock, the scope of political arrangements is restricted to the domain of mutual advantage. What individuals already have, quite apart from the justice of their holdings, is simply not up for grabs, except insofar as each individual might agree to take or exchange part or all of his prior holdings in return for something of equal or greater value.

There is in fact no way of defining constitutionally the scope of public policy that would guarantee that no public measures ever affected any individual's prior or preconstitutional holdings. Even relatively uncomplicated policy affects individuals' current assets as well as their expectations of future levels of welfare and resources. To say, however, that preconstitutional entitlements are not up for grabs is not to say that those assets are frozen. Individuals may exchange what they have acquired preconstitutionally. The key here is that any redistribution must be agreed to by those affected by it. Each person has in effect a veto over the transfer of his preconstitutional entitlements. No one can obtain them other than by his consent.

The exchange model suggests a way of protecting preconstitutional holdings against public measures that would encroach upon them, namely by constitutionally providing that in order to be adopted policy measures must be unanimously agreed upon. Though there is no way of separating at the constitutional level objects in the domain of collective policy from those outside the domain, there exists in the unanimity rule a guardian of preconstitutional holdings. Policy that encroaches on someone's preconstitutional holdings, that fails, at least in that person's eyes, to confer sufficient offsetting benefits, is subject to veto. The unanimity rule ensures that, once set, the domain of collective policy is properly maintained.

The plausibility of the unanimity rule is not limited entirely to its role in protecting preconstitutional holdings. There is a forward-looking aspect of unanimity that also connects to the general economic framework used to set the scope of collective policy. The domain of collective policy is coextensive, in this view, with the realm of mutually advantageous cooperation. Political arrangements may then be modeled within cooperative game theory, in particular as involving certain kinds of bargaining games. Voting is not just a way of protecting preconstitutional holdings that are beyond the realm of collective action; it is also a way of securing a "bargain"; and like a two-person exchange or bargain, it requires everyone's consent. Voting is the n-person surrogate for bilateral exchange. And like mutually advantageous exchange, acceptable public policy, which, given the framework, must also be mutually advantageous, must secure the agreement of each person to the bargain.

The argument for the unanimity rule squarely places it within a particular economic-contractarian framework. In this framework, solving structural problems of human interaction like the Prisoner's Dilemma motivates political arrangements. The "solution" is defined in terms of other models, like that of the perfectly competitive market in which individual "competitive" utility-maximizing behavior produces socially optimal equilibria. The problem is the logical structure of the state of nature. The solution is the stable, optimal equilibria of the perfectly competitive market. In this abstract model, political institutions occupy the "space" between the state of nature and perfect competition. The contractarian aspect of the argument consists in the self-interested rationality of cooperation to overcome the Prisoner's Dilemma structure of human interaction in the state of nature; the economic aspect of the argument derives from the model of the perfectly competitive market that provides the "ideal" toward which political institutions strive. The liberal or consensual aspect of the argument derives from a combination of both. Though it is in each person's interest to cooperate, no person will forgo what he can secure noncooperatively unless he stands to secure even greater gain by doing so. Unanimity provides the veto against policy that would impose net costs on any particular person.

The liberty element of the unanimity rule can also derive from the market model that provides the ideal toward which political institutions strive. Among the properties of competitive markets in equilibrium is Pareto optimality. Moreover, in markets rational exchanges are made only if they are mutually advantageous, that is, Pareto superior. In the economic model of political institutions the market with regard both to the optimality of the outcome of exchange and to the liberty of exchange requires that public measures pass the unanimity test. Only unanimity could possibly guarantee both that no person is made worse off by collective policy and that the outcome of collective policy is stable.

By applying an economic-contractarian argument to the problem of justifying democratic rule, one can give a plausible defense of certain sorts of democratic decision rules (e.g., unanimity) that also takes seriously the idea of a constitutionally limited domain of application. However, the argument rests on morally controversial premises and gives rise to equally problematic conclusions.

Though the idea of a constitutionally constrained domain of application of coercively enforceable collective decisions is attractive, the fact that in this model that domain is coextensive with each person's preconstitutional holdings may be considerably less attractive – at least from a moral point of view. Moreover, the unanimity rule that gives each individual absolute control over his preconstitutional holdings may merely place a moral gloss (of voluntary assent) over a morally unappealing state of affairs (entitlement to preconstitutional holdings). After all, one's preconstitutional holdings may be secured by force and fraud.

The underlying problem is in the economic-contractarian framework's commitment to rationality as both necessary and sufficient for justifiable authority. The advantage of rationality is that it is adequate to justify mutually advantageous schemes of cooperation. And given the logical structure of human interaction, there will almost always be good reason for cooperation. However, rationality appears inadequate to justify the redistribution of holdings obtained noncooperatively. If these preconstitutional holdings are redistributed, at least some individuals will be made worse off. A reduction in welfare will be irrational for at least those persons. The problem with rationality as the only criterion of justification, then, is that it apparently cannot provide a criterion of assessment for what most needs moral assessment, that is, pre-social-contract holdings.

As long, therefore, as we are committed to the criterion of rationality alone, we can assess the fairness of schemes of political cooperation, but not the states of affairs on which those schemes are constructed. This is precisely the same problem as political redistributions under conditions of perfect competition. Under perfect competition any set of factor endowments – regardless of their "fairness" – leads to individually and collectively rational outcomes. The role for politics – as opposed to economics – is to adjust the set of factor endowments so that the economy yields *just* as well as *optimal* outcomes. This involves tinkering either ex ante or ex post with individual holdings. Politics requires a coercive redistribution that is not individually rational for everyone, because it imposes net costs on some. If rationality is the principle of justification – as it is in the economic- or market-contractarian framework – then all such tinkerings, because they are irrational, will be arbitrary and unjustified. The set of initial factor endowments, like the set of preconstitutional holdings, is beyond the apparent reach of rationality and thus beyond the reach of justified redistribution.

There are two ways out of this dilemma. One is to bite the bullet of rationality. If rationality is in fact the principle of justification in one's theory – as it is in economic or market contractarianism – then preconstitutional holdings are not themselves suspect. If they are the outcome of an equilibrium secured by the interplay of *rational* defense and attack strategies, then the holdings are rational and therefore fair. There simply is no other applicable standard of justification or of fairness.

The second strategy is both more complicated and more appealing. Here I can only outline how it might play itself out. The key is to draw a distinction between perfect and imperfect competition regarding the reach of the principle of rationality. The result of perfect competition is a *stable* optimal outcome. That outcome obtains regardless of initial holdings, so no considerations of rationality reach the set of initial endowments, and redistribution is necessarily and always unjustifiably coercive.

The same argument may not obtain under conditions of market failure. There collective action is necessary to capture the cooperative surplus. One might think that the domain of legitimate political activity is coextensive with specifying the terms of cooperation alone. If that is correct, preconstitutional holdings, like initial factor endowments, are beyond the reach of rationality. But there may be an important difference between the *stability* of rational competition and that of rational cooperation. Rational cooperation requires voluntary agreement to the imposition of *constraints*. Unanimous acceptance of these constraints is necessary for the cooperative venture to succeed. Each person is always considering alternative schemes of cooperation potentially more beneficial to him than the plans offered by others. In contrast, everyone in a market is a price taker. There is no pressure to form coalitions, to demand renegotiation, or to pursue exit options. The *stability* of cooperative ventures is far more fragile than is the *stability* of perfect competition. If this is so, one might construct an argument of the following sort: It is rational for each actor to be concerned about the *stability* of cooperation; the stability of cooperation depends on the fairness of its terms; fairness in turn is a function both of the terms for distributing the cooperative surplus and of the distribution of precooperative holdings. Thus, rationality may reach into preconstitutional holdings. The question that remains is whether this line of argument, in which the fairness of preconstitutional holdings becomes a dimension of rationality through the concern for stability, can be made plausible. This task, too, however, is left for another occasion.

This essay is drawn from a paper presented at a conference on democracy. Since then, I have had the opportunity to construct a more rigorous version of some of the arguments. For example, see chap. 12 (written with John Ferejohn) of Jules L. Coleman, *Markets, Morals and the Law* (Cambridge University Press, 1987).

Notes

1   Jules L. Coleman, *Markets, Morals and the Law* (Cambridge University Press, 1987), chap. 10.
2   Douglas Rae, "Decision-Rules and Individual Values in Constitutional Choice," *American Political Science Review* 63 (1969): 40–56, at p. 40.
3   William Riker, *Liberalism Against Populism: A Confrontation Between the Theory of Democracy and the Theory of Social Choice* (New York: Wiley, 1982), p. 5.
4   Ibid.
5   Ibid.
6   Ibid., p. 7.
7   Ibid.
8   Ibid., p. 37.
9   Kenneth O. May, "A Set of Necessary and Sufficient Conditions for Simple Majority Decision," *Econometrica* 20 (1952): 680–4.
10   Riker, *Liberalism Against Populism*, p. 244.
11   Ibid., p. 245.
12   Rae, "Decision-Rules and Individual Values."
13   James Buchanan and Gordon Tullock, *The Calculus of Consent* (Ann Arbor: University of Michigan Press, 1982).
14   David Gauthier, *Morals by Agreement* (Oxford: Clarendon Press, 1986).
15   Coleman, *Markets, Morals and the Law,* Chaps. 10, 11, 12, and 13.

CHAPTER 10

The morality of democracy and the rule of law

Shirley Robin Letwin

"At the bottom of all the tributes paid to democracy," Churchill said, "is the little man, walking into the little booth, with a little pencil, making a little mark on a little bit of paper" (speech to House of Commons, October 31, 1944). Almost everyone would agree with Churchill that democracy means rule by the people. And until recently, rule by the people would have been assumed to entail the rule of law. But in the past few decades that assumption has gone. Instead, it has become fashionable to insist that democracy is quite distinct from the rule of law, indeed hardly compatible with it.

This way of thinking about democracy is not, of course, new. Aristotle was opposing a similar view when he distinguished between just and unjust governments according to whether the rule of law prevailed. That the people decide, Aristotle argued, cannot in itself secure justice. If the people answer every question just as they please without being bound by standing rules, they are no better than a many-headed tyrant, because their decisions are wholly arbitrary. In Aristotle's world, the rule of law was rare and regularly attacked, and its friends were not likely to forget that it needed defending. But now in the West, the rule of law has for so long been taken for granted that the attempt to sever democracy from law has gone unnoticed.

What is the relationship between democracy and the rule of law? To answer that question, we have to consider first of all why admirers of democracy attach such importance to the little man with the little pencil. We have to consider what it means to say that democracy is rule by the people.

The only precise and consistent meaning attached to "rule by the people" is that of a government constituted in a particular fashion. In other words, democracy is a form of government in which the authority to determine who is to govern is taken to belong collectively to all adult subjects. To constitute a government, they have to delegate their authority to some of their number. That delegation takes place in elections in which all adults vote to select those who shall serve as officers of the government. A democratic government thus acquires its authority by being composed of officers chosen by a majority in the universal suffrage of its subjects. Just how the election is conducted and just how a majority is constituted may vary. What makes a government "democratic" is the plausible appearance of its authority having been genuinely delegated by all adults subject to it.

That in a democracy authority belongs collectively to all adults has two corollaries. First, an office of government can be held only for a limited time. The delegation of authority has to be periodically reaffirmed because the authority to govern has been only delegated, not surrendered. And the formal method of ensuring that authority has been conferred on the government by the subjects at large is voting at regular intervals to elect officers of government. Second, a democratic government has to conduct public affairs in a manner that, to the degree that prudence permits, makes that conduct visible to its subjects. In a democracy, those who come to be officers of government, far from being expected to be ideal, are assumed to be neither as clear-headed, as prudent, nor as dedicated to the public good as one might wish. It is not supposed that any procedures can protect the public perfectly against greed, stupidity, and incompetence. But making the deliberations of government visible to the public is designed to ensure, as well as it is possible to do so, that those entrusted with authority will not be distracted or seduced by irrelevant considerations.

The public airing of disputes in a democracy has an unintended consequence of great importance. The prevalence and toleration of disagreement are so well displayed that it seems plausible to describe democracy as a "neutral" or "open" way of organizing communal life. Many have concluded from this that democracy is compatible with every view of what is possible and desirable and that its "openness" or "neutrality" accounts for the liberty enjoyed in the most successful democracies. It is the view expressed by E. M. Forster when he said that "two cheers" for democracy, "one because it admits variety and two because it permits criticism," were "quite enough; there is no occasion to give three" ("What I Believe," in *Two Cheers for Democracy,* 1951).

Forster was mistaken. To see why, we need only ask, Would we want democracy if we had access to indisputable knowledge of what ought to be done? The answer is, of course, no. Whether such knowledge were derived from God, history, science, or nature, it would be folly if not sacrilege to let the ignorant decide. Any reasonable person would want to hand over all public decisions to the sages or technicians who knew the truth. Even if something called a parliament were retained, it would cease to be the source of legislation; it might serve as a line of communication between oracles and subjects. Though judges might don wigs and robes and decide cases, their decisions in effect, if not literally, would be churned out of a computer programmed by experts. All debates about the justice or expediency of proposals would disappear, bringing the blessings that have for so long been commended by the apostles of certainty. In short, if individuals had access to indisputable knowledge about how to organize their communal life, democracy had better be consigned to the dustbin of history because it would be merely an obstacle to getting things right. We would be obliged to agree with Nietzsche that only a blind, mean refusal to acknowledge our superiors can sustain a preference for democracy.

If there are no indisputable answers to our controversies over public affairs, learned and sensible people can in good faith and with good reason disagree about what the right answers are. But that is not the only postulate of a preference for democracy. It assumes in addition that we wish to settle our disagreements peacefully rather than to repress them by force or to dissolve them by trust in a charismatic leader. This attitude toward disagreement springs from a distinctive conception of human beings. They are taken to be intelligent agents who can interpret their experience and respond to it in an unlimited variety of ways. In exercising this capacity, human beings shape their individual personalities. In other words, the power to choose how they will see the world and what they will make of it is one with the rationality and individuality of human beings. And when we insist on resolving disagreement peacefully instead of repressing or dissolving it, we are declaring our respect for human rationality and individuality.

What enables democracy to resolve disagreement without annihilating it is accordingly of the utmost importance. Why is democracy not, as Lenin said, an organization for the systematic use of violence by one part of the population against another? The answer is: Because a democratically constituted government is subject to the rule of law. This follows necessarily from understanding democracy as a form of government in which the authority to govern is delegated to chosen officers by those who wish to be associated under one government. Without rules defining the powers of those who occupy the offices, a democratic government could not exercise "authority," that is to say, be recognized to "have a right" to make certain decisions for the community as a whole. Nor could anyone be acknowledged as an officeholder unless there were rules defining the authority that the holder of that office was entitled to exercise. Such limitations may or may not be articulated in a written constitution. What matters is that there should be some formal definition of the powers that belong to the various offices of government. That in normal circumstances formal rules restrain a government from assuming every possible power is acknowledged by the fact that Western constitutional law always provides in some fashion for "emergency powers."

Governing in a democracy means exercising the sole authority to make and administer the general rules and arrangements of an association of persons who, whatever else they may have in common, are associated in terms of recognizing this authority. The government of a democracy is accordingly engaged in the care, custody, and administration of the law. It enacts or repeals current rules and penalizes actions that fail to subscribe adequately to the conditions stipulated by the established rules.

That disagreements in a democracy can be settled peacefully without being either repressed or dissolved is due to a particular attribute of the rule of law, what might be called its "formalism." This attribute is overlooked nowadays or even deliberately repudiated. But unless the law had this quality, it could not save rule by the people from being merely an exercise in repression of the few by the many.

The formalism of the law is most obvious from the fact that rules of law are general and impersonal, referring to classes of persons, actions, or relations. And these categories are abstractions invented by the human makers of law. The "debtor" who appears in statutes and cases is neither a poor man unable to pay his grocery bill nor a rich man in dispute with the jeweler; indeed, he is not any natural person but an abstract, formal category created by law. When "murder" appears as a legal category, it excludes some kinds of killing, indeed many kinds of killing, and nobody qualifies as a murderer unless he fits within the definition established in the law. In the same fashion all legal categories, such as fault, duty, privilege, right, property, contract, or gift, abstract from human actions and relations and are established by and within the rules that constitute a legal system. And whether a particular person, Jones, is a debtor or murderer in relation to Smith is a relationship to a legal category that has to be determined by a judge according to the established rules. "Formalism" is of the essence of law because all legal categories, whether persons, actions, or instruments, radically abstract from the everyday world.

The formalism of law also appears in the fact that rules of law are "noninstrumental." Unlike orders or commands, rules of law do not tell anyone to perform some action; they set out the manner in which certain activities are to be conducted by anybody who wishes to engage in them, with sanctions for failures to comply. When, for instance, the law prescribes that a will cannot take effect unless there have been two independent witnesses to its signing, that does not command anyone to make a will at a particular time or ever, to bequeath his property to anybody, or to accumulate property in order to bequeath it. The subject of a command must either obey or disobey because when an officer shouts, "March!" he necessarily indicates who must do what, where, and when. The subject of a rule of law is not obliged either to obey or to disobey, because a rule of law states a condition that he must take into account when engaged in an activity affected by that rule. Moreover, a rule of law may not be relevant to any of his activities: He may never contemplate killing anyone or ever be affected by the laws concerning divorce, hunting, or marine insurance.

Because rules of law do not designate outcomes that must be achieved, they are noninstrumental. Rules of law are like the rules of a game, which indicate conditions to be observed by the players but neither compel anyone to play nor dictate the players' performance in the course of the game. Just as the rules of a game "aim" only at making it possible to play the game, so the law "aims" at making possible a certain sort of association. Of course, law may have other consequences, and considerations of prudence and public policy enter into the framing and administration of laws. Such consequences and considerations are, however, incidental. They do not define the object of law because, insofar as it retains its formalist character, law neither "cuts up the pie" nor "satisfies interests," but rather defines conditions that its subjects ought to observe when choosing what to do. The law of contract does not oblige anyone to make any agreements; it stipulates what must be done when making an agreement in order to be able to sue in a court of law for redress should the agreement be violated.

Because the law is supposed to provide standing rules that enable its subjects to know what is expected of them, the judge has a carefully circumscribed function. When he is asked to decide a case, his office obliges him to inquire only how the concrete circumstances and characteristics of the litigants fit into the abstract forms of the law or laws at issue. If an accident is at issue, the judge must determine who was at "fault," what were the "damages" recognized in the law, and what kind of "restitution" is required by law. In arriving at these determinations, he has to be guided by the relevant legislative rules, as well as by prior decisions of courts, indicating how those terms are to be understood. He may not import into his decision his own view about what would be a desirable outcome. Should he believe that the borrower of a car needs it more than its lawful owner, he may not for that reason transfer title from one to the other. Should he be persuaded that the legislature has acted unwisely, he may not on that account overlook violations. Should he believe that a rule of long standing is unjust, he nevertheless lacks authority to repeal it. In short, the judge is obliged to interpret the law as it stands even though he may wish it were otherwise. His proper concern is with the law as it is and not with the law as he thinks it ought to be. Unless adjudication is kept separate from legislation, no one could know who has a right to do what. There could be no limit on how or when rules of law might be changed and, therefore, no standing system of rules.

Only laws and decisions made in accordance with the rules that constitute the legal system are authentic and carry an obligation to be observed by all subjects and officers. The obligation to abide by authentic law flows not from the subject's or officer's assent to the content of any law or of all the laws but rather from his recognition that the law has been made by those whose right to do so he has recognized. In other words, form, not content, determines a law's authenticity and the obligation to abide by it.

Much of the confusion about the character of law arises from the fact that many activities of government, though regulated by rules, are concerned with promoting and achieving certain substantive conditions. All governments must, at the very least, acquire the means to maintain themselves, to operate the rule of law, and to finance their policies; that is to say, they must levy taxes and provide for protection against unruly subjects and hostile strangers. Sometimes governments undertake also to provide substantive services, to engage in commercial and industrial enterprises, or to mount military expeditions. For such purposes, governments promulgate laws that in effect order their subjects to perform certain actions, such as making payments or enrolling for military duty. Laws that impose a tax or conscription are not, however, laws in the strict sense, because they are not formal abstract rules. They are rather commands, albeit general commands dressed in statutory terms. To the degree that the statute book contains such rules, it departs from the formalist character of law. Nevertheless, even where there are many such rules, the formalism of the law pervades all the offices of government, because the occupants of those offices exercise authority not in their natural character of individual persons with interests and purposes of their own but only insofar as their offices are created and defined by the law.

It is the formalism of law that offends the advocates of participatory democracy. What is at issue here appears in the contrast that Sir Henry Maine drew between the jury as we now know it and what he called the "old adjudicating" democracy from which both the modern jury and modern democracy emerged. What went on in the earlier form was very simple. The question was, Maine says, "guilty" or "not guilty". The old men of the community give their opinions in turn; the adjudicating democracy, the commons standing round about, applaud the opinion which strikes them most, and the applause determines the decision. The popular justice of the ancient republics was essentially of the same character. The adjudicating democracy simply followed the opinion which most impressed them in the speech of the advocate or litigant. Nor is it in the least doubtful that, but for the sternly repressive authority of the presiding judge, the modern English jury would, in the majority of cases, blindly surrender its verdict to the persuasiveness of one or other of the counsel who have been retained to address it. (Sir Henry Maine, *Popular Government*, London, 1886, p. 91)

But the modern jury operates in a very different fashion:

It is the old adjudicating democracy, limited, modified and improved, in accordance with the principles suggested by the experience of centuries, so as to bring it into harmony with modern ideas of judicial efficiency. . . . The Jurors are twelve, instead of a multitude. Their main business is to say "Aye" or "Nay" on questions which are doubtless important, but which turn on facts arising in the transactions of everyday life. In order that they may reach a conclusion, they are assisted by a system of contrivances and rules of the highest artificiality and elaboration. An expert presides over their investigations – the judge, the representative of the rival and royal justice – and an entire literature is concerned with the conditions under which evidence on the facts in dispute may be laid before them. There is a rigid exclusion of all testimony which has a tendency to bias them unfairly . . . their inquiry concludes with a security unknown to antiquity, the summing up of the expert president, who is bound by all the rules of his profession to the sternest impartiality. If he errs, or if they flagrantly err, the proceedings may be quashed by a superior court of experts. Such is popular justice, after ages of cultivation. (Ibid., pp. 90-1)

To the advocates of participatory democracy, the rules that distinguish modern democracy from the "old adjudicating" democracy are nothing but a sinister barrier to the execution of the people's will. They believe that, by voting directly on all issues, the members of a participatory democracy possess a greater degree of "self-determination" and are less subject to the will of others in the conduct of their lives. Those who admire participatory democracy make the mistake of supposing that, because in a democracy the authority to govern belongs in the first place to all the adult subjects (or to a majority of them), the authority to govern belongs to them as natural persons. But authority cannot belong to natural persons, because no one is born with authority over someone else. Authority has always to be bestowed by those subject to it. When it is said that in a democracy the authority to govern belongs in the first place to all adult members, it is assumed that by some means, such as a contract, each has given authority to each. And it is authority not to do just anything but to do something quite specific – to make the rules for the proposed association. When authority is conferred by a rule designating an office, it is not a natural person, but the occupant of an office who has authority to take the required actions.

In addition, the advocates of participatory democracy overlook the practical impossibility of submitting public decisions directly to a great mass of people. In a modern state that is much larger and more heterogeneous than the ancient republics, participatory democracy becomes a device for enabling small factions, disciplined enough to manipulate a crowd, to impose their will on the majority. In no other way could participatory democracy in a modern state avoid chaos.

A quite different sort of objection to the formalism of law accuses it of making government inflexible and indifferent to suffering by turning it into a monster of rectitude obsessed with inhuman technicalities. Regard for the formalism of law is dismissed as a pretense that conceals the power of the strong to dominate the weak. Thanks to advances in moral sensibility, this party argues, we have learned to replace worship of rigid rules of law with a concern for the substantive outcomes of judicial decisions. Judges have come to interpret laws in a manner calculated to accomplish desirable results. Whereas suits concerning contracts used to be resolved by ascertaining the obligations entered into by the parties, now they are, and increasingly should be, determined with compassionate regard for the needs and interests of the weaker party. Controversies at law between trade unions and employers, for instance, are and should be decided so as to adjust more equitably the relative power of the two sides. In short, laws should be used as an instrument for promoting equality. And this follows, we are told, from recognizing that legal decisions are necessarily political decisions about who is to get what. To attempt to distinguish law from politics, as the formalism of law pretends to do, is a "legalistic" illusion that should be abandoned.

A similar attack on the formalism of the law is launched from an opposite direction by those who believe that they have access to a standard of justice that is universal and anterior to the law. Whether they appeal to natural law or natural rights or to economic efficiency, they argue that, unless law conforms to that standard, it is nothing more than an instrument of power, serving the interests of the strongest. Therefore, no one should feel bound to observe the law as it is when he finds that it violates the higher standard of justice.

However different their demands, all the critics of formalism attack democracy by promoting a view of justice that is incompatible with the morality of democracy. They have no regard for the formalism of the law because they assume that there are indisputable answers to public questions. In making that assumption, they deny that human rationality is a power to make distinctive, personal responses to experience, and in doing so they abandon the understanding of human beings postulated by democracy.

The critics of formalism not only reject that understanding but also fail to recognize that it constitutes a "morality." Their charge that regard for the formalism of law is amoral sounds plausible because, though disagreements about whether a certain kind of conduct is "moral" are familiar enough, we are less aware of another kind of disagreement at a more abstract level about the nature of morality. What we commonly think of as "morality" stipulates something to be achieved, and the moral quality of an action, person, or institution is taken to depend on its conformity to something outside itself, rather than being intrinsic to it. What makes an action virtuous is therefore generally supposed to be that it secures the right consequences. In other words, we generally accept a consequentialist or utilitarian conception of morality. But there is an alternative, what may be called a noninstrumental conception of morality. According to that, what makes a person good is not *what* he does but *how* he goes about doing it, whether he acts out of the right motives rather than whether he achieves desirable results. In a noninstrumental morality, a good person disdains to deceive others not because it will get him to heaven, make him happy, healthy, or helpful to others, but because "that is not the way a person like me behaves." What matters is not whether he works as a carpenter or philosopher but whether he works "conscientiously"; not how much he gives but whether his giving is prompted by "generosity." In other words, virtue is identified not with the performance of certain deeds, the pursuit of correct objectives, or the achievement of designated consequences but with a manner of conducting oneself. The reasons a person considers it right to behave as he does constitute his manner of conducting himself. The right manner of conducting oneself consists in taking into account, when deciding on performances, the considerations that belong to a proper understanding of human conduct. Therefore, a person's moral quality rests on how he understands himself and his relations with the world that he inhabits.

For the purpose of practical instruction it might be convenient to reduce an understanding of human conduct to a catalogue of specific virtues, a rule book or guide indicating how to do the right thing. But any such device is necessarily an abridgement of a morality that consists in the abstract ideas that become incorporated into habits and dispositions to shape decisions about what constitutes good conduct.

Just as the moral quality of a person resides in the understanding of the human world that shapes his conduct, so does the moral quality of an institution. What makes a law "just" is not that it conforms to a transcendent pattern or law or that it achieves good results but rather that it rests on and is justified by a proper understanding of human beings. In the same way, the moral quality of democracy resides in the abstract understanding postulated by it. The morality of democracy is neither a program for action nor a set of first principles for the deduction of syllogisms but a way of seeing the human world that explains a preference for democracy.

Though real enough, the morality of democracy is exceedingly difficult to identify. The greatest impediment to recognizing it is the perpetual and troublesome disagreement among the members of any democratically governed community; for that suggests not only that all moralities are equally compatible with a democracy and that moral relativism is its hallmark but also that democracy thrives in a moral vacuum. Nevertheless, acceptance of the morality of democracy not merely is compatible with disagreement about other matters but even requires it. Because the agreement is about highly abstract ideas, which are not teleological principles that can be used as the premises of demonstrative syllogisms, fundamental moral agreement in a democracy is compatible with many different conclusions at a less abstract level. For instance, the morality of democracy does not commit us to any particular view on whether divorce should be allowed or on what conditions, whether murder should be punished by death or twenty years, whether the government should derive its revenue from a tax on income or a sales tax or whether taxation should be progressive, who should be allowed to become citizens, how we should govern our relations with Albania, or whether we should concentrate our resources on balloons or bombs. In Communist countries, where conclusions about what is desirable and possible are supposed to be deduced from a general theory, disagreements are necessarily construed as "deviations" from true doctrine. But because the moral premises of democracy do not entail assent to any particular conclusions about public policy, the members of a democracy can subscribe to the same morality and yet consistently disagree on public issues. The perpetual public disagreement in a democracy testifies to a moral consensus, not to moral relativism.

The members of a democracy can enjoy a peaceful communal life even while disagreeing, because the formalism of the law translates substantive disagreement into procedural agreement by disengaging the procedures of deliberation from the outcome. The unity secured stems from common subscription to a set of procedures. It is accordingly a formal unity that does not require the members of the association to renounce their divergent beliefs and preferences, any more than observing the rules of a game prevents players from competing with one another or performing different actions. The members of a democracy can agree on the procedures for electing legislators even though they disagree about who is best qualified for the office. Legislators can agree on the procedure for deciding whether a measure should be promulgated as law though they may differ about what the law should prescribe. In the same way, the subjects of law can recognize a duty to observe authentic law even when they disagree about whether a given law is desirable.

It is a common but gross error to conclude that respect for the formalism of law makes justice an irrelevant consideration for a democracy. Of course, when legislators deliberate about proposals to modify the existing arrangements, they are obliged by the rules of their office to conform to certain procedures and to take into account a variety of considerations. Some of these are prudential, concerned with questions like, Will it work? What will it cost? But in addition there is always a concern with the "justice" of a proposal: Is it right to make the proposed change? In a democracy, that question can be answered only by considering whether the proposal is acceptable in terms of current moral beliefs, assuming, of course, that it is compatible with the morality of democracy. The answer will be expressed in the form of specific requirements rather than in an abstract formulation, and it will be expected to change over time. But that does not render the answer amoral. On the contrary, the obligation to consult current beliefs about what is right or fair is imposed by the morality of democracy. Because that morality excludes the possibility of discovering indisputable knowledge, legislators in a democracy are obliged to recognize that they cannot claim any other justification for their view of what is just. And that different legislators will reach different conclusions that have to be defended and rebutted is only to be expected by those who appreciate the morality of democracy. Nor should it be surprising that a democracy may at different times and places hold different views of what justice requires in the way of practical policies.

In private lives, diversity may be even more marked than in public life. Because the moral agreement of members of a democracy is at such an abstract level, their substantive moral beliefs will be shaped by tradition, family, religion, and education in a variety of ways. There is no saying whether they will choose to live in rustic villages or skyscrapers, or will prefer more or less propriety, homogeneity, or equality.

The diversity that distinguishes democracy has inspired proposals for filling what is regarded as a moral vacuum with a program for instilling the beliefs and practices that constitute the "good life." Whatever else may be said about such proposals, it must be recognized that, far from endowing democracy with a moral quality, they reject the morality on which democracy rests; for we can believe in the possibility of discovering a pattern of life that is universally ideal only by assuming that human beings are in essence members of a species and that the requirements of the species define what is best for each of its members. Once we accept that assumption, we deny that each human being is a species in himself, that is to say, an independent rational agent responsible for making and saving his own soul. We thereby cease to attach supreme value to the individuality of human beings and renounce the morality of democracy.

If we take individuality seriously, we do not want a government to impose a pattern of life. Moreover, insofar as the moral quality of individuals has to do with the motives that constitute good conduct, it necessarily cannot be imposed by any government, democratic or other. And any such attempt would necessarily entail abandoning the rule of law and embracing some form of despotism. A democratic government can promote the moral quality of its subjects' lives only by providing security for a generous space within which people can shape *a* good life for themselves. For more direct assistance, the subjects of a democracy can draw on one or more of the institutions and activities that the formalism of the law enables to flourish.

Recognizing these limitations does not reduce democracy, as some would have us believe, to a set of institutional arrangements for imposing a bureaucratic unity on a society that lacks a genuine moral consensus. Although the particular content and degree of the consensus that prevails in any existing democracy is bound to vary with historical circumstances, any community committed to maintaining a democratic form of government shares a moral commitment. That it entails respecting and maintaining diversity need not in the least deter anyone from recognizing the possibility and desirability of distinguishing between learning and ignorance, beauty and ugliness, truth and falsehood, good and evil, civilization and barbarism. Human inventiveness is expressed not in crude denials of such distinctions, but in explorations of the nuances of established distinctions and the elaboration of new ones or ways of making them. Although some democracies may be careless about maintaining the quality of their civilization, it is a fallacy to associate democracy, as Tocqueville did, with the particular culture of a particular historical community. The fallacy arises from failing to recognize that the virtues of a democratic government depend on preserving a sharp separation between the manner in which the government is constituted and all other ingredients of a good life. And the formalism intrinsic to the democratic way of constituting government necessarily allows for a great variety of natural cultures as well as political practice.

That democracy is inseparable from diversity should make it obvious that a true democrat cannot believe in vox populi, vox dei, because that belief assumes, as Sir Henry Maine pointed out, "that a great number of people on a great number of questions can come to an identical conclusion and found an identical determination about it" (*Popular Government*, London, 1886, p. 88). Given the room that democracy allows for individuality, the more successful the democracy, the less likely are its members to reach unanimity. But that need not prevent them from enjoying a fundamental agreement at a fairly abstract level.

The moral agreement essential to a democracy is maintained not by uniformity but by skill in distinguishing between agreement on principle and agreement about policy, and between more and less fundamental disagreements about either. Making such discriminations enables the members of a democracy to acknowledge the authority of their government while retaining their independence of opinion about its performance. They can entertain doubts about the justice of a policy without concluding that it is iniquitous and rushing into revolution.

It is essential also to distinguish the dependence of democracy on a commitment to value self-determination from the expectation that the activity of voting bestows self-determination. In a democracy, as in all modern states, public decisions have to be made and enforced by a few for the rest. The only regular way in which public decisions can be directly affected by the opinions of individual subjects is by allowing officers of the government to be removed when they are deemed to be performing their duties unsatisfactorily. But this control is necessarily rough and remote, and to identify it with self-determination is a dangerous delusion. In any case, complete self-determination is impossible in any civilized community, let alone a modern state. But a government can be more or less responsive to public opinion. This responsiveness, however, has serious drawbacks. It may as easily threaten self-determination as protect it; for public opinion is the opinion of the majority or of the most vociferous, who may be mistaken or ready to give up independence for more "security." The only thing that a government can do to promote self-determination is to refrain from directing the lives of its subjects and to protect an area within which individuals can pursue their own projects without fear. In short, the only genuine safeguard for self-determination is the rule of law. Although universal suffrage and regular elections cannot bestow self-determination, they can make it easier to detect, avoid, or remedy misconduct among the officers of government. That is the great virtue of democracy.

But democratic procedures do not operate equally well in all circumstances. Where special interests become powerful and cunning enough to distort the judgment of the electorate, universal suffrage may be more a threat than a safeguard for the morality of democracy. The many can be corrupted at least as easily as the few, and corruption in a democracy may be more readily available and more various than in an oligarchy.

Paradoxical though it may seem, the morality of democracy gives the rule of law priority over the democratic way of constituting a government. Though democracy is inseparable from the rule of law, the converse is not equally true; for it is conceivable that the rule of law may flourish, perhaps even more effectively, under other forms of government. Where the greatest danger lies has to be decided for every set of circumstances. It is a prudential judgment that cannot be determined in advance for all times and places. It follows that a commitment to the morality of democracy obliges us to decide whether democracy should be preferred here and now not on grounds of lofty moral principle but on hard considerations of expediency.

Index

235